Routledge Revivals

Bringing up Children in Ghana

Bringing Up Children in Ghana (1962) covers a whole spectrum of child training from birth to maturity, including nursing and feeding, sibling relationships, parental discipline, sexual behaviour, puberty rites, children's household chores. The studies were conducted by the Child Development Research Unit at the Institute of Education, University College of Ghana, and presents an in-depth survey of the intimate life of the young in Ghana.

Bringing up Children in Ghana

An Impressionistic Survey

Barrington Kaye

Routledge
Taylor & Francis Group

First published in 1962
by George Allen & Unwin Ltd

This edition first published in 2026 by Routledge
4 Park Square, Milton Park, Abingdon, Oxon, OX14 4RN

and by Routledge
605 Third Avenue, New York, NY 10017

Routledge is an imprint of the Taylor & Francis Group, an informa business

Publisher's Note

The publisher has gone to great lengths to ensure the quality of this reprint but points out that some imperfections in the original copies may be apparent.

Disclaimer

The publisher has made every effort to trace copyright holders and welcomes correspondence from those they have been unable to contact.

A Library of Congress record exists under LCCN: 62006774

ISBN: 978-1-041-30428-9 (hbk)
ISBN: 978-1-003-77452-5 (ebk)
ISBN: 978-1-041-30432-6 (pbk)

Book DOI 10.4324/9781003774525

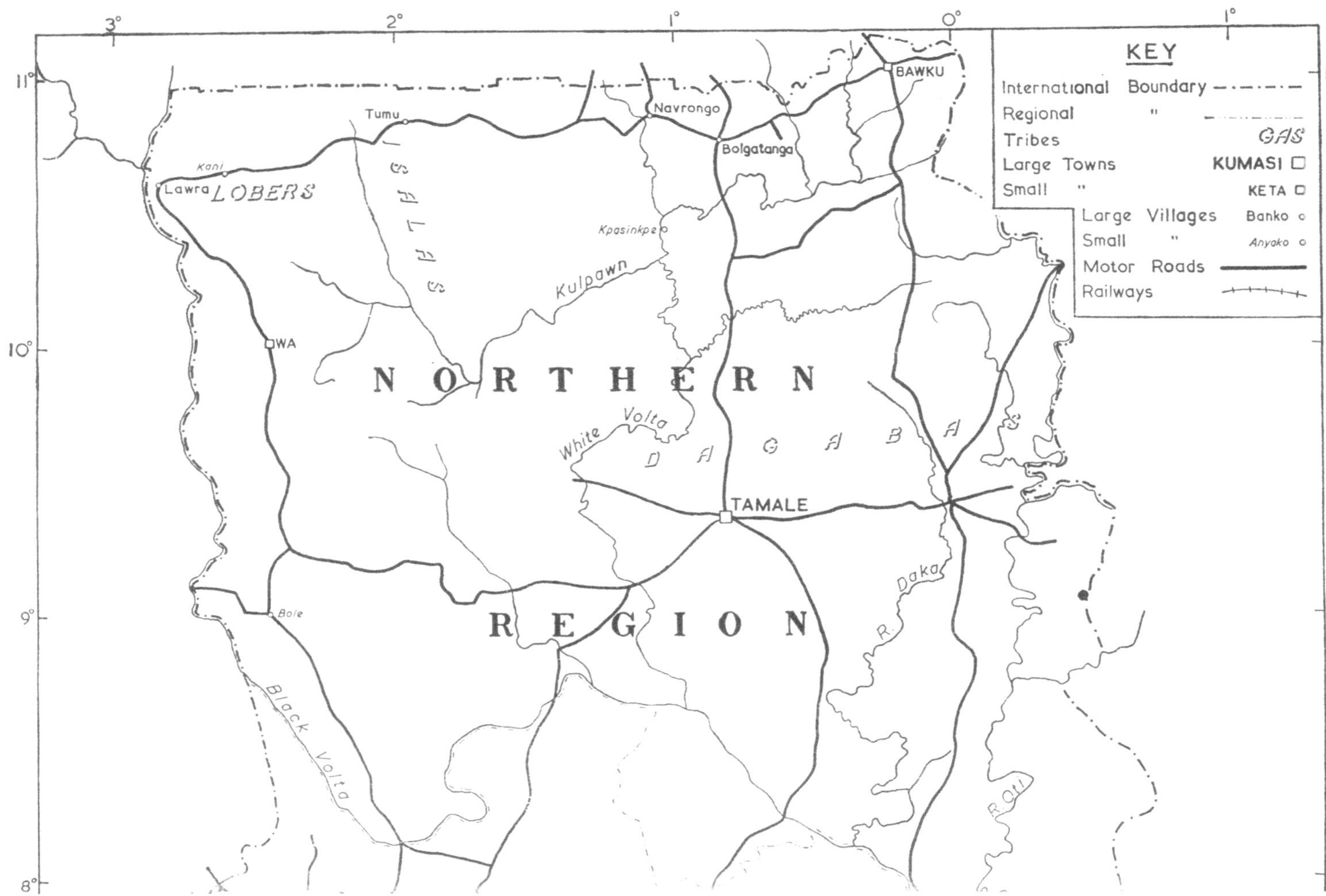
KEY
International Boundary
Regional "
Tribes GAS
Large Towns KUMASI
Small " KETA
Large Villages Banko
Small " Anyako
Motor Roads
Railways
NORTHERN REGION
BAWKU
Navrongo
Bolgatanga
Tumu
Kani
Lawra
LOBERS
ISALAS
Kpasinkpe
Kulpawn
WA
White Volta
DAGABA
TAMALE
R. Daka
Bole
Black Volta
3°
2°
1°
0°
11°
10°
9°
8°

Bringing Up Children in Ghana

AN IMPRESSIONISTIC SURVEY

BARRINGTON KAYE

B.Sc. (Econ.), Ph.D.

Senior Lecturer in Education
University College of Ghana

ILLUSTRATED

London

GEORGE ALLEN & UNWIN LTD

FIRST PUBLISHED IN 1962

DEDICATED

TO THE STUDENTS UPON

WHOSE FIELDWORK THE

FOLLOWING PAGES ARE

BASED

PRINTED IN GREAT BRITAIN
in 11 *point Bell type*
BY C. TINLING AND CO., LTD.
LIVERPOOL, LONDON AND PRESCOT

PREFACE

THIS book is a condensed version of a longer work, *Child Training in Ghana*,[1] which is itself an impressionistic survey of the field, based upon a number of reports of field investigations carried out by students of the Institute of Education, University College of Ghana, as part of their course. *Child Training in Ghana* is intended to serve as a sourcebook for social scientists planning research into the field of child development in Ghana. For the general reader and for the student, however, it is too detailed; much of it is repetitious and there is, necessarily, a fairly lengthy discussion of the methodological problems involved. It was felt that, in view of the almost total absence of books in this field, there was room for the publication of a condensed version, to serve as a handbook for students and to meet the needs of the general reading public.

The aim of the present book, then, is to give an impressionistic picture of the way in which children are brought up in Ghana. The word *impressionistic* must be emphasised. The following pages cannot be regarded as in any way definitive. While the students[2] who undertook the investigations were, of course, given some instruction in the techniques of social research fieldwork, it cannot be pretended that they were trained social scientists, nor can the material they gathered be claimed as equivalent to data obtained by modern rigorous methods of investigation. This is not said with any intention of disparaging the valuable contributions made by these students to our pitifully inadequate store of knowledge concerning the whole field of child development in West Africa; it is only to make clear that the generalizations presented in this book are essentially impressions and constitute what scientists call a first approximation only.

It cannot be stressed too strongly that the process of social research is by stages, or approximations. A full and reliable picture of a community can be built up only by degrees. First impressions are recorded and analysed; from them, rough generalizations are made. From these generalizations working hypotheses are derived,

[1] *Child Training in Ghana: an Impressionistic Survey*. Institute of Education Child Development Monograph No. 1. Legon, 1960. Obtainable from the Institute of Education, Legon, price (bound in hard covers) £G3 10s 0d, post free in Ghana.

[2] A list of the names of those students whose field studies were used in the original analysis, together with the towns and villages in which they worked, will be found in Part I of the Bibliography, pages 213-16.

tested, modified, tested again and modified again until they can be used in conjunction with other hypotheses, similarly arrived at, to construct a very tentative picture of some part of the society under study. This picture is itself tested for contradictions. Predictions are made from it and compared with the facts to test its validity, and the final picture is obtained only after many years of painstaking and often laborious fieldwork.

Thus, the more rigorous research projects of fully-qualified social scientists cannot be undertaken until first impressions have been recorded and an impressionistic survey has been made of the field. The first stages of scientific research can then proceed on hypotheses that will not be too wildly remote from the truth. It was to provide a sourcebook for such hypotheses that *Child Training in Ghana* was written, and similarly the main value which is foreseen for the present book for students, and particularly for student-teachers, is to provide a source of hypotheses for their own further research, and to act as a starting-point for discussions.

Hence, the present text can in no way be regarded as authoritative. Nonetheless, it is still legitimate to ask: How far are the methods of bringing up children given here typical of Ghana as a whole? Are they the same in the Northern Territories as in the south? Are they the same in matrilineal tribes as in tribes practising patrilineal descent? Is there no difference between the way a child is brought up by an illiterate family in a small fishing village, say, and the methods employed by parents, both of whom are university graduates, living in the well-to-do residential area of a large town? Are there no differences, in this respect, between the various tribal groups? Does religious affiliation not have a bearing on the subject? Are there no individual variations, from one family to another, in the same community?

To answer this question accurately one would have to have completed the research projects to which this study is itself a preliminary. However, it is possible to give a very tentative and impressionistic answer. To begin with, and taking the last point first, there is almost certainly no such thing as a 'typical' Ghanaian family, any more than there is a 'typical' French family or a 'typical' Chinese family. Families and households are made up of individuals, and individuals are infinitely varied. Hence, at best, it is possible to talk only of a family *norm*, meaning by this that there is an observed tendency in a given community for families to act in a certain manner, but that there will be many deviations from this norm.

A second qualification that must be made is that deriving from the distinction between normal and ideal behaviour. By *normal* behaviour is meant what most people in fact tend to do; this behaviour constitutes the norm. By *ideal* behaviour is meant what they think ought to be done, both by themselves and by others. But often, of course, what people think they ought to do, and what they in fact do, are two different things. Unfortunately, when they are asked what they in fact do, they very often tell the inquirer what they think they ought to do; that is, they report ideal instead of normal behaviour. Fully-trained and experienced social scientists are well aware of this possibility and they use various techniques to ensure that the data they obtain relate to normal behaviour. But in the present case it is possible that some of the reported actions and attitudes relate to ideal rather than to normal behaviour. However, it is unlikely that the reporting of ideal behaviour in place of normal behaviour was widespread, as it would have revealed itself by inconsistencies within the data, and also between what was reported and what was observed (since the students were required to observe as well as to interrogate). In fact, the few obvious cases of ideal reportage (one or two of which are included in the extracts given in this book) are so patently instances of pious hope rather than of practical experience, and so demonstrably conflict with the other extracts, that it seems reasonable to assume that this source of error was probably of little importance.

A third consideration which may serve to prevent a misleading interpretation being placed on the material presented here, is the fact that no attempt was made to record the frequency with which any particular method was employed. For example, references are made, in the section on parental discipline, to the behaviour prescribed of a son who has incurred his father's formal curse, and who subsequently seeks forgiveness. The form of behaviour is given in some detail in many of the investigations, even to the amount considered to be a suitable pacification fee. However, it must not be supposed that this ceremony is a commonplace in the villages in question. It is quite possible that, in any given area, years may pass without a single instance of its performance. In other words, the fact that a form of behaviour is well-known and even prescribed in some detail, is no indication of its frequency.

Bearing these three qualifications in mind, individual variations, the possibility of the data relating to ideal rather than to normal behaviour, and the fact that no inferences can be made about the frequency of reported behaviour, it is possible to venture an impressionistic answer to the question asked above: How far are the methods of bringing up children given here representative of those practised in the whole of Ghana? Of the thirty-seven investigations included in the original study,[1] only two were carried out in the Northern Territories, and of these two, one leans fairly heavily on other published material. Even if the Northern Territories are

[1] Listed in Part I of the Bibliography, pages 213-16.

excluded from the purview of the question, it will be seen that some parts of Ghana are better represented than others; the Akwapim Ridge, for example, the Fante coast, the Ga States, Mampong-Ashanti, Akpini State, are all over-represented compared with other parts of Ghana. It is clear that faithful representation on a geographical basis cannot be claimed. What may be claimed, however, is that most of the different types of community to be found in Ghana have at least *some* representation; there are both small isolated villages and large towns included in the areas of investigation; both matrilineal and patrilineal tribes; both fishing or farming communities and industrialized areas; both villages whose adult populations are almost all illiterate and areas with a long tradition of formal education; both pagan communities and old-established mission centres; and while it is true that the areas of investigation tend to be clustered together, yet several of these clusters more or less coincide with areas of dense population. Thus, while it is not possible to claim proportional representation in this study for the various kinds of community in Ghana, it can be said at least that they all have *some* representation, and this is as much as it is reasonable to expect from an impressionistic study of this kind.

It would be both tedious and improper to inquire any further here into the general validity of the material presented in the following pages, the more so since such inquiry can only for the most part be met with further disclaimers as to any pretence of methodological rigour. Details of the content-analysis itself, further source material, and the description and results of a very rough reliability check are given in the longer work, *Child Training in Ghana*, to which the more specialized reader is referred. For the general reader, however, and for students interested in the field of child development in West Africa, it is hoped that the present compilation will be of value, as a starting point for both discussions and further fieldwork.

The research scheme for the students' investigations was originally drawn up by Dr. A. Taylor, now Professor of Education and Director of the Institute of Education, University College, Ibadan, Nigeria, and he was also responsible for the supervision of several of the investigations.

Finally, the writer would like to express his gratitude to the Ford Foundation, United States of America, for a generous grant towards publication.

Child Development Research Unit.
University of Ghana,
Legon, 1961.

CONTENTS

ILLUSTRATIONS

All the photographs were taken by the author, using a Kine-Exacta camera with a Tessar f2·8 lens, on Ilford FP3 film.

CHAPTER ONE

THE PEOPLE OF GHANA[1]

THE people of Ghana can be divided roughly into five language groups, each of which approximates to a geographical area. These are the Akan, the Ga-Adangme, the Ewe, the Guang and the Gur language groups.[2]

Akan-speaking people occupy the southern and central part of Ghana, from the Ivory Coast on the western boundary to the River Volta, with the exception of the Ga and Adangme States in the south-east, and of isolated Guang-speaking villages on the Akwapim Ridge and along the southern coast. Ga is confined to a small area along the south-eastern coastal plains, approximately from Accra to Kpone; Adangme is spoken from Kpone to the River Volta, and north to Krobo Hill. Ewe-speaking people inhabit the southern part of Trans-Volta Togoland, which constitutes east Ghana. To their north are speakers of the so-called 'Togo remnant languages', which have a number of affinities with Guang. The Northern Territories of Ghana, including the northern part of Togoland, can be divided linguistically into two parts; the tribes in the southern part, which reaches very approximately from the Black Volta River to the Kulpawn River, speak a Guang dialect, while those in the northern part speak one or other of the Gur languages.

There are pockets of Gur language-speaking tribes in the Guang area at Bole and Daboya. The Tchakosis, an Akan-speaking tribe, live in northern Togoland among Gur-speaking tribes. The Bussansis, who speak Bisapele, a Mande dialect, occupy the extreme northern tip of Togoland. The Guang-speaking pockets among the Akans have already been mentioned.

[1] This chapter is based on Manoukian's three volumes in the Ethnographic Survey of Africa; see (25), (26) and (27).

[2] This division is Manoukian's. Westermann, however, includes Guang in his Akan 'language group'; see (37) 78.

The main language groups are thus the Akans, inhabiting south, south-west and central Ghana; the Ewes, inhabiting east Ghana; the Ga-Adangmes, inhabiting a small area in the south, between the Akans and the Ewes; the Guangs, to the north of the Akans; and the Gurs, inhabiting the whole of north Ghana.[1]

It must be emphasized that this distribution is very approximate. In addition to isolated villages where migrants from one language group have settled among those speaking a different language, there are various other factors that go to confuse the picture. The cities and bigger towns are polyglot; they attract migrants from every part of the country. Then the tribes of the Northern Territories are traditionally the source of recruits for one branch of the police force, and they are found in every town in Ghana. Migrant labourers from the Northern Territories are also employed on the cocoa farms in central Ghana, by Akan-speaking farmers. Schoolmasters, born on the Akwapim Ridge, may be sent to teach in Government schools in the north, and in general, administrators of every kind may be sent to live in areas far from their native towns. The overall picture presented in the first two paragraphs of this chapter must be regarded as very roughly approximating to the pattern of settlement only.

The following approximate percentages have been calculated from the figures obtained at the 1948 Census for the distribution of the population according to 'tribal division'.[2]

(*Akan*)			
Akwapim	2%		
Asante	14%		
Brong	3%		
Denkyera	0.4%		
Fante	11%		
Kwahu	2%		
Nzima	2%		
Other Akan	9%	Total Akan	44%
(*Ewe*)			
Ewe	13%	Total Ewe	13%

[1] See the map at the end of this volume.
[2] See Table 23 (17), 367.

(Ga-Adangme)			
Ga	4%		
Adangme	3%		
Krobo	2%	Total Ga-Adangme	9%
(Guang)			
Cherepon	0.4%		
Efutu	0.6%		
Other Guang	0.4%	Total Guang[1]	1%
(Northern Territories)			
Dagaba	3%		
Isala	1%		
Other N.T.s	28%	Total N.T.s	32%
		Grand Total	100%

The Akan-Speaking Peoples

The Akan dialects spoken in Ghana may be divided into two groups: Twi and Anyi-Baule.[2] Twi is the generic name for such dialects as Akwapim, spoken by the inhabitants of the Akwapim Ridge, rising out of the Accra Plains; Asante, spoken by the Ashantis, who inhabit the central forests of Ghana; Akyem, spoken by the Akims, who live between the Akwapims and Ashantis; Fante, spoken by the inhabitants of the coastal towns, roughly from Accra to Sekondi; and Kwahu, spoken by the inhabitants of the country lying between Ashanti and the River Volta, to the north of Akim. Other neighbouring tribes, such as the Denkyeras, speak variants of Twi; all Twi dialects are more or less mutally intelligible.

The second group of Akan dialects are those termed Anyi-Baule, comprising, among others, Nzima, spoken in the extreme south-western corner of Ghana; Ahanta, spoken to the west of Sekondi; and Anufowo, which is the dialect of the Tchakosis, who live among the Dagombas in the Northern Territories.

The Akans are a matrilineal people; that is, inheritance and succession follow the female line. They belong to one or other of a number of exogamous matrilineal clans, the members of

[1] Excluding Gonja, a tribal division included among 'Other N.T.s'.
[2] But Westermann adds Guang; (37) 78.

each of which are believed to be descended from a common ancestress and therefore to be related by blood.

With matrilineal descent, the mother's brother stands in a special relationship to the child, as he is the child's nearest adult male blood relative, and he represents for the child the authority of his clan. The tie which binds a child to his or her own father depends upon totemic membership, inherited patrilineally. The totemic groups are also exogamous in theory, but allegiance to these groupings has waned very rapidly in recent years.

Traditionally, in so far as the children born to a marriage belong ultimately to their mother's clan, the husband's interest in them is limited. This is particularly true of daughters, who are highly valued by the mother and her clan relatives, as they ensure the continuance of the lineage. The upbringing and domestic training of daughters are the responsibility of the mother, who often enlists the help of her female clan relatives. The relationship between a father and his son is closer, as the father is responsible for his care and training from young childhood until marriage. Traditionally, he should provide for his son's adult status by giving him a gun and finding him a wife; nowadays, instead of a gun, a cocoa farmer may present his son with a cocoa farm. Trades, such as that of weaving and gold-smithery are also handed down from father to son.

All debts and legal obligations of a child, other than those arising from sexual misconduct, are traditionally the responsibility of the child's clan; the father is responsible only for those arising from sexual misbehaviour. On the other hand, in so far as the father is responsible for the training of his children, the arrival of formal education with its attendant fees and expenses has often proved a point of dispute between a child's father and the maternal uncle, each arguing that the privilege of paying for the child's education lies with the other.

Except in so far as he was discharging his traditional responsibilities, the father used to be unable to give property to his children without the consent of his own clan relatives, as a man's property ultimately belongs to his own clan. However, in Ashanti, since 1942, it has been permissible for a father to give up to half his property to his children without the permission of his clan.

On their father's death, it is the duty of his children to provide a coffin, and this obligation is regarded as a very serious matter.

In addition to his role as the father of his children, an Akan male family head will also fulfil the role of maternal uncle to his sisters' children, to whom he is bound by the lineage ties of his own clan, a position which entitles him to considerable respect from them. If the father of his sister's children is unable to give them an adequate upbringing, the maternal uncle has the right to remove them into the care of his own clan. While the children are under the care of their father, however, their maternal uncle may punish them only with their parents' consent. In the past the maternal uncle had the power to compel his sister's children to marry his own children; this cross-cousin marriage has always been regarded as an ideal by the Akans. A maternal uncle had also the right to 'pawn' his sister's children to pay for clan debts, and this extended even to the right to compel his niece to divorce her husband, so that he could pawn her. The custom of pawning is now illegal and it is difficult to say to what extent it survives. Pawns often led their whole childhood in the service of the creditor. The apparently widespread practice of entrusting a middle-school child to the care of a literate guardian, often a non-relative, in return for the child's services, may descend from the custom of pawning.

Polygyny is allowed among the Akans; the extent to which it is practised is difficult to say. Formerly, cocoa farmers regarded a large number of wives as an economic asset in so far as their labour force was primarily drawn from their own children. With the spread of full-time schooling and its cost, both directly in fees and expenses, and indirectly in the loss of labour, there are signs that limits are being set on the preferred size of families, and this may well affect the attitude towards the desirability of several wives.

The typical dwelling house is an enclosed rectangular compound, round which rooms and open sheds are grouped. Dwelling groups vary considerably; they may consist only of members of a single clan; of married couples and their children; of groups of clan relatives, married or unmarried, of the same sex; of polygynous households; or of a mixture of two or more of these.

The Ewe-Speaking Peoples

Ewe is the term used of a group of dialects spoken in Ghana by the inhabitants of Trans-Volta Togoland. Anlo is spoken in Keta and in the surrounding area. Other Ewe dialects are used by the inhabitants of the country to the north of the Anlos, up to Kpandu and Bakwa.

Descent among the Ewes is patrilineal, and local communities are divided into a number of patrilineages, each claiming descent from a common ancestor. Inheritance varies, some patrilineages following the male line, others the female. In the former case, lineage and clan exogamy is the rule, while in the latter there is further variation, though among the Anlos clan (but not lineage) endogamy is preferred. The Ewes practise polygyny, though its incidence is difficult to determine.

The responsibility for the upbringing of young children rests wholly with the mother, who continues to be responsible for her daughters' care and training until they are married. Sons, after circumcision at about the age of five or so, come gradually under the surveillance of the father. Children often go to stay with relatives, particularly their grandparents, both paternal and maternal.

There is very little data available regarding the domestic organisation of the Ewes; such descriptions as exist generally relate to particular areas, and may well not be typical of the Ewes as a whole.[1]

The Ga-Adangme-Speaking Peoples

The Gas. Ga is spoken in the coastal towns and villages from Accra to Tema, and to some extent in the villages on the plains behind.

Succession and inheritance among the Gas are by patrilineal descent. Men and women live in separate compounds; in general, men's compounds are restricted to members of the same patrilineage, while women's compounds contain members of various patrilineages, though all are related by kinship ties. Children live in the women's compounds, in the case of boys until they are judged old enough to join the men, and in the case of girls until they marry, and often for their whole lives. Wives bring or send food to their husbands' compounds, and visit their rooms at night. Polygyny is practised among the Gas.

[1] See Manoukian (26) 28-9

The Adangmes. Adangme dialects are spoken in the coastal towns and villages from Kpone to Ada, at the mouth of the River Volta, and inland to Krobo Hill. The various dialects, which are mutually intelligible, include Krobo and Shai. Ga and Adangme are not completely mutually intelligible.

There is very little material relating to the domestic organization of the Adangmes. They appear to be grouped into a limited number of patrilineal clans.

The Guang-Speaking and Gur-Speaking Peoples

Despite differences in language and dialect, there is a high degree of cultural uniformity among the tribes of the Northern Territories of Ghana. It should be noted, however, that those pockets of Guang-speaking tribes to be found in southern Ghana, while retaining the language of their groupings (though they normally also speak the local dialect), have adopted many of the customs of their neighbours, and the generalizations given here are strictly applicable only to the Northern Territories.

Inheritance and succession are determined by patrilineal descent, except for a few cases where inheritance of property is matrilineal. The majority of tribes are organized into exogamous patrilineal clans. Polygyny is practised among all the tribes; estimates of its frequency vary.

Dwellings consist of groups of circular or lozenge-shaped mud huts, arranged round walled compounds. A dwelling group normally consists of a patrilineal joint family, comprising two or more men of the same patrilineage, with their wives and children. Each wife has her own quarters, including a bedroom for herself and her children. Unmarried men normally have rooms in their mothers' quarters. Husbands do not usually have rooms of their own, but sleep in one or other of their wives' bedrooms.

CHAPTER TWO

ATTITUDES TOWARDS HAVING CHILDREN

> 'Love and romance are things of a sophisticated society.'

THE attitude in Ghana towards the having of children appears to be universally positive. Children are wanted by every married couple; they are regarded as 'better than riches', as 'gifts from God'.[1] In many towns and villages it is said that to have children is the main, or even the only purpose of marriage. In TUTU (Akwapim)[2] it is said that children are greatly valued, since they help in the house and on the farm, they serve visitors, they support their parents in old age and are their heirs. In BANKO (Asante) children perpetuate the clan. Both boys and girls are of economic value, and they support their parents in old age. They are a source of social prestige, and parents who have ten children or twins, are greatly respected and addressed by special titles. Such parents are believed to be holy, and free from the evil effects of witchcraft. Since one is sent into the world to have children, a large family is evidence that one is loved by gods. Moreover, children are a source of wealth, since a high proportion of the bride-price goes to the girl's parents. In BENIM (Asante) child-bearing is the most important aspect of marriage, if not the sole aim, since without children a lineage comes to an end.

In BOSOFO (Asante) children add to social prestige, prove their father's manhood and remove the stigma of barrenness. In DWINYAMA (Asante) 'they regard the possession of offspring

[1] Fortes says that the Tallensis believe 'it is better to die in poverty and leave children than to die childless but rich'; (14) 136.

[2] On this and the following pages are given examples and instances from students' theses to substantiate the generalizations made. All such examples are preceded by the names of the towns or villages in which the investigations were made, and the predominant dialects used there are given in parentheses.

as the supreme purpose of life'.[1] Children are a source of prestige. They mean more hands on the farm. In the old days they could be pawned by the maternal uncle to pay off a debt. They provide care for old age, and ensure their father a fitting burial, especially since his wife's relatives do not feel obliged to contribute to the funeral expenses if there are no children to share the cost. In BEREKUM (Brong) the aim of marriage is procreation. Children are a source of social prestige, and a woman with ten children is very highly regarded. An illiterate farmer with five wives and twenty-seven children, on being asked whether he wanted any more children, answered: 'Definitely. I wish I had even double the number of children I have at present. They are a real blessing from God. There would be no need to engage labourers to weed my cocoa farm and to help in the plucking and in carrying the dried beans to the nearest weighing station if I had more children.' In SUPOWMU DUNKWA (Fante) 'material progress and ease in life are dependent upon having children'. Among the KWAHUS a large family is a source of honour and prestige, and perpetuates the father's name. In GBLEDE (Ewe) 'marriage is solely and purposely for bringing forth, what the inhabitants value as the greatest priceless possession on earth—children'. In CENTRAL ACCRA (Ga) social prestige and progress depend upon the possession of children, and to have many children is 'a major type of material wealth'. In TESHIE (Ga) a woman's status depends upon her child-bearing. 'Material progress and ease in this life, security and peace in the next life, are dependent upon having children.' In OTROWE (Adangme) they are regarded as a means of support in old age. 'Parents gain social prestige according to the number of children they have.' In WINNEBA (Efutu) children ensure the continuance of the family, create more hands for domestic and other work, provide a guarantee of security for old age, dispel loneliness and show that the home is a living place. It is thought better to have children than to have wealth. Among the DAGABAS 'the procreation of legitimate children is the most ardently desired of all ends. The consensus of opinion was summed up by the chief at Jirapa in the following words: "If

[1] Direct quotation from the original theses are enclosed in quotation marks as here; the author of the relevant thesis can be identified by reference to Pt. I of the Bibliography, pages 213-16. No page references are given to these theses, which are in manuscript. All the theses used in the compilation of this book have been deposited in the Library of the University of Ghana, Legon.

you have no children, who will farm for you when you are old and infirm? If you do not farm you will never be able to obtain food to eat and if you do not get food to eat, you will die." '

Children are valued for many reasons. Those most often given are: (i) they perform domestic tasks, such as helping in the preparation of food, gathering firewood, sweeping the rooms and the compound, washing the dishes, looking after smaller siblings and running errands; (ii) they are a source of labour on the farm, and assist their fathers in fishing and other occupations; (iii) they are a form of security for old age, when they are expected to support their parents;[1] (iv) they ensure their parents a fitting burial and guarantee that sacrifices will be made to their spirits;[2] (v) they are a universally-recognized source of social status and prestige; (vi) they guarantee the continuance of the family line, whether patrilineal or matrilineal;[3] (vii) they enable proper courtesy and respect to be shown to important visitors, by serving and waiting on them; (viii) they uphold their father's dignity in public by carrying his stool and other possessions, and by running errands for him.

The advantage most often mentioned of having children is that to have a large family ensures high social status to the parents, and is a source of much prestige. After their first child, a couple will cease to be addressed by their own names, but will instead be referred to as 'Kofi's father' and 'Kofi's mother'. Special titles may be used to address the woman who has brought forth ten children or twins, who are regarded as exceptionally auspicious.

Very few informants could be found who were able to think of any disadvantages to having children. In ABURI (Akwapim) 'the older people think the modern women prefer property in the form of clothing and ornaments to having children. They do not want to stay with one man but with several others at the same time, and a woman who practises that is childless generally. They want to avoid the care of children. If a young woman happens to have a child she does not like it much because she wants to be free to attend dances and other functions.' In

[1] Fortes observes that, among the Ashantis, the more sons a man has, the more secure he feels; (11) 269.

[2] Rattray quotes a Gurensi informant as saying that the desire to have sons who will sacrifice to him when he is dead and thus keep his memory alive is the reason why a Gurensi man 'is fonder of having children than anything else'; (32) 160.

[3] Fortes says that, among the Ashantis, the passing on of the names of forbears is regarded as an important filial duty; (11) 266.

APIREDE (Cherepon) 'children are such important products of marriage that no one would think of the possession of them as being a liability'. In WINNEBA (Efutu) it is agreed by some informants that it may be difficult to maintain children if one is poor. 'A certain old man explained that the question of marriage and child-birth is best likened to a small bush animal called Santrofi, which has within itself potentialities both for good and evil. This odd creature is rare and if, by chance, a wanderer comes across it he is faced with the problem of either bringing it home, in which case he brings in an insidious creature to wreck the entire household, or he may decide to leave it alone and then lose all possible chance of fortune for ever. The explanation is that married people without children cry bitterly to get children, while those who have them also meet such reverses that they are forced to regret having got them. "Some of the difficulties," the old man went on, "are that people are poor and cannot afford to maintain their children or to care for their schooling. In some cases, too, the children imbibe evil tendencies and behave in ways which bring headaches to their parents." '

While there were few informants who could think of any disadvantages to having children, there is some evidence that the cost of educating children is beginning to become a factor in the attitude towards birth control, particularly in the educated classes, among the members of which a family of six children is often stated to be the ideal. The trials and anxieties of child-rearing are sometimes mentioned as disadvantages to having children though not, of course, sufficient to dissuade one from doing so.[1] Among the illiterate farmers and fishermen no limit is given to the preferred size of the family, and the various advantages already mentioned to be derived from the possession of children are used to justify the frequent response, 'the bigger, the better', in reply to the question, 'What size of family would you prefer?' It should be added that this attitude extends naturally to polygyny; many informants found in the possession of several wives and their numerous offspring the true source of economic security, social status and spiritual content. In ABURI (Akwapim) the preferred size of the family,

[1] Fortes says that, while the Tallensis regard children as the chief reward in life, nevertheless they stress the tribulations involved in child-rearing, and the heavy responsibility attached to it; (14) 163 and 168.

having regard to the high cost of living, is said to be from four to six children. In MAMPONG (Akwapim) there are no limits to the preferred size of family. 'Many of the elders who are illiterates, and farmers by profession, have many wives. Some have as many as eight or even more. Asked whether it was convenient for them to have such a number of wives, one of them roared with laughter and replied that he wanted helpers for his farm work.' In BANKO (Asante) while it is recognized that child-birth shortens the mother's life, yet the larger the family, the better the father is pleased. If, after nine or ten children, the mother wishes not to have any more, then that is allowed. But it is recognized that schooling and other costs are high, and nowadays 'both the younger literate and illiterate wives and husbands prefer to have 3-5 children at most, provided that at least there are boys and girls together'.

In BOMPATA (Asante) with the rising cost of living, most Christian men want from four to six children. Some pagan families want at least ten, from fear of child mortality, and others have no limits. In BOSOFO (Asante) when the old men pour a libation, they ask for thirty children. The women hope for the honour of becoming a mother of ten children, when a public ceremony is held, during which two sheep, one from the mother's clan and one from the husband's, are slaughtered and eaten by all. If the tenth child is a girl, she becomes the chief's wife. The young men, however, feel the responsibility of too many children. In JAKOBO (Asante) the general opinion is that one should have as many children as possible, but some girls say for economic reasons it is better to have only from four to six children, especially if there are no matrilineal uncles to look after them. In KOMENDA (Fante) there are no limits to the size of families among the illiterates, but among the professional classes four to five children are preferred, so as to give them a secondary education. In KPANDU (Ewe) 'the more wives one has, the more he is respected, and his influence is the more felt by the number of children born for him by the wives'. In AYIKAI DOBORO (Ga) the majority of informants want as many children as possible, though some say eight children (four boys and four girls) are enough because of the high cost of living. In TESHIE (Ga) it is said the more children the better, since it is certain that some would survive to help with the fishing. In APIREDE (Cherepon) one may have any number of children. 'This is the statement made by an old man: "I feel I am the happiest man in the village for at present I have thirty children. You would like to see me with my three wives and thirty children around us in the evening, telling Ananse stories. Again, because of my children I scarcely work on the farm and, above all, I am highly respected in the village." ' Among the ISALAS, 'since children are considered as constituting a labour force, they are regarded as assets. Hence the more of them one has the better. The fact that the more of them there are, the more mouths there are to feed is hardly realized and even if it were realized it is never considered a problem since they themselves always produce the food. Female children are equally welcome in numbers for they serve as a means of obtaining money and cattle when they marry.'

The attitude towards childlessness follows from the high store set upon the possession of a large family. It is widely said that to be childless is the most serious misfortune that can befall a woman. The childless man, and even more the childless woman, are everywhere treated not merely with pity, but with scorn and abuse.[1] They are mocked and jeered at; their barrenness is continually thrown in their faces. They have no one to run errands for them, or to carry their stools before them to a public ceremony, and if they attempt to bribe other peoples' children to perform these tasks, they are likely to be abused both by parents and children. The procreation of children being the main aim of marriage, it follows that suspected sterility is accepted as sufficient grounds for divorce.[2] A man who suspects his wife is barren may marry another to prove his potency. A wife who on her part thinks that the source of their childlessness lies with her husband, may take secret lovers to become pregnant, or may even be allowed by her husband to do so.[3] Alternatively, her relatives may insist that she divorce him and marry another.

Sterility being in many cases attributed to youthful promiscuity, the attitude towards it often includes moral condemnation. Childless adults have little or no social status; they are not invited nor expected to comment on public affairs. They are

[1] Fortes says that in Ashanti, 'childlessness is felt by both men and women as the greatest of all personal tragedies and humiliations'; (11) 262.

[2] Wartemberg says that, in Elmina, a divorce on account of sterility requires the consent of both spouses and their family clans; (36) 121.

[3] Fortes notes this custom among the Tallensis, where a man may depute a kinsman not of his own clan to impregnate his wife; (14) 23.

accorded no respect by either relatives or strangers, and are equally despised by young and old. Barren women are sometimes given a special, disgraceful, form of burial, to prevent a recurrence of the unfortunate situation in a reincarnation. A few cases of suicide were attributed to despair at being sterile, and among the advantages of having children, one often mentioned was the avoidance of the disgrace of being found barren. In MAMPONG (Akwapim) childnessness is attributed to witchcraft, or to an irregular life, and is regarded as very unfortunate. It is a cause of divorce. In APA (Asante) to be childless is a disgrace, and a reason for destooling a chief. Barren women are despised by young and old. In BOSOFO (Asante) childlessness is regarded as a great misfortune, and attributed to witchcraft or fornication. In JAKOBO (Asante) 'a sterile man is not half as much subjected to ridicule as a sterile woman'. Sterile women are mocked and neglected; no proper burial rites are performed for them. They are regarded as useless, and can be divorced. In KOFORIDUA (Asante) six cases were counted by the investigator of women who left their husbands 'because "he is not a man", as one said, and "I cannot go on wasting my strength and energy on that man," said another'. In SUPOWMU DUNKWA (Fante) it is regarded 'as a grievous fault and short-coming. The barren woman is despised, sometimes ridiculed and calumniated; and should she be involved in a quarrel, the keenest insult that could be thrown at her is that she is sterile.' Among the DENKYERAS a childless person 'is regarded as a social nonentity'. In VAKPO (Ewe) 'a childless woman is an outcast. Her own husband gives her no respect. She is spoken of as "cook" in the house. The husband's relatives give her no respect and very often they plot to make her a public ridicule with a view to driving her away.' In CHRISTIANSBORG (Ga) childlessness is regarded 'as a great misfortune indeed, and every married man tries to do all he can to avoid dying childless'. A childless Christian is thrown into a dilemma when his relatives insist on his marrying a second wife to prove that he is not impotent. In TEMA (Ga) 'shortly after the marriage the woman is expected to be pregnant. She is regarded with suspicion and contempt and she becomes a figure of ridicule if there is no sign of this. Her friends and other women snub her and openly attack and blame her for her childlessness. Sometimes scandalous stories are spread about her, that either she has bewitched her own womb or she led an immoral life before she was married. If she happens to be the wife of a polygamist, she suffers the more from her co-wives; they will not allow her to ask any of their children for any services. She is openly challenged to have her own children. Much of the insult is launched by her husband's sisters who complain that their brother has purchased "worthless goods".'

In AGOMANYA (Krobo) childlessness is attributed to pre-marital sexual intercourse, or to fate, and is greatly deplored. In WINNEBA (Efutu) childless men have little social prestige, and are snubbed. Several cases of suicide have occurred. In one 'a young woman who had lived with her husband for over three years without issue looked upon the man as the guilty partner and began to nurse feelings of separation. One morning, in answer to certain demands made by her husband she burst out: "Oh, don't worry me. Aren't both of us the same sex? My equals who married are all bearing children. What have you done for me? I'm fed up with foolish work." Silence reigned, tears followed; the rest was suicide. The husband was so profoundly hurt that he decided at once to end his life. So the next morning, he washed himself, combed and brushed his hair, powdered his face and neck and armpits and dressed up gorgeously in his Asafo uniform.[1] Then he fetched a strong fishing line and hanged himself round the neck in his own room.' Among the ISALAS 'childlessness is regarded as a curse. The fact that a couple have no children is regarded as proof that they are bad people and they are being punished with childlessness by God.'

Innumerable remedies are practised for overcoming sterility, the simplest and most widely recommended being for a barren woman to bury the placenta of a newly-born baby, and then urinate over it.[2] In most places a distinction is made between sterility attributed to physical causes, and that attributed to witchcraft or the displeasure of spirits or gods. In the former case, which may be the result of a congenital abnormality, of the abuse of one's genital organs in childhood and adolescence, of too frequent abortions or of failing to wash thoroughly, a herbalist is customarily consulted, who may prescribe vaccina-

[1] The Asafo companies are the traditional tribal military organizations of the Ghanaian people; see (5) Chapter VI for a description of the Asafo organization among the Fantis.

[2] Mentioned in (25) 89.

tions, usually at the waist and joints, medicinal potions, herbal suppositories, taboos, charms and amulets. For cases of sterility attributed to supernatural causes, such as witchcraft by or on behalf of a jealous rival, the resentment of a spirit-husband or spirit-wife, displeasure of totemic or tribal gods, resort may be had to a witch-doctor or to a fetish priest. The remedy usually consists of propitiating angry spirits or driving away evil ones by means of various rites, offerings and sacrifices.[1] In some areas, public ceremonies are conducted for sterile participants, sometimes without their prior consent. The essential ingredient of such ceremonies is usually the humiliation of the sterile person, who may be stripped and led about on a rope. The spirit possessing a barren woman may be driven out by gongs and shouts at the end of a purifying ritual. In ABURI (Akwapim) barrenness is sometimes attributed to witchcraft, and cured by a herbalist. Alternatively, the barren women may appeal to the python fetish, by standing on a sacred python which will emerge from a lake when summoned by a flute. To urinate on a buried placenta is also recommended. In TUTU (Akwapim) 'among married couples it is the man who is always suspected of sterility . . . The two major causes of sterility are venereal diseases and undeveloped uterus. This is believed to be prevalent among members of a rich family, beautiful girls, and those belonging to a royal family, owing to the fact that such people tend to lead reckless, licentious lives.' Other minor causes are believed to be slave descent, marrying girls before their puberty rites, and witchcraft. The following authorities are usually consulted in this order: (1st) the witch-doctor, who may prescribe medicines and enemas; (2nd) the fetish priests; (3rd) the priests attached to the Tigare cult; (4th) the *Kotekrawa* custom, in which the suspected sterile man is led about naked on the end of a rope, beaten and abused. Barren women are also recommended to urinate over a buried placenta, for which the usual charge is threepence, and having done so, to go away without looking back. In BENIM (Asante) particular stress is placed upon the husband's *ntoro*.[2] If a woman fails to keep the taboos of her husband's *ntoro*, then conception may be hindered. Witchcraft is also suspected. In the past, men who had been married for a year without sign of children were

[1] See (8) 161 for a description of such a rite.
[2] Or totem; see (29) 45 *et seq*, and (5) 77 *et seq*.

subjected to the *Krawa* ceremony. Stripped naked and smeared with sheep's blood mixed with powdered charcoal, they were dragged through the streets by a rope round the waist while the onlookers shouted: 'Krawa, we demand your child!' If there were still no children at the end of a second year, such men were divorced. In BOSOFO (Asante) women are more often suspected of being the cause of childlessness than are men. Barrenness is attributed to (i) disease, when a herbalist is consulted; (ii) promiscuity, for which there is no treatment; (iii) misconduct towards parents, for which the parents' spirits must be propitiated; (iv) failure to observe the husband's *ntoro* taboos, for which propitiation must be made; or (v) witchcraft, which 'is believed to be the chief cause of sterility, and nearly every barren woman interviewed in Bosofo suspected that some old person in her family had bewitched her'. A well-known remedy for barrenness is to take the placenta of a newly-born baby to the outskirts of the town, to bury it under a tree, and to urinate over it. In JAKOBO (Asante) it is believed that if there is a long wait after the first menstruation before marriage, that may lead to barrenness, and consequently early marriages are recommended. Barrenness is also attributed to the activities of a witch, who looks in women's wombs, and eats their unborn children. To avert this, witch-doctors are consulted and sacrifices made. In KOFORIDUA (Asante) herbal remedies are used. Persistent cases are attributed to witchcraft. Married women who are childless may have extra-marital affairs secretly in order to become pregnant. This custom, which 'has become a common practice', is called 'jolly-making', and has extended to some younger married women with children. In APAM (Fante) the wife is usually suspected. Her barrenness may be attributed to physiological causes, to witchcraft (in which case a witch-doctor is consulted) or to pre-marital promiscuity. In GBLEDE (Ewe) sterile men are given medicines and vaccinated by the herbalist, while women are told to keep various taboos. 'In very extreme cases she has to subject herself (especially those whose husbands have divorced them) to being "reinvigorated" by sexual intercourse with the sorcerer.' In CENTRAL ACCRA (Ga) barrenness may be attributed to any of the following causes: (i) witchcraft by evil-minded or jealous persons, in which case recourse is had to a medicine man to prepare counter-spells; (ii) an 'unwholesome life' in youth, during which venereal disease may have affected reproductive capacity, in which case nothing can be done; (iii) infidelity after marriage, in which case the husband may be appeased (since it is the wife's in-infidelity which is thought likely to lead to sterility) by gifts; (iv) not having informed the tribal gods of the marriage according to custom, in which case they may be appeased by suitable ceremonies and offerings; (v) the jealousy of the wife's spirit-husband, in which case ceremonies and sacrificial offerings may be made. The source of childlessness is usually attributed to the wife, rather than to the husband. A popular remedy for barrenness is for the woman to obtain the placenta of a newly-delivered child (which may be had for a penny, or for twopence in the case of a twin), to bury it and then to urinate on its burial place. In KORDIABE (Shai) sterility in men is attributed to evil spirits, or to the effect of jealous spirit-wives. The witch-doctor is consulted, who prescribes vaccination, purification baths, and carries out exorcising rites. In APIREDE (Cherepon) barrenness is attributed to disease, in which case suppositories are prescribed by the herbalist; to witchcraft, in which case various sacrifices are offered; to too many abortions during adolescence; to an abnormal-sized womb; or to indulgence in sexual intercourse before the first menstruation. The *Dwobofo* custom is practised for sterile men, who may also be treated by rectal suppositories if the cause of sterility is believed to be physiological. Barren women are often recommended to buy and bury the placenta of a new-born infant.

While there seems to be some indication that public ceremonies for the treatment of sterility are dying out, the belief in witchcraft as a prime cause of barrenness appears to be both vigorous and widespread. Often childless adults will consult all the various practitioners in the village—herbalist, witch-doctor, fetish priest, cult priest, patent medicine pedlar and hospital clinic—either successively, or at the same time.

Contraception is little practised. It appears to be unknown by the majority of illiterates and is used chiefly by educated persons, and particularly by schoolgirls, who also are said to procure abortions. In many places any attempt to limit the size of the family is regarded as a public offence.[1] However, in cases

[1] Fortes notes that when he told members of the Tallensi tribe 'that Europeans often refrain deliberately from having children, they were either sceptical or appalled', (14) 169. At the same time, a Tallensi woman may try to procure an abortion if she conceives before her youngest child is weaned; see (27) 71.

where a mother habitually undergoes exceptionally difficult and painful delivery, permission may be given by one or both sides of the family for child-bearing to cease after a specified number of children. In such cases, various rites may be performed, herbal potions taken, or complete abstinence may be practised.[1] Also, since it is believed that it is undesirable for children to be born too close together, *coitus interruptus* may be practised by husbands during the early months of nursing, or marital intercourse may be confined at that time to what is believed to be a safe period. An abortion may be procured if a mother becomes pregnant again too soon after the birth of her last child. In polygynous families, a wife who has given birth may not be expected to resume marital intercourse for a year. In monogamous families, three months after the birth of the last child is an often-quoted time for the resumption of intercourse. In MAMPONG (Akwapim) there is no desire to limit the size of the family, though 'what usually happens during the nursing period is that the parents practise what is called the "safe periods". The intercourse takes place on the third or fourth week after the last menstrual flow. No conception is expected at this time.' In BOMPATA (Asante) there was no apparent knowledge of contraceptive techniques among the informants, though there was a vague idea that the herbalist had some potions, believed to have very unpleasant after-effects. The only recognized means of limitation is for a woman's eldest daughter to stand in front of her immediately after her last delivery, and before the navel cord is severed, and to protest. In DWINYAMA (Asante) abortions were sometimes procured by women in the old days, to conceal the results of adultery. 'A knowledge of abortifacients is, as far as I could gather, unknown to the younger people, but some elderly men and several women mentioned seven types obtained from herbs, the most powerful being *sedua sebama*,[2] a kind of herb used to help a woman having a miscarriage.' Contraceptives have been heard of, but it is thought strange that they should be used. 'Nevertheless, two men admitted having practised *coitus interruptus* when their wives were nursing their children.' In JAISI (Asante) in cases of difficult child-birth where the mother's life has been at

[1] Rattray describes an abortifacient used in Ashanti if a pregnant woman's life is in danger; (31) 55.

[2] *Sic; asedua, asebuam?*

stake, and provided the consent of her brother has been obtained, a secret herbal potion is given to the mother, and a blacksmith's hammer is placed lightly on her belly, while an invocation is made to the gods to prevent any further conception. The effect of this remedy is believed to last for life. An abortifacient made from certain leaves is used if pregnancy has occurred too soon after the last birth. In KOMENDA (Fante) contraception is not practised among the illiterate people, but the professional classes use the safe period and contraceptives. In KPANDU (Ewe) 'to limit the family by birth control, the woman has to annoint her forehead with the blood from the placenta and strike the floor with her palm three times, saying that she wants no more children. The husband is then called to shake her and to repeat the same words that he does not want any more children. This ceremony is strongly believed to be a never-failing remedy in stopping child-bearing. Abortion, contraceptive medicines and other crooked ways of birth control are abhorred in the clan and are punishable.' In CENTRAL ACCRA (Ga) a few educated persons, especially schoolgirls, practise contraception. In APIREDE (Cherepon) in cases of difficult labour, and where the consent of the relatives of both sides of the family has been obtained, the family may be limited by (i) sacrifice and libations, (ii) abstinence for three years or (iii) contraceptive tablets or the procuring of an abortion. In LARTEH KUBEASI (Guang) 'the procuring of abortion is a growing evil among schoolgirls in the whole town. Such girls consult dispensers who administer drugs to effect abortion.' Among the DAGABAS 'the idea of limiting the size of the family is entirely foreign; to them it is inconceivable that a married couple should, for economic or personal reasons, deliberately seek to restrict the number of its offspring'.

The attitude towards illegitimacy in Ghana is widely permissive; in many places it is said that, in so far as all the children born in the clan are of equal standing, the word has no meaning. The positive attitude shown towards children in general is extended to those born out of marriage, and in some areas such children are regarded as lucky and well-destined.[1] In many cases, the child of an unmarried girl is adopted by her family or clan.

[1] Manoukian observes that, among the Adangmes, fathers encourage their daughters to have children before they marry, because such children become their property and work on their farms; (25) 108.

The child's father may subsequently claim it; he will then be required to pay the estimated cost of its upbringing so far. The unmarried mother's children who are adopted by members of her clan are treated in all respects the same as other children in the clan, and are not discriminated against in matters of succession and inheritance.[1] Among patrilineal tribes, the 'legitimacy' of a child depends primarily on the mother's having undergone her puberty rites. If she has not done so, her child can never become legitimate by its father's acknowledgement; such a child is openly derided.[2] An unmarried mother may subsequently marry the father of her children, in which case they are regarded as no different from any children she may subsequently have. Alternatively, she may marry another man, who may or may not adopt the children. If he does, he may discriminate against them. The children of a married woman by a lover may be adopted by her husband, on payment of a pacification fee.[3] A man who has children by a woman other than his wife may bring them home to be brought up with his other children. It is generally believed that such children will be discriminated against by their stepmother. Moreover, in a matrilineal tribe, they are not members of their stepmother's clan, and are therefore not entitled to inherit any of the family property. For this reason, their fathers during their lifetime may compensate them with gifts of land and other property. In ABURI (Akwapim) an illegitimate child may be claimed by its father, or alternatively, adopted by the girl's own father or by her maternal uncle. In these last two cases, the child's real father may subsequently claim it by asking pardon, and by repaying the cost of its upbringing. In a family 'all the children are regarded equal'. In TUTU (Akwapim) illegitimate children are often badly treated in their father's home by their step-

[1] Rattray observes that among the Ashantis 'an illegitimate child (by a free woman) will of course always have its mother's *abusua*, and hence may inherit almost equally with a legitimate child'; (29) 39. Fortes agrees that an illegitimate child's status within the *abusua* is secure, but says that it may carry a stigma in later life if its natural father does not acknowledge it as his child at the eighth day out-dooring ceremony; (11) 266. Christensen confirms Fortes's view as also applying to the Fantis; (5) 100. Among the Tallensis, an illegitimate boy may be treated as inferior in the clan in so far as he cannot inherit from his foster-father. In the case of an illegitimate girl, no difficulties arise. See (14) 22-3.

[2] See (9) 23-4.

[3] Tait says that, among the Konkombas, 'children born to a woman by a lover belong to the woman's husband and are accepted by him as his children. I know of no differentiation between children begotten by a lover and those begotten by the husband'; (34) 221.

brothers. They are given small shares of food, and referred to as 'children to be pushed out of the way'. They are not entitled to any claim on the father's property. For these reasons they are often handed over to their father's sister to be looked after, and are 'showered with gifts' during the father's lifetime, to make up for their loss of inheritance. In BENIM (Asante) all children are provided for by their mother's brother, and 'no difference is made between children born outside marriage or inside it', as matrilineal descent is more important than any ties outside the clan. In BEREKUM (Brong) the father of an illegitimate child may exercise some control over it, provided that he makes at least some contribution towards its upbringing, even if it is no more than a token contribution of, for example, one cloth a year. Then no decision affecting the child can be taken without his consent, even if the child's mother has meanwhile married someone else. If the father has made no provision for its upbringing, however, then he loses all right over it. All children are felt to be the responsibility of the maternal uncle, and 'in every home there is scarcely any difference in the attitude of the people towards the legitimate and the illegitimate children'. In APAM (Fante) illegitimate children are accorded full rights with the other children in the family, and are regarded as 'gifts from God'. In GBLEDE (Ewe) the child of an unmarried mother is adopted by her parents unless its father comes to claim it and pays for the cost of its upbringing. In GOVIEFE (Ewe) illegitimate children are regarded as belonging to their natural father, by whom they are treated as equal to their legitimate offspring, though they may be discriminated against by their step-mother. In CHRISTIANSBORG (Ga) the children of an unmarried girl are adopted by her family and named by her father. Even if the father of such illegitimate children is known, he is ignored. Such children are believed to be lucky, and will make good in the world. In the case of a married woman who has a child by a lover, her husband may agree to adopt the child, but he will demand a pacification fee from its father. In KORDIABE (Shai) an unmarried girl's child is adopted by her father; a married woman's child by a lover is adopted by her husband. 'The care for an illegitimate child compares favourably with that given to the real descendants in many families.' In LARTEH KUBEASI (Guang) 'whether the illegitimate child is claimed by the father or left alone with his mother, his position as far as inheritance is concerned, is precarious'. Among the DAGABAS 'there are no special arrangements for illegitimate children, who are called "lovers' children". Public opinion does not attach any stigma either to the "lovers' child" or to the mother. Although the Dagaba disapprove of a girl bearing a child before she is legally married, such a woman would experience no difficulty in obtaining a husband and the children would enjoy the same status as any children in the family unit to which they belong.'

Orphans are almost always adopted by relatives, often their uncles, aunts or grandparents; on the mother's side in matrilineal areas, on the father's side in patrilineal areas, though this is by no means an invariable rule.[1] In almost all areas it is believed that the spirit of the dead parent, particularly that of the mother, is watching to see how the child is treated, and will reward with misfortune and calamities those foster-parents who neglect their charges. For this reason it is often claimed that orphans are better treated than their foster-siblings.[2] Sometimes orphans are given to childless members of the clan to bring up. In cases where only one of a child's parents has died, the child may be claimed by the dead parent's relatives if the surviving parent remarries. In patrilineal tribes, for example, the children of a widow who remarries may be claimed by the dead husband's relatives; sometimes the children are left with their mother until, say, the age of six before they are taken away. Conversely, in matrilineal tribes, the children of a widower are claimed by the dead wife's clan. The responsibility for the upbringing of a dead man's children may fall on the inheritor of his property, who may also be expected to marry his widow.[3] However, in some places this leviratic practice is said to be dying out. Apart from the adoption of the orphans of relatives, and a few cases in which childless relatives may be permitted to

[1] Fortes reports that, among the Ashantis, motherless orphans are generally brought up by the dead mother's sister; (11) 264. Manoukian says that, among the Ewes, such children will be brought up by an aunt on either the father's or the mother's side; (26) 28. Among the Tallensis, very young motherless orphans may be sent to their maternal grandmothers; otherwise they will be brought up by their dead mothers' co-wives; (14) 130.

[2] But the Tallensis say that the lot of an orphan 'is always a hard one. An orphan never receives the devoted attention and the selfless love which can be given only by its own mother.' (14) 130.

[3] Among the Ewes, if a man marries his dead brother's widow, he is expected to adopt her children; see (26) 28. This is also reported of the Kusasis, (32) 385, and the Tallensis, (14) 4-5. According to Fortes, out of a random sample of 111 Tallensi married men, no less than 21 had inherited wives; (14) 71.

adopt clan children, there is virtually no adoption in Ghanaian society. Children are regarded as too valuable for the parents' rights over them ever to be completely abandoned, though children are often lent for shorter or longer periods to help in the house or on the farm of a relative, or as a mark of respect to an elder, or to receive some special kind of training, or to benefit from being brought up in a literate household. Such cases are not of adoption proper, however, but of temporary guardianship.[1] The only exception to the rule of no adoption outside the family is that where certain children are destined for office by virtue of the circumstances of their birth. In Ashanti, for instance, twins are regarded as sacred, girls being trained as wives for the chief, boys as his personal servants. In ABURI (Akwapim) the inheritor of a dead man's property also inherits responsibility for his children. In TUTU (Akwapim) orphans are 'well cared for by either the wife's or the husband's relatives, because it is the general belief that if such children are not well treated the spirit of the dead will let misfortune befall them'. In BOMPATA (Asante) orphans are brought up by the dead mother's relatives, usually her sister. Orphans are treated with great care, since it is believed that kindness to orphans is well rewarded. However, there have been several cases of cruel foster-mothers, especially where the latter already have large families of their own. The responsibility for an orphan's upbringing is inherited along with the dead man's property, but it is said that few inheritors carry out their responsibilities in this direction fully, many contenting themselves with merely giving a few presents at Christmas. In JAISI (Asante) orphans are the responsibility of the dead woman's brother, who will ask a sister or an aunt to look after them. Orphans are usually brought up in ignorance of their true birth, and regarded as the children of their guardians. Fatherless children may be taken on by the dead man's inheritor. The care with which orphans are treated tends to depend upon the closeness of the ties between their guardians and their dead parents. In SUPOWMU DUNKWA (Fante) orphans are well cared for. 'The foster-mother, if she has children of her own, does not differentiate between her own children and the orphan. Often, the orphan may never know that the guardian is not really his or her own mother, and anybody who reveals to the child his real parentage is severely

[1] See below, pages 183-4, for a fuller description of this practice.

reprimanded and scorned for being a gossip-monger.' In GOVIEFE (Ewe) fatherless children are adopted by the dead man's relatives. His widow may be marries by his brother. Orphans are well looked after, for fear of the dead mother's spirit. In DOME (Ga) orphans are taken over by members of their father's family. They are often given to childless women to look after. In AGOMANYA (Krobo) orphans belong to their father's family. Hence, if a widowed mother remarries, the younger brother of her first husband will claim the children, though he may wait until they are six. Great care is taken of orphans for fear of the anger of their dead mother's spirit. In LARTEH KUBEASI (Guang) a dead man's heir inherits also his widow and children. A child whose mother dies within seven days of child-birth is expelled from the town, from fear of the local fetish. Fortunately, there lives on the outskirts of the town a good woman, Madam Akosua Ansaa, who has made it her duty to adopt such expelled children and look after them in addition to her own children. This she has been doing for the last thirty years.

CHAPTER THREE

ATTITUDES TOWARDS PREGNANCY

> 'It is abominable to expect the outcome of an event so dangerous and uncertain.'

PREGNANCY is universally regarded throughout Ghana as a joyous event, though any joyous feelings on the part of the pregnant woman herself may be tempered as time goes on, particularly in the case of a first baby, with anxiety regarding the approaching delivery. Child-birth is thought of as so beset with dangers, both physical and supernatural, that during the process the woman is often said to lie 'between life and death'. And to the natural anxiety at an event with so uncertain an outcome is attributed the irritability which everywhere in Ghana is said to be characteristic of pregancy. In MAMPONG (Akwapim) anxiety is said to be the typical state of mind of pregnant women. In TUTU (Akwapim) their thoughts are dominated by the fear of child-birth, 'which is assumed a great struggle between life and death'. In DWINYAMA (Asante) the pregnant women rejoices for her lineage, and she anticipates with pleasure the praise she will receive from both her own and her husband's clans. In GBLEDE (Ewe) pregnant women are anxious and irritable, a state which is often made worse by the jealousy of their co-wives. In TEMA (Ga) the pregnant woman 'rejoices over the fact that she will be honoured as a begetter of children and not scorned'. She is expected to be very irritable and impatient. In KORDIABE (Shai) pregnant women are happy when they are first pregnant. In the third or fourth month they become gloomy and irritable; later they are depressed and bully their children. By the ninth month they have become happy again. In WINNEBA (Efutu) the initial happiness is succeeded by anxiety and irascibility. Among the ISALAS 'the typical feeling of a pregnant woman is one of happy expectation of a child if she has been faithful to her husband. If she should have had sexual intercourse with any other man, then there is fear of hardship or even death at birth.'

Innumerable precautions are taken by the pregnant woman to guard against illness, bad luck, witchcraft, the resentment of spirits and gods and the evil practices of ill-wishers. These precautions range from certain foods and activities to be avoided, well-known to everyone, to various herbal and ritual prescriptions taken under the instructions of a herbalist, witch-doctor or fetish priest. Various changes in diet are recommended; the most widely cited being an avoidance of sweet foods, such as sugar-cane, mangoes and ripe plantains, which are believed to cause miscarriage, particularly in the early months of pregnancy.[1] Certain foods are avoided because of their supposed effect on the growing embryo; eating fresh snails, for instance, is widely believed to lead to the birth of a baby with a slimy mouth. Special soups or stews, made from a mystical number of ingredients, are often prescribed. Food fads are widely recognized, and a liking during pregnancy for the white clay used in building appears to be widespread. In APA (Asante) pregnant women have food fads, including the eating of white clay. They should not eat ripe plantains, for fear of a miscarriage. Monkey and rabbit meat are to be avoided, lest the baby looks like a monkey or has rabbit's ears. In BOMPATA (Asante) pregnant women may eat rats, mice and white clay. They should not eat in public, and should also avoid eating from a cooking pot, which might lead to the baby's having convulsions. A special soup made with seven times seven nuts is often prescribed by the herbalist, as is also meat of the heads of mudfish; this latter dish is believed to result in the baby's head being flat like that of the mudfish—a widely admired shape in Ashanti. In BOSOFO (Asante) rats, mice, squirrels, snakes and clay are among the food fads recognized. Palm-nut soup made with seven times three nuts or nine times three nuts, seven peppers, smoked fish, dried snails, green herbs and fufu[2] are

[1] This is confirmed of the Ashantis by Rattray; (31) 54. Fortes mentions honey as one of the foods to be avoided by a pregnant Tallensi woman, otherwise the baby will be born with a catarrhal snuffle; (14) 166; see also (15) 273. Honey is also forbidden among the Birifors; (27) 69.

[2] Fufu is made from yam, cocoyam or plantain, first boiled and then pounded into a thick, glutinous paste.

all recommended dishes. Pregnant women must not allow anyone else to share their meals, and they should finish everything set before them. They should not eat mushrooms, lest the child be born with a large navel. Pawpaws should not be eaten in public, and plantains and roasted groundnuts should be avoided. In KPANDU (Ewe) among the foods prohibited to pregnant women are hedgehog meat (which causes the baby to be born with a soft skull and a wide fontanelle), honey (which may close the baby's nostrils), too much beef (which might lead to excess of phlegm in the baby's nose) and monkey meat. In APIREDE (Cherepon) the food fads of pregnant women include a liking for building clay. They should not eat groundnuts, ripe plantains (which may weaken the child), pineapples (which remove the child's skin) or chew sugar-cane (which might cause a miscarriage). Among the ISALAS 'since pregnancy is not regarded as something extraordinary, the pregnant woman is not given any special diet and she feeds with the other females in the large family'.

In nearly all the areas studied, women are urged to carry on with their normal domestic duties throughout pregnancy. This is believed to ensure an easy delivery and a strong, active child, just as idleness is believed to lead to a difficult labour and a weak, lazy child. In some areas, however, strenuous or violent exertions are to be avoided. Certain tasks should not be undertaken for fear of their sympathetic or magical effect; no pregnant woman, for example, should help another pregnant woman with her head-load, for fear that the latter's misfortunes will be transferred to the helper. Splitting firewood is widely thought to lead to the baby being born with a very soft skull, or a wide fontanelle. A pregnant woman's body, particularly in later pregnancy, is said to become very hot; for this reason, she should not make matters worse by working near a large fire. In MAMPONG (Akwapim) pregnant women should carry on with their domestic duties to strengthen the muscles and ensure an easy delivery. In TUTU (Akwapim) they work hard after the first two months of pregnancy. Firewood should not be split with an axe, lest the baby's head be born split open. Pregnant women should avoid helping others to lift up their head-loads, and they should not fire pots nor burn weeds. In JAKOBO (Asante) pregnant women should work hard to ensure an easy delivery and a strong baby, but they should avoid lifting heavy things during the first three months of pregnancy, and not wash clothes nor use laundry blue, which might turn the baby blue. They should not split firewood, nor use oil for frying (or the baby will be born with black patches on its skin), nor nurse anyone with a sore (or their own birth sores will be long in healing). If a pregnant woman carries vegetables and other things purchased in the market, the child is likely to turn out a thief. In VAKPO (Ewe) hard work is said to ensure a strong baby and an easy delivery. In AYIKAI DOBORO (Ga) they should carry on with their domestic work to ensure an easy delivery. They should not split firewood in the open, however, lest they are seen by a sorcerer, which might lead to the baby's head being split open at birth. To wash clothing in the open is believed to turn the unborn baby blue, and lead to its death. Care should be taken not to use a new earthenware pot, lest the baby be born with black marks on its skin. Fowls and game should not be prepared by pregnant women, or they may die in child-birth. A pregnant woman should particularly avoid helping another pregnant woman to carry her head-load, for if the latter has not taken the proper precautions to ensure an easy delivery, her misfortunes may be communicated to the helper, who will have a miscarriage. Among the ISALAS a pregnant woman 'is supposed to go about her duties normally. The local midwives insist upon this and their reason being that it reduces the amount of bleeding during child-birth. From about the seventh month of pregnancy and onwards, the expectant mother is not allowed to do hard work. She should not lift heavy weights nor should she bend downwards and remain in that position for a long time.'

The wearing of new or gorgeous clothes during pregnancy is often discouraged, and pregnant women should leave off their jewellery and ornaments. Care is taken by a pregnant woman not to expose her belly or breasts, for fear a witch-doctor might be looking and thereby cause a difficult delivery. In TUTU (Akwapim) pregnant women dress shabbily and leave off their jewellery, for fear of exciting the jealousy of the spirits of women who have died in child-birth. In BOSOFO (Asante) pregnant women should cover their breasts and bellies in public, lest their babies get ill, or they have a miscarriage. They should not wear gold ornaments or beautiful clothes, partly because it is a solemn time when vanity is inappropriate, and partly because the excessive heat from a pregnant woman's body wears out clothes more quickly. In BEREKUM (Brong) pregnant women keep their bellies and breasts covered, lest they be seen by a witch-doctor, which might result in their having a miscarriage. In APIREDE (Cherepon) to dress up while pregnant is an invitation to evil spirits.

The attitude towards marital intercourse during pregnancy varies. In many places it is believed to be beneficial, since it widens the birth passage, and since the semen is thought to be important or even essential for the well-being of the unborn child. For these reasons, unmarried girls who become pregnant may be allowed to have their lovers to stay with them until their confinement. It is often said that pregnancy is accompanied by increased sexual desire, particularly in the early months. It is also said that husbands sometimes find intercourse with their pregnant wives unpleasant. In a few places, however, marital intercourse is thought undesirable during pregnancy, or even harmful, especially in the early months, when it might lead to a miscarriage. The attitude towards its cessation also varies; in some areas marital intercourse continues until delivery, in others it ceases after the sixth month. Adultery during pregnancy, either by the husband or the wife, is generally regarded as more serious than at other times;[1] one reason is that it is thought that the embryo's development may be harmed by contact with a different semen. Husbands who commit adultery during their wives' pregnancies, are expected to allow one or two days to elapse before resuming marital intercourse. In BANKO (Asante) marital intercourse is considered important for the formation of the baby, and also to keep the birth passage open, especially with a first baby. Care must be taken during the ninth month, however. In BOMPATA (Asante) pregnant women have an increased desire for sexual intercourse, especially up to the sixth or seventh month. It is believed that it is good for the unborn child, hence divorces are postponed if the wife is pregnant, and lovers are permitted to visit girls whom they have

[1] Rattray notes that among the Isalas, although it is a recognized institution for a wife to have a lover, the fact being well known to her husband, who refers openly to the man as ' my wife's lover', once a woman has become pregnant she may not have sexual intercourse with anyone except her own husband. Should she do so, it is supposed that she will have difficulty in bringing forth, unless she confesses; (32) 497-8. Among the Ashantis it is thought that if a woman who commits adultery during pregnancy does not confess, it may result in miscarriage or even death; (31) 55.

made pregnant, even if they are married men, and anyone who tries to prevent their doing so is condemned. Adultery with a pregnant woman is considered a very serious offence, almost tantamount to murder, since it will probably lead to the death of the child. Fines ranging between £40 and £100 may be imposed, in addition to one or more sheep. In DWINYAMA (Asante) it is said that sexual intercourse is essential for the well-being of the child. The semen acts as a lubricant and eases delivery; it is also necessary for the strength of the baby. In BEREKUM (Brong) 'marital intercourse is considered indispensable during the prenatal period', otherwise the mother may have a difficult delivery, and a husband who refuses may be fined or divorced, up to the eighth month. In GOVIEFE (Ewe) marital intercourse continues until the seventh or eighth month. The semen is belived to be good for the unborn child, and hence an unmarried girl who is pregnant is allowed to have her lover to stay. In TESHIE (Ga) pregnant women have strong sexual demands 'and are a source of worry to husbands. This was confirmed by many of the men.' Some confine their sexual activities to the first three months of pregnancy; others continue until delivery. Many cases were reported in which intercourse had taken place less than twenty-four hours before delivery. In APIREDE (Cherepon) sexual intercourse is avoided in the early weeks of pregnancy to avoid a miscarriage. After three months, it is allowed. Some believe that the semen is good for the unborn child, and hence intercourse often continues until the day of delivery, and unmarried girls are allowed to visit their lovers if they are pregnant. Among the DAGABAS 'it is taboo for a pregnant woman to commit adultery'.

Various other taboos concerning pregnancy are widespread, the most often reported being: for the pregnant woman not to look at ugly animals or things, or deformed persons, lest the baby resembles them;[1] not to allow anyone to pass behind her, or jump over her legs, while sitting down, which might lead to a miscarriage or difficult delivery; to avoid quarrelling; to have nothing to do with wounds, corpses and suicides;[2] and to respect her husband's totemic taboos.[3] The consultation of

[1] Mentioned also by Rattray, of the Ashantis, (31) 54, and by Field, of the Gas, (8) 165.

[2] The sight of blood is mentioned by Rattray, (31) 54, as something to be avoided.

[3] Confirmed by Fortes, of the Ashantis, (11) 267, and by Christensen, of the Fantis, (5) 83.

herbalists, witch-doctors and fetish priests by or on behalf of pregnant women appears to be very widespread in Ghana. These prescribe vaccinations,[1] herbal baths, enemas and potions, and provide magic amulets to be worn. One prescription against witches is for the pregnant woman to bathe in water to which has been added fragments of every possible foodstuff.[2] Among some tribes of the Northern Territories, no one should mention the fact of her pregnancy to a woman until she has been ceremonially splashed with water by a relative.[3] Various taboos relating to diet, clothing and behaviour are also prescribed. In ABURI (Akwapim) pregnant women are vaccinated to ensure good health during pregnancy, and various rites are performed. They should not quarrel, and should sit against a wall in case a bad child should walk behind them. No one should jump over their legs while they are sitting down. In BENIM (Asante) pregnant women are advised to keep within their compounds as much as possible, and to avoid travel and public ceremonies. They should not quarrel with their husbands, nor think evil of others, particularly their co-wives. The sight of blood should be avoided, for fear of a miscarriage, and so should ugly people and monkeys, lest the baby look like one. The herbalist prescribes vaccinations and amulets. In DWINYAMA (Asante) a pregnant wife does not make any preparations for the baby, as 'it is abominable to expect the outcome of an event so dangerous and uncertain'. She is kind to beggars, lest they are gods in disguise sent to tempt her. She does not allow anyone to pass behind her, nor to jump over her legs while she is sitting down. She is vaccinated, and various herbal mixtures are prescribed for use as medicines, enemas, douches and ointments. In JAKOBO (Asante) anyone who tells a pregnant woman to her face that she is pregnant may be held responsible for her miscarriage, and fined. She should avoid seeing monkeys, deformed persons or badly-carved statuettes, for fear the child is born deformed. A beautifully-shaped doll, *akua ba*, is worn to ensure the child's beauty of form. She should always sit on a stool and never squat, or the baby will have a perpetual head cold. She should not quarrel with her husband, nor lie on her face nor on her back. She is vaccinated and given amulets to wear. In KPANDU (Ewe)

[1] It should be noted that, here and elsewhere in this book, by 'vaccination' is meant the application of a local medicine to cuts, usually made on the joints.
[2] Mentioned by Field; (8) 164.
[3] Noted of the Dagabas and the Isalas by Rattray; (32) 417 and 497.

a pregnant woman should not allow her tears to fall on her belly, or she will have a miscarriage. People should be prevented from stepping over her legs. The witch-doctor is consulted for taboos and other prescriptions. In AYIKAI DOBORO (Ga) no preparations are made for the coming baby, or it may not survive. The pregnant woman is careful not to sit in the unswept yard in the morning after rising, or the birth will surely be delayed. Herbal baths and various potions are prescribed by the herbalists, and it is said that all women in this district follow these prescriptions. In TESHIE (Ga) a pregnant woman takes a special bath, to which pinches of every possible kind of food have been added, in order to preserve her from witches, who feed on the spirits of unborn children. While a child inherits the soul of an ancestor, its physical appearance depends upon chance factors. Hence the pregnant woman is careful not to look at ugly animals such as pigs and monkeys, or the child may resemble one. Similarly if she sees a furry animal, the baby will be born hairy. She should be the first in the house to have her bath, or she may catch the complaints of those who have bathed before her. She should sit with her back against a wall, lest someone walk behind her, in which case her child may turn out wicked. No one should step over her while she is lying down, or his misfortunes may become hers. Among the DAGABAS 'dancing, running and tree-climbing are forbidden, and mothers are discouraged from looking at ugly animals such as monkeys, or at ugly persons such as hunchbacks, or from crossing their shadows else they may bear distorted children'. With a first pregnancy it is taboo to mention a woman's pregnancy to her, and she must pretend to be ignorant of it, until a custom of pouring cold water over her has been performed. This is done during the night by the relative appointed for the purpose, who hides behind the door and pours water over the pregnant woman who is enticed out of her bedroom with some fictitious story. 'At an advanced stage of her pregnancy, a woman may use some black concoction as a protection against evil eyes and bad mouths. Some women consult soothsayers continually to inquire what sacrifices are required by the earth-god or the ancestral spirits to facilitate prompt and easy delivery.'

The pregnant woman's husband is expected to ensure that she carries out the various instructions, to satisfy her sexual demands and to avoid quarrelling with her; he may also perform special rites.[1] In TUTU (Akwapim) quarrels with the pregnant woman are avoided. Her husband takes care not to commit adultery, lest the baby be contaminated. In BANKO (Asante) the husband avoids provoking or beating his pregnant wife. He also drinks the powder used to vaccinate her, in a glass of whisky. In JAKOBO (Asante) a pregnant woman's husband takes special care not to eat foods tabooed by his *ntoro*, nor to have sexual intercourse on the same day with his wife as with another woman. In CENTRAL ACCRA (Ga) a pregnant woman's husband may take on him minor ailments for her. She transfers these to him by stepping over him while he lies in bed in the morning. Feelings of somnolence and lethargy may also be passed on in this way, and for this reason drowsy men are often asked if their wives are pregnant. Among the ISALAS, after the water pouring ceremony has been performed, another ceremony is held in which boys from both the woman's and her husband's families wrestle, and gifts are exchanged. At the wrestling, the husband's family contestant always succeeds in winning the fight. 'From this time onwards the husband is prohibited from destroying the life of any animal or insect. Even if he sees a snake coming into the house he must call someone else to kill it. It is believed if he kills any animal or insect his wife will give birth to a dead baby. If, however, he is a hunter, he is permitted to kill bush animals with his gun. In such a case he eats the boiled liver and intestines of the animal with a mixture of medicine with his pregnant wife.'

[1] One such Ashanti rite is described by Rattray, (29) 50-2; a rite for Ga men of rank is described by Field, (8) 162-3. Various activities, such as cutting a new bush farm, hunting certain animals, participating in funeral rites, are prohibited to husbands of pregnant women in the Tallensi and Gurensi tribes; (27) 70.

CHAPTER FOUR

CHILD-BIRTH

'The stranger who has come, his back is towards the darkness. Amen. His face is towards the light. Amen.'[1]

THE period of confinement is regarded by everyone in Ghana as a solemn and anxious time. As has been said before, a woman in labour is said 'to lie between life and death'. In some places, women are urged to bear their pains with fortitude, and it is considered humiliating to cry out.[2] In ABURI (Akwapim) 'the labour pains should be borne courageously without telling anybody at first till it is really time for the child to come. She should not shout for pain when the child is coming. If she does it shows her weakness; besides, strangers like the Ewes do that and as a result lose their self respect.' In BENIM (Asante) excessive pains and a difficult delivery are attributed to infidelity. Her husband or father may be brought into the room if labour pains are prolonged. The husband pats her belly, and says: 'If you are my child, come forth'. If delivery is still delayed, adultery is suspected, and the wife is urged to confess, so that the child may be born. In JAISI (Asante) prolonged labour is attributed to infidelity, and the woman is urged to confess in order to lessen her pains and bring about the child's birth. In VAKPO (Ewe) 'the period of labour is regarded as the most critical period in the life of a woman'. A woman who dies in child-birth or within eight days is accorded a disgraceful death. In AYIKAI DOBORO (Ga) a woman is said to lie between life and death during the period of her confinement. All her friends and relatives are anxious about the outcome; her husband is said often to absent

[1] From a chant given by Field in (8) 172.
[2] Fortes notes the solicitude of Tallensi husbands for their wives in labour; (14) 164.

D

himself from the scene to save himself the anxiety of it. In TESHIE (Ga) it is said that if a woman in labour calls out the name of the child's father, it will move towards the birth passage. This belief is often used in cases of disputed paternity, when the child may not move until several names have been called. Women are sometimes gagged during their confinements by relatives to prevent disclosures. It is believed that children conceived in adultery are born only after a prolonged and difficult labour. Among the ISALAS 'the whole family is plunged into a state of terrifying suspense during labour pains. The suspense is so great that no food is prepared for the rest of the family until the woman gives birth. The elderly people in the family remain outside in front of the compound with solemn faces. They remain outside even throughout the night if labour should continue overnight.'

Difficult or protracted labour is widely attributed to the woman's infidelity to her husband, and the universally-accepted remedy is for her to make a confession.[1] In some cases, if the woman is obstinate, the names of suspected lovers will be recited by the midwife, and the man whose name is being uttered when the child is finally delivered, is assumed to be its father. Generally, however, delivery is said to follow the husband's forgiveness after his wife has made her confession. Various other devices are used, partly to alleviate the pains, but mostly to hasten the process of delivery; these include drugs, ointments, purges and blowing into an empty bottle. The midwife sometimes assists delivery by thrusting her hand into the woman's vagina to see if the child is stuck, or by pulling it forth as soon as its head appears. There is some evidence of attendance at hospitals and clinics, though often this is regarded as a last resort in difficult cases, when other methods have failed. In TUTU (Akwapim) palm soup and kernels are given to the woman shortly before delivery is expected, to ensure an easy birth. In a case of protracted delivery, medicine is given, or the mid-

[1] Rattray notes that among the Ashantis resort is made to confession by pregnant women whose labour is prolonged, if herbal remedies fail, (31) 57-8; this is confirmed of the Fantis by Christensen, (5) 83. Rattray says that, among the Birifors (Lobers) it is believed that a woman who has been unfaithful to her husband and has not confessed, will die in child-birth, (32) 438, and this belief is widespread in Ghana. Field says of the Gas that 'an adulterous woman enters her confinement in secret terror', and she describes a confinement which she attended in which the woman, after being in labour for about a week, eventually confessed to having committed incest with her brother, after which confession the child was almost immediately delivered; (8) 168-9.

wife will feel for the child and pull it out. Alternatively a fetish priest may be sent for as an oracle, to hear confessions of adultery. In BOSOFO (Asante) in cases of difficult delivery, the pregnant woman is given a medicine, which is squeezed into two tiny cuts on the forehead, and then drunk. Her husband makes presents of gold nuggets and pieces of white calico, which are placed before the woman. The child is then told to come out for these presents. If these measures fail, the woman is urged to disclose the names of the lovers she had during her pregnancy. If she refuses, the midwife addresses the womb, saying, 'If your father is So-and-So, then come out', running through a list of all the possible fathers. He whose name is pronounced when the child is delivered is assumed to be its real father. Nowadays, however, difficult cases are often rushed to Mampong Maternity Hospital. In JAKOBO (Asante) a difficult delivery may be attributed either to cruelty on the part of the husband's *ntoro*, in which case herbal remedies are applied, or to adultery, in which case confession must be made. In GBLEDE (Ewe) in cases of difficult delivery, the woman is given a bottle to blow into, or she is forced to vomit by having a hand or stick thrust down her throat. In TEMA (Ga) the liquid strained from an infusion of silk cotton tree leaves is given to the woman in labour to drink, and various medicines are smeared on her belly to facilitate delivery. An enema is given. In TESHIE (Ga) to place a fishing net and a grinding stone in the doorway of a woman in labour prevents any abdominal pains possessed by other women entering the room from passing into the pregnant woman's body. If birth looks difficult, one of the midwife's first remedies is to fetch a broom and sweep her body clean of evil influences. Some women are given castor oil or pawpaw root boiled in water. A bottle is provided for the woman to blow into during labour. In APIREDE (Cherepon) medicines are given to hasten delivery. Prolonged cases are attributed to adultery, and the woman urged to confess.

Delivery takes place at the woman's house, or in her mother's house, or in the midwife's house. In Ashanti there is a tendency for women to return to their clan homes for their confinements, often several weeks before delivery is due.[1] The reason usually

[1] According to Rattray, Ashanti women return to their clan homes for their confinements at about the eighth month of pregnancy. (31) 56. That women return to their mothers' homes for their confinement is confirmed of the Ashantis by Fortes, (13) 63; of the Fantis by Christensen, (5) 83; and of the Gas by Field (8)

given for this is that, should a deformed child be born, it can be destroyed without it being known outside the clan.[1] Formerly, the woman was delivered by her mother, or by another old woman of the family; nowadays there is a growing tendency for the village midwife to be called in. She is not necessarily a qualified midwife, however, and may even be a male herbalist. In any case, the herbalist is usually sent for in difficult cases. Even if the woman's mother does not act as midwife, she is usually present to assist, and so are one or two other female relatives.[2] If labour is prolonged, the husband is sent for to hear the woman's confession. Apart from him and the herbalist, men are usually excluded from the birthroom,[3] as are also children and young women who have not yet borne children. In cases of difficult delivery, however, the room may quickly fill with various persons, some to give professional advice, others to hear the confession and some simply to avoid accusations of witch-craft. In MAMPONG (Akwapim) pregnant women are sent to live with their mothers two or three months before delivery is due, partly on account of bashfulness in the presence of a pregnant woman's mother-in-law, which might impede delivery, and partly in case the child should prove to be deformed, which fact would have to be concealed from her husband's family. The midwife and the woman's mother deliver the child. In BOMPATA (Asante) delivery formerly took place in the bathroom, or on the porch, but nowadays a bedroom is prepared. The woman is attended by a midwife, her mother and two or three helpers. In cases of difficult delivery, the husband is called in to forgive her if she should confess to adultery. If

169. On the other hand, Manoukian says that the belief that a child should be born under the roof of its father is general throughout the Northern Territories, though occasionally among the Dagabas pregnant women go to their mothers' homes for their confinement. Among the Tallensis and the Gurensis it is taboo for a child to be born in its maternal grandfather's house, (27) 70; this is confirmed (of the Tallensis) by Fortes, (14) 28-9. Among the Kusasis, a woman takes care not to be confined inside a room, according to Rattray; (32) 386. Tait says that, among the Konkombas, children are born in their mothers' rooms near a ritual hole in the floor, into which young children urinate, and into which the birth blood is allowed to flow; (34) 335.

[1] Confirmed of the Ashantis by Rattray; (31) 56. Among the Gas, a woman returns to her mother's home because 'it would not be seemly for her mother-in-law to assist at the birth', according to Field; (8) 169. Among the Tallensis, women deliver their children in their husbands' homes so that the spirits of the paternal ancestors may guard them; (14) 28-9.

[2] Among the Gurensis and the Tallensis, the pregnant woman's own relatives are not allowed to be present during her confinement, and she is attended by her mother-in-law and other female relatives of her husband; (27) 70.

[3] Confirmed of the Ashantis by Rattray; (31) 56.

delivery is prolonged, everyone collects in the room, as exclusion from it is tantamount to an accusation of witch-craft. In JAISI (Asante) birth takes place in the woman's home. She is attended by the village midwife, and other old women, who have the task of holding her by the arms and waist. She is urged to bear down, and beaten if she refuses. The woman is then given a bottle to blow into, to deliver the placenta. Infants who have not cut their teeth are not allowed to be present at birth, as it is believed that they can communicate with unborn babies, and tell them the troubles of this world. This would lead to difficult labour. Women who have never given birth are not allowed to be present, for fear they are scared. Only close relatives are allowed in, in case a monstrosity is born, which must be hushed up. In KOFORIDUA (Asante) delivery usually takes place in the woman's mother's house, though in some cases the husband may invite his mother-in-law to come and live with them for the purpose. 'Nowadays the tendency is for many of the women to attend the child welfare clinic or maternity hospital during pregnancy and child-birth.' A few women relatives attend during delivery; 'the mother in most cases acts as the midwife'. In SUPOWMU DUNKWA (Fante) the woman does not normally go to her mother's house. 'There is no qualified midwife in the village, and babies are normally delivered by an experienced old woman in the family, or the patient's mother, who in any case is usually present to assist.' In GBLEDE (Ewe) delivery takes place wherever the pregnant woman finds herself; at home or on the farm. 'The ideal even at home is for a woman to bring forth quietly on her own.' However, she is usually attended by her mother, a midwife, the medicine man, and close female relatives. Her husband is brought in if there is a crisis. In CHRISTIANSBORG (Ga) the pregnant woman is delivered in her own family house, and is usually attended by a trained midwife. Formerly, children were delivered by the old woman of the family. In LARTEH KUBEASI (Guang) the woman is attended by a midwife, her mother and one or two others. 'If the labour is prolonged, the attendants become alarmed and very soon many people flock to the place of delivery.' Among the ISALAS 'at birth, the midwife, who is generally an old lady, with two or three elderly women, is present in the room with the expectant mother. The midwife is not trained for her work but has learned her art through the experience of child-bearing herself. Birth may take place in any room in the large family compound. As soon as the child is born, one of the women assisting the midwife gives an alarm in the form of a yell—a sound very much like the whistling of a train—announcing the arrival of the child. And one of the women goes out to the men waiting outside the compound and informs the father of the sex of his new-born baby.'

The birth of deformed children is generally regarded as inauspicious; children with six fingers on a hand were instanced in many of the villages studied. Formerly, the practice in most areas has been to destroy such children; nowadays in some villages they are allowed to survive after the superfluous digit has been amputated; they continue to be regarded as unlucky, however.[1] Abnormal positions in delivery, such as limb-foremost, are also said in some areas to be ill-omened.[2] In ABURI (Akwapim) children born with six fingers were formerly destroyed at birth. Nowadays the extra finger is cut off, but they continue to be regarded as ill-omened. Similarly, a child who is born arm- or leg-first is regarded as unlucky and is never loved, and may even not be named. In BENIM (Asante) deformed children are thrown away. 'The toes and fingers are counted. In some families, the child is thrown away if they see that it has got more than five fingers or toes on each limb. Other people nowadays just cut off the extra fingers or toes and keep the baby.' A child born with a closed anus is also destroyed; hence care is taken to ensure that the child's anus is open at birth. Children born buttocks first are expected to die; cases in which a child's arm or leg is delivered first are believed to involve certain death of both mother and child. Normal birth involves a delivery head first, with the child in a praying position, as God has asked, 'What are you going to do in the world?' and the child thus answers, 'I am going to pray'. In OTROWE (Adangme) if the baby has six fingers on one hand, or is born with teeth, or has a long body like a snake, it is not fed and allowed to die.

[1] Rattray mentions traditions of women having given birth to children with such deformities as six toes, three breasts, or to hermaphrodites; all such would be destroyed at birth; (31) 56. Among the Isalas, according to Rattray, children born with teeth, or with one eye or ear, were formerly killed. Children with six fingers are supposed to become hunters when they grow up; (32) 499. Among the Dagabas, a child born with any teeth has them pulled out before the father sees them; (32) 417-8.

[2] Rattray says that, among the Dagabas, it is thought unlucky for a child to be delivered feet first; (32) 417.

Safely delivered, the child is slapped or splashed with cold water to make it cry; if this fails, peppers may be rubbed over its body, and a basin beaten over its head. Importance is attached in several areas to the placenta; the mother is often not allowed to see the baby until it has been delivered, and sometimes it is said that if it is not safely buried, the child will become a vagabond. Alternatively, it may be sold to a barren woman.[1] Great importance is attached to the newly-delivered infant's first bath, as it is believed that the birth-odour will persist throughout life if not removed on this occasion. Hence, the first bath may be given three times, or the baby may be rubbed down with kerosene.[2] Another precaution widely taken is the 'clearing' of the baby's throat by giving it a few sips of gin or rum or lime juice.[3] Among the Ashantis the shape of the head is considered an important criterion of beauty, and infants of both sexes have their heads shaped with hot towels by the midwife immediately after birth, and daily for several weeks thereafter. The limbs of infants are massaged and stretched to ensure their strength. Most babies are also vaccinated[4] by the herbalist against convulsions and other misfortunes. In ABURI (Akwapim) the baby is carefully bathed to prevent a body odour that will last throughout life. Its head is shaped by the midwife. 'As soon as the child is born he should cry. If he fails to do this he is slapped. If that also fails, pepper and ginger are ground together and applied to the body. He is then put under a big basin or pan, and the back of the bowl beaten very hard till

[1] See page 29 above. Rattray notes that, among the Ashantis, the placenta is thrown away on the midden; (31) 57. Among the Gas, according to Field, the placenta is buried in the bath-house; a barren woman who then urinates on it will become pregnant; (8) 169. Rattray says that, among the Gurensis, the placenta is placed in a pot and buried at the foot of the kitchen midden, (32) 133; that, among the Kusasis, it is buried in a pot on the compound farm, and covered by another pot, (32) 386; that, among the Birifors (Lobers), it is burned outside, (32) 438; and that among the Dagabas, it is put in a pot and buried behind the compound, (32) 418.

[2] Rattray notes that the Ashantis believe that new-born infants should not be bathed with water that has been boiled; (29) 54. Among persons of rank in the Ga tribe, it may be necessary for a new-born infant to have a special herbal bath, prescribed by the herbalist; (8) 169-70. A course of extremely hot baths, for both mother and child, is regarded as conducive to good health during the days following confinement in many parts of Ghana; Fortes records the practice among the Tallensis, (14) 166-7. Manoukian notes the bathing of a new-born infant among the Ewes in a 'leafy concoction' to protect it from witches and sorcerers; (26) 42.

[3] Confirmed of the Ashantis by Rattray; (31) 57. Among the Tallensis, some of the very hot herbal water used to bathe infants is forced down their throats, and this is thought to be very important, according to Fortes; (14) 166-7.

[4] That is, a dried and ground herb is rubbed into cuts made on the forehead and joints.

he begins to cry.' In BENIM (Asante) a premature baby is bathed in hot water. All children are bathed carefully after birth, and their limbs are rubbed with a towel to strengthen them. The mouth is washed out by the midwife with her fingers, and the back of the throat touched with gin or rum to clear it. It is vaccinated to avoid the influence of evil spirits. In JAISI (Asante) a newly-born child is given pepper fumes to inhale if it fails to breathe; its body is rubbed with pepper if it does not cry. It is then thoroughly washed with kerosene and palm-oil, and its navel dressed. The placenta is thrown on the women's latrine if it is a girl, on the men's if a boy; otherwise the child will become a vagrant. It is vaccinated on the forehead and joints, and given medicine made with gin and the herbs which have been carried in the waist-band of its mother during her pregnancy. In SUPOWMU DUNKWA (Fante) the newly-born baby is very carefully bathed, otherwise it will have a foul odour that will last throughout its life. It is vaccinated. The placenta is buried to prevent white ants from eating it, and giving the child stomach pains. In GBLEDE (Ewe) the placenta is buried under a long-living tree. During child-birth, the father takes a compulsory three day holiday, lest he should cut a worm while tilling the soil, and by so doing prevent the navel from healing. In CENTRAL ACCRA (Ga) the child is slapped at birth to make it cry. The navel cord is dressed with a paste made from ground snail-shells and kernel oil. The new-born baby is washed very thoroughly, especially its orifices, to clear away the bad smell, which otherwise will persist all its life. The placenta is buried. After its first bath, the baby is powdered with its mother's old chewing-sponges. In APIREDE (Cherepon) if the baby does not cry at birth, it is given a cold water douche, a bowl is beaten over its head and its body rubbed with ginger. It is then bathed three times, and its throat cleared with lime juice or diluted rum.

It is widely believed among people in Ghana that a newborn baby may in fact be a spirit-child, and not a human child at all. If it is a spirit, it will return to the world of spirits before a week is out, so for the first seven days after the birth[1] the

[1] In the Northern Territories this period varies; among the Birifors (Lobers) it is six days, (32) 438; among the Dagabas, three days, (32) 418; among the Isalas, it is three days for a boy, four for a girl, (32) 498. According to Manoukian, three days for a boy and four for a girl is the custom throughout the Northern Territories, with the exception of the Walas, among whom the child comes out on the seventh day; (27) 71.

Attitudes of parents. 1. Maternal pride in Lawra.

2. Paternal pride in Bowiri.

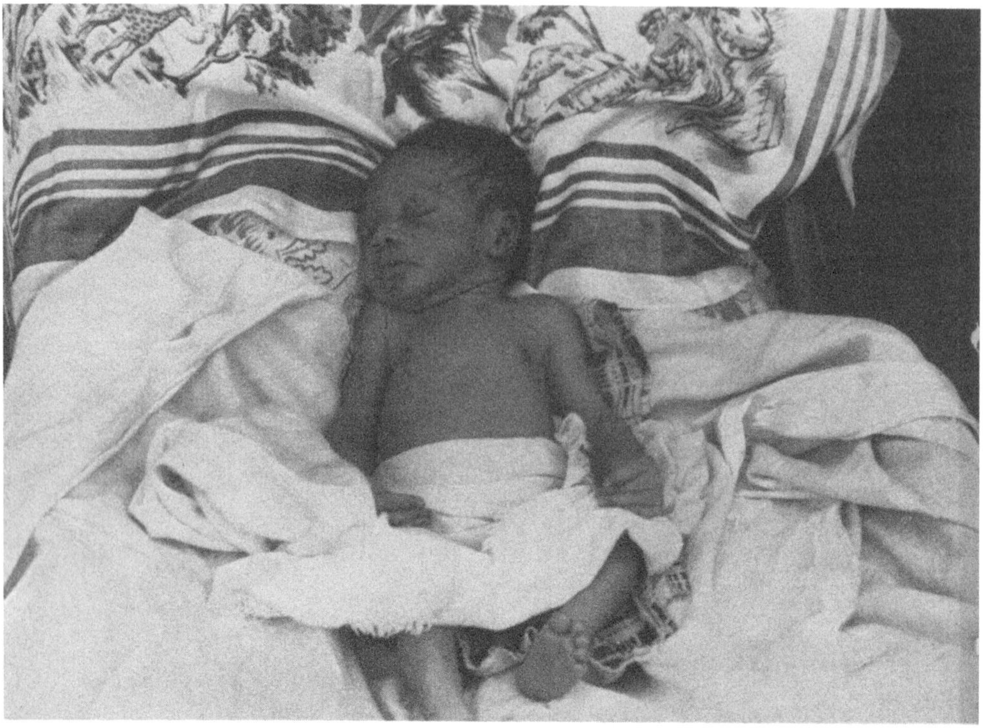

Out-dooring. 3. A three-day-old baby, sleeping on a bed made of pillows and cloths. This baby has been kept indoors from birth, and will not be allowed out until its out-dooring ceremony is celebrated. Taken in Gblede.

4. A baby, twelve days old, whose out-dooring ceremony had not been celebrated because the father had not returned from a journey. The baby was therefore being kept indoors until the father returned, when the ceremony could be performed. Also taken in Gblede.

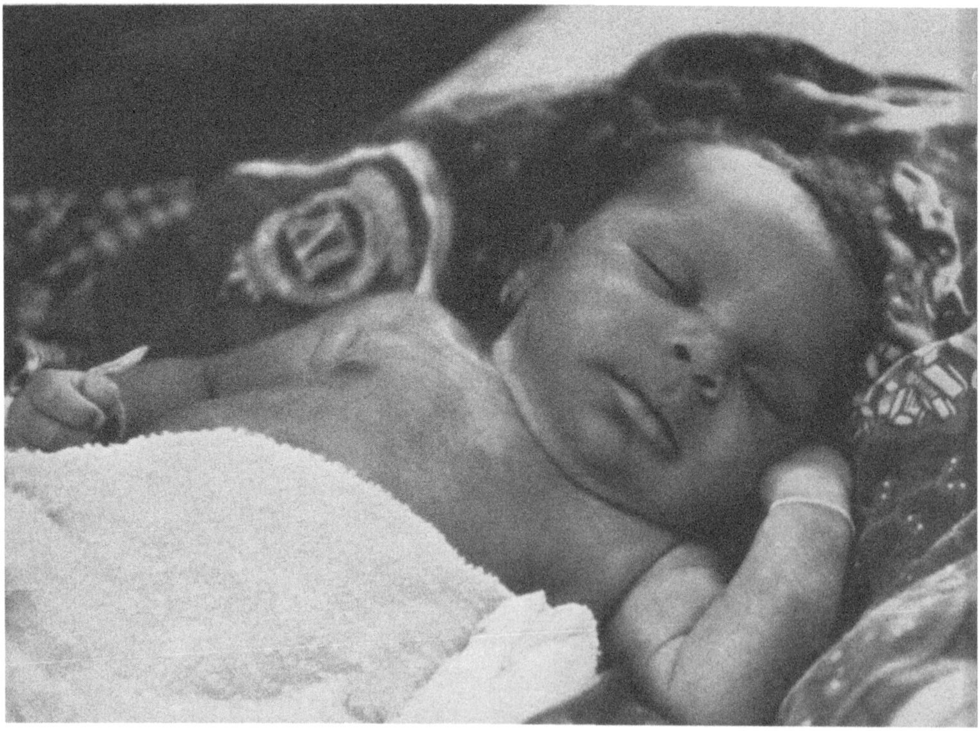

Begyina children. 5. A *begyina* child, plastered with clay as additional markings, said by her mother to be four years old. Taken in Apam.

6. Another *begyina* child in Apam.

Babies being suckled. 7. This mother, surrounded by her large family, is suckling her last-born twins. Taken in Winneba.

8. A young mother giving the breast to her first-born. Notice the elaborate dressing of the mother's hair. Taken in Teshie.

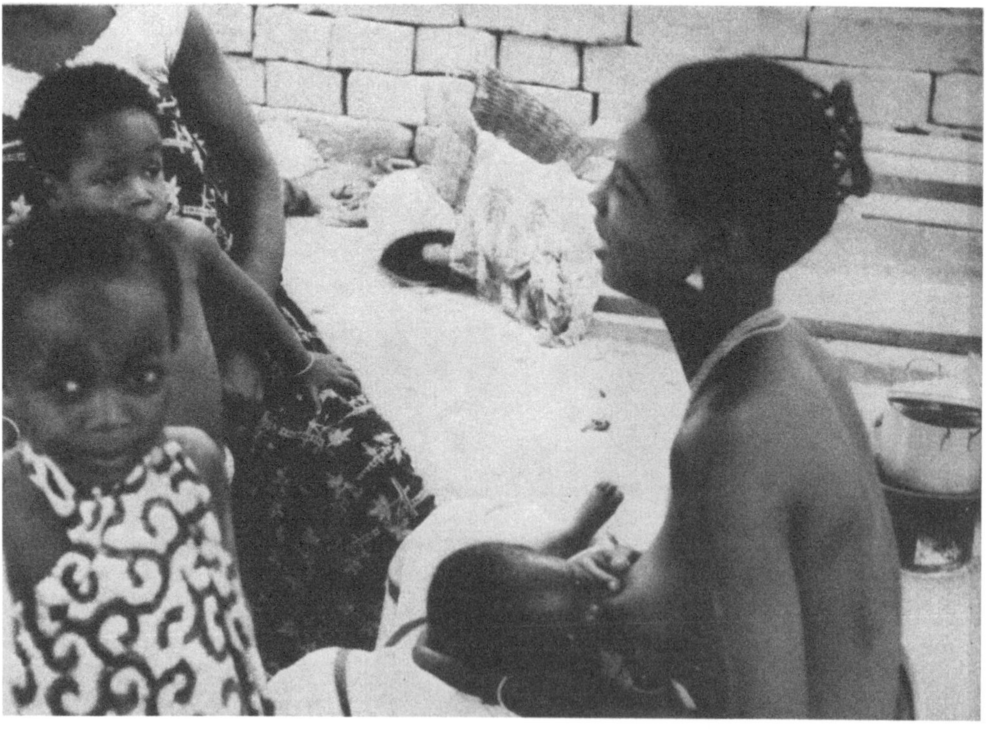

mother and child are confined to the room in which the birth took place, or at any rate to the house. If the child dies during that time, it is assumed that it was in fact a spirit-child. The body is mutilated and buried in a pot, to prevent its return in similar circumstances. The parents are not allowed to mourn its loss, but should show signs of joy at being rid of such an unwelcome guest.[1] Similarly, if a woman dies in child-birth or during late pregancy, the unborn baby is removed and treated in the same way. The woman herself may also be given a disgraceful burial.[2]

After seven days have elapsed, however, it is considered that the child is human, and it is 'out-doored', or brought into the open for the first time.[3] This is usually done early in the morning (the air being then considered very beneficial), and the child is placed on the ground, under a basket or under the eaves of the house. A second ceremony, which may be performed concurrently with this, is the naming ceremony. The first name of most, though not all, Ghanaians is chosen according to the day of the week on which they were born; thus Kofi is the name of a boy born on a Friday, Ama that of a girl born on a Saturday, and so forth. The child is given a second name at the naming ceremony. This may be the name of an ancestor, of some hero, or of some relative, whose character the father of the child admires. In the latter case, the chosen relative attends the naming ceremony, and exhorts the child to become like himself. He may step over the child three times, carry it in his arms, or spit into its mouth, as a means of ensuring that this happens. In most places these ceremonies are usually accompanied or followed by a public presentation and appraisal of the gifts to the mother and child from the husband. Drinks are served, libations poured, the ancestral spirits and gods prayed to, and donations called for.[4] In the Northern Territories, the child is carried

[1] This custom is confirmed of the Akims by Field, (7) 136; of the Ashantis by Rattray, (29) 54 and (31) 59-60; of the Akans generally by Manoukian, (25) 51.

[2] Among the Gas, according to Field, a woman who dies in child-birth before the child is delivered is held to have murdered the child and she is buried secretly in an accursed grove. If she dies after delivery, however, she is merely accounted unlucky; (8) 59. Rattray notes that, among the Dagabas, a stillborn child is buried on the kitchen midden, (32) 418; among the Kusasis, a stillborn child is given an ordinary funeral if formed, but is buried in a pot on the kitchen midden if unformed, and a woman who dies in child-birth is buried in the bush, (32) 387.

[3] See Plates 3 and 4.

[4] Field describes an out-dooring ceremony among the Akims in (7) 135-7; Rattray describes that of the Ashantis in (31) 61-6; Christensen that of the Fantis in (5) 83-5; Wartemberg that of the Elminas in (36) 123; Field that of the Gas in (8) 171-7. Manoukian gives a brief description of that of the Ewes in (26) 42.

on to a flat roof of the compound to celebrate its out-dooring in some tribes. It is often several months before the child leaves the compound itself, and this may be done by a mock kidnapping of the child by a relative.[1] In BENIM (Asante) 'for the first eight days of a child's life, it is regarded as a temporary being, not fully human, not fully spiritual. If it dies before the eighth day, it is considered as the exit of a visitor, and there is no weeping. So the eighth day of a child's life is an important occasion. On that day the child is admitted as a full member of the family. He assumes a personality and is given a name. From that day he is no more considered as a stranger. This day is celebrated with various important celebrations.' In BOSOFO (Asante) 'the eighth day after child-birth is a great day for the mother. She dresses in her best cloth and looks gay and very cheerful with her shoulders, arms and breasts smeared over with slightly scented white clay, a symbol of victory. The infant is also given her bath and given a good toilet. Then she is put to sleep on the new mat and new pillow laid in the sun. This is the first occasion on which the child is taken out of doors by daylight. After being thus exposed for a short time, it is removed and carried back indoors, to be named. The naming of a child in Bosofo follows the general Akan pattern. The father names his children after his own parents, grandparents, uncles and aunts as well as his friends. This is done by a sister of the father, who brings the gift to the mother and tells the people present the purpose of her visit. Very often, the child is later presented to the old man after whom he is named, and there the person spits into the mouth of the child to bestow upon him his virtues. He prays that the child shall grow to be like him.' In APAM (Fante) 'on the eighth day of the birth of the child, there is a full gathering of the two families—the husband's and the wife's. "When we meet on such an occasion, we have two main things in mind—to welcome the 'stranger', and to give it a name." It is the name which gives it full membership of the family. It is also the occasion that the husband presents gifts to the wife. The size of the gift depends upon the elasticity of the husband's resources, so that in addition to things used by women such as a piece of cloth, head-kerchief and powder, the husband may

[1] See Manoukian, (27) 72-73, for a general account, and Rattray, (32) 498, for an account of the customs of the Isalas; *ibid.* 438, for those of the Birifors (Lobers); *ibid.* 133, for those of the Gurensis.

include a sheep, goat or fowl. The husband's family may present gifts of kerosene, cloth, powder, comb, pomade, scents. The wife's family also presents similar gifts. This closes the birth ceremony.' In GOVIEFE (Ewe) 'the eighth day after the birth of a child is always a great day, a day of out-dooring'. In CENTRAL ACCRA (Ga) the naming or out-dooring ceremony, called *Kpodziemo*, is performed eight days after birth. 'So essential is the *kpodziemo* ceremony, and so much place does it occupy in the child's life, that an unnamed child is mocked at.' During the seven days preceding this ceremony, the child remains indoors and is regarded as possibly a spirit-child. If it dies during this time, it is thought of as never having been born. Among the ISALAS a few days after the birth of a child, the husband presents his wife's parents with a white cock or hen, according to the sex of the child, in the exchange for which they give him some medicine. This medicine is used by the child's mother to smear over herself while standing on the roof of the house, at a time when there is dead silence in the village. The new baby is then ceremonially presented to the mother on the roof, after which it may go out of doors freely. A week or two after birth the baby is given a name at a ceremony at which sacrifices are made.

Twins are especially honoured in nearly all the villages studied, and so are tenth children. Special ceremonies may be performed for them, and special tasks reserved for them on public occasions.[1] There is no general preference for children of either sex. It is widely said that mothers prefer the first-born to be a girl, so that she can help with the household tasks, while fathers prefer a boy, to help on the farm or with the fishing. In matrilineal tribes there is some preference for girls, and in patrilineal tribes for boys, but it is generally agreed that to have several children of each sex is the best, and parents who have had a succession of children of one sex only may on that account consult the witch-doctor or herbalist. In TUTU (Akwapim) mothers prefer girls since they help in the house; fathers prefer boys since they help on the farm, and since succession is patrilineal. 'When the mother is pregnant it is the ardent wish of each parent that birth is given to a child of his or her own

[1] See Field, (8) 179-184, for a description of such rites among the Gas; Rattray, (31) 66, for those among the Ashantis. Manoukian says that twins are given special consideration and care among the Gurensi, Tallensi, Konkomba, Birifor and Wala tribes; (27) 73. Wartemberg mentions the expensive customs relating to twins in Elmina; (36) 122-3.

sex.' In BENIM (Asante) 'it is considered very unfortunate to give birth to boys only because without a daughter the mother's line comes to an end, the worst that can befall any Akan family'. If a couple produce more than three boys without any girls, they may consult a fetish priest. Twins and tenth children are sacred persons; a special ceremony is performed at their birth, and their mothers are sometimes exempted from taxes and communal labour. In BOSOFO (Asante) no preference for either sex is given unless the parents already have a large number of one sex. Twins and tenth children have a special ceremony performed for them at birth. In GOVIEFE (Ewe) parents prefer the first-born to be of their own sex; thereafter an equal number of each sex is desired. In AYIKAI DOBORO (Ga) for the first-born, fathers prefer boys, mothers girls. To have a family of all one sex, however, is regarded as unfortunate. In LARTEH KUBEASI (Guang) boys are preferred on the whole, on account of the system of patrilineal descent. But mothers are pleased if their first-born is a girl, since she will help to look after her younger siblings. Among the ISALAS 'each parent favours having children of his or her sex'.

When a child is born after several preceding children have died, either in child-birth or subsequently, special precautions to outwit the spirits and gods are taken in most of the villages studied. The face of the new-born infant is disfigured with cuts, often radiating from the corners of the eyes and mouth; it is ostensibly neglected, its parents taking care not to make any show of affection towards it, and it is clothed in old rags. It is often given a slave's name and its hair is left unkempt, or tied up with charms. This treatment is intended to persuade the spirits that it is unwanted, and to lessen thereby the danger of its sharing the fate of its siblings, since the spirits would get no satisfaction from depriving anyone of something that he did not in any case value.[1]

In those villages in which tribal marks are used, they are made either at birth or during the naming ceremony.[2]

[1] Such children are called *begyina* among the Ashantis, *kosamba* among the Elminas, *gbobalo* among the Gas; the custom of the first is described by Rattray in (31) 65; of the second by Wartemberg in (36) 121; and of the third by Field in (8) 177-8. The custom is mentioned by Manoukian as being practised by the Ewes; (26) 42. See Plates 5 and 6.

[2] For a general account of tribal marks in Ghana, see (2). See Plates 44 and 77.

CHAPTER FIVE

NURSING

> 'A young mother told me that she was so happy when she fed her baby that she wished she had nothing to do besides baby-feeding.'

BREAST-FEEDING is almost universal in Ghana. In a few cases bottle-feeding is used temporarily if the mother is sick, or has insufficient milk, but it is commoner for the baby to be handed over to the charge of a nursing relative in such cases. In several areas, the idea that bottle-feeding was bad, either for the child's health or for its manners, was expressed.[1] In BANKO (Asante) 'mother's milk alone should be the baby's food'. The use of artificial baby food is regarded as an indication of the mother's laziness. In BOSOFO (Asante) if a mother has no milk, the child may be given diluted tinned milk. This practice, however, is widely believed to prevent the child from growing up into a normal sensible adult. In JAISI (Asante) children are breast-fed. The bottle may be used for supplementary feeding sometimes if the mother has not enough milk herself, or if she has an abscess on the breast. But bottle-feeding is said to be unnatural, to lead to constipation and furthermore it is thought that children do not receive so much satisfaction from it. 'The mothers will never exchange breast-feeding for bottle-feeding. They say they do not have any enjoyment if they feed their babies by the bottle.' In GBLEDE (Ewe) 'children are bottle-fed in some cases'. In AYIKAL DOBORO (Ga) children are breast-fed, but they are bottle-fed in cases where the mother dies after birth. In WINNEBA (Efutu) some mothers, especially if they have too little milk, bottle-feed their children. Among the ISALAS 'babies

[1] Fortes says that among the Tallensis artificial feeding is unknown; (14) 272. Grant notes that in Ayeduase village, Ashanti, only two women had used evaporated milk for their babies; (20) 44.

are all breast-fed. Artificial feeding is absolutely unknown among the tribe.'

The period that elapses between birth and the new-born baby's first feed varies. In some areas the first feed is given as soon as the child has been bathed; if the mother has no milk herself, a nursing relative takes over. This may happen in any case, as some people believe that the colostrum is harmful for the infant. In other areas, the baby does not receive its first breast feed until the second or third or even the fourth day after birth; in the meanwhile it is given sugar-water, or sometimes coconut milk. In ABURI (Akwapim) the newly-born infant is fed on sugar and water for the first day as it is believed that the mother's milk is at first impure. In DWINYAMA (Asante) the baby is given its first feed a short while after birth. The colostrum is considered unfit for children and a nursing relative suckles the baby until the colostrum is milked out. In AYANZILI (Nzima) newly-born infants are fed on water for the first three days. In CHRISTIANSBORG (Ga) the newly-born baby is given its first feed as soon as it has been bathed. In APIREDE (Cherepon) infants are fed on sugar water for the first day or two as the mother's first milk is considered impure. Among the DAGABAS 'the first breast feed is given about ten to twelve hours after birth and by another woman with a baby of the opposite sex'.

The normal position for nursing is for the mother to sit with the baby across her lap, supporting its head with one hand or arm, and using the other hand to direct the nipple into its mouth.[1] The way in which the infant is held during nursing is considered a matter of importance in some areas, and the new mother is carefully instructed by her own mother or an experienced female relative. In some of the villages studied it is thought that for the mother to lie down to feed a young baby of under three months is bad for it; in others it is thought better to feed a new-born baby in this position. Older children may be suckled in other positions; while the mother is standing or walking or even working, the infant may be tied to her side by the cloth, within reach of her breast.[2] In ABURI (Akwapim) babies are nursed on their mothers' laps. Inexperienced mothers are taught how to hold the babies properly and how to present the breast so that the child can suck properly. 'Mothers say

[1] See Plate 8.
[2] See Plates 9 and 10.

this teaching is very necessary because inexperienced mothers push the nipple too much into the child's mouth. This may result in the child developing a wide mouth, make him take in too much breast-milk at once and vomit, or the breast will cover its nose and suffocate him.' In DWINYAMA (Asante) the newly-born baby is at first fed on the ground, its mother lying beside it, since too much picking up is considered bad for it. Later on, it is nursed on its mother's lap. The baby may also be fed while the mother is walking along, when it is held in place by a cloth. In TEMA (Ga) the baby is fed on its mother's lap; she uses one arm to support its head, the other to direct the nipple into the baby's mouth. Among the ISALAS when a mother breast-feeds her baby, she sits on a stool and 'holds the baby on her lap with its head raised towards her breast in a caressing fashion to feed it'.

Demand-feeding is almost universal. Virtually no attempt is made to establish regular feeding schedules, and babies are fed whenever they cry.[1] A woman who allows her young baby to cry for more than a few minutes is accused of heartlessness. Infants may also be fed when they wake, whether they cry or not, and when their mothers feel that their breasts are full. During the night, immediate attention to a crying baby is considered very important, for fear its cries attract the attentions of witches or evil spirits. In ABURI (Akwapim) 'the child is fed when he cries even if the interval is not long. If the mother refuses to feed him, she is said to be a wicked woman who wants to underfeed her child. A few educated mothers try to feed their children at regular intervals but they are not allowed to do so. Their mothers and husbands keep on quarrelling with them till they give in. So the more the child cries, the more he is fed. Apparently there are some children who do not cry very much because they sleep a lot. If such a child sleeps for a long time, he is woken by his mother and fed.' In BANKO (Asante) babies are fed when they cry, unless they have just been fed, when their crying is attributed to stomach pains and they are given an enema. Mothers are especially careful to feed their children the moment they cry during the night, lest they attract the attention of witches and evil spirits. 'It is regarded as harmful

[1] Manoukian says that, among the Ewes, for the first two or three years of their lives children are breast-fed whenever they are hungry; (26) 42. Fortes says that, among the Tallensis, babies are fed whenever they cry or fret or their mothers feel inclined to nurse them; (14) 187-8.

and unnatural for an infant to cry when hungry for more than a short period. Many mothers therefore will stop everything they are doing in order to feed their babies at once. Neglecting to feed her baby at the proper instant is a just cause for the husband to beat the wife, because this may make the baby ill and hospital expenses will be paid by the man.' In AGOMANYA (Krobo) 'the baby is nursed whenever it cries, frets, or whenever the mother is inclined to nurse it. Whenever the mother sits down to rest or has nothing else to do, her baby is at her breast sucking or maybe just playing with the breast with the mouth and fingers. It is allowed to nurse as long as it wishes. No attempt is made at regularity. Babies sleep with their mothers and are often lulled to sleep with the breast in the mouth. Feeding at night is at any time the child wakes up from sleep.' In APIREDE (Cherepon) 'every time the baby whimpers, he is lifted, jogged up and down, smiled at and given the breast'. In WINNEBA (Efutu) among the illiterates, babies are fed when they cry. In some literate families, babies up to two months old are fed two-hourly; older babies four-hourly.

Infants are allowed to suck for as long as they please, and efforts may be made to induce them to take more after they have finished. If the child refuses to suck at all, it causes great anxiety in the mother who suspects some illness. She may examine the child herself, or consult an elderly woman or the village herbalist. If some form of stomach trouble is suspected, the usual treatment is for an enema to be given. Attempts may also be made to force the child to take the breast. In MAMPONG (Akwapim) when the baby stops sucking it is assumed that it has had enough. In BANKO (Asante) the mother may urge her child to take more after it has stopped feeding, if she is to be away for a while. Vomiting is regarded as a sign of over-feeding. In DOME (Ga) the baby may be encouraged to take more once it has stopped; there is a saying that a lazy infant does not suckle continuously. Among the ISALAS 'each time the child stops feeding, the mother waits a while and tries to feed it again. A second refusal shows that it has had enough.' In BANKO (Asante) during the first two days after birth any refusal to feed is attributed to the shock of birth and nothing is done. After this, a refusal to feed is attributed to illness and the fetish priest may be consulted. The child's desire to feed is associated with the size of its fontanelle, and in cases of refusal

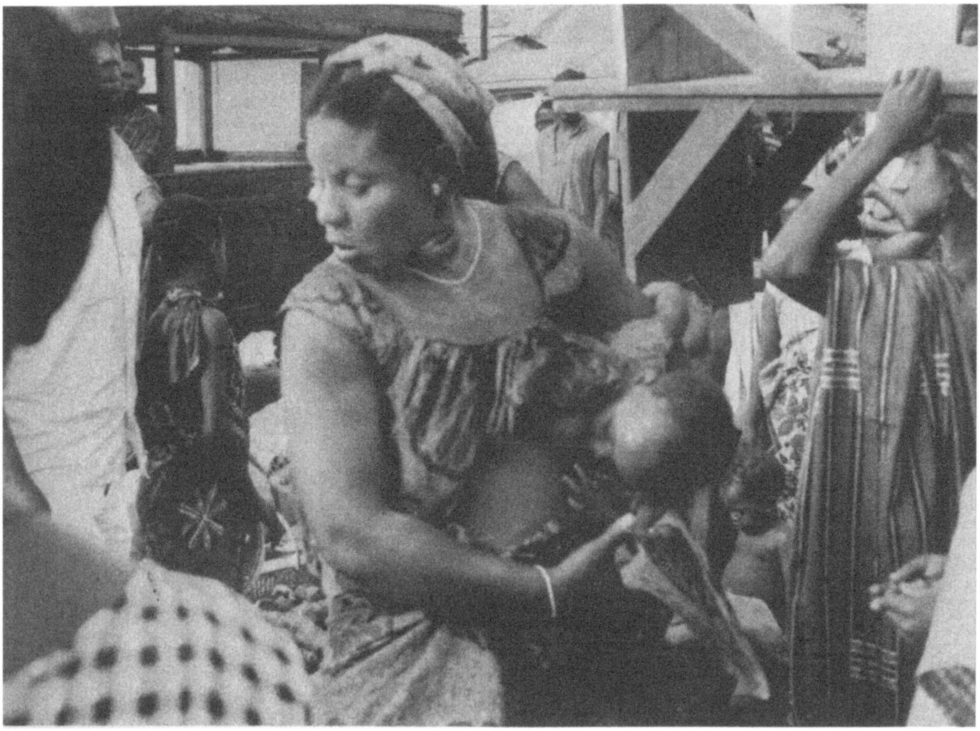

Babies being suckled. 9. This nursing mother sells fish in the market and she is here suckling her baby, while watching a customer selecting his purchase. After the photograph was taken, she took the money, paid out the change and wrapped the piece of fish in a sheet of newspaper, all without disturbing the infant at her breast. Taken in Salaga Market, Accra.

10. This mother is nursing her baby while standing. The baby's age was three weeks, five days, according to the mother. Notice the *oware* board in the background. Taken in the compound of a house in Teshie.

Children feeding. **11.** A young child eating with a fork. Taken in Winneba.

12. A child eating from a bowl. While children normally sit round a bowl to eat, they may take snacks at all times. Notice circumcision, and absence of girl's pad. Taken in Tamale.

Children feeding. 13. An adolescent girl having her breakfast by herself. Taken in Tamale.

14. Young child finishing up the scraps. Taken in Winneba.

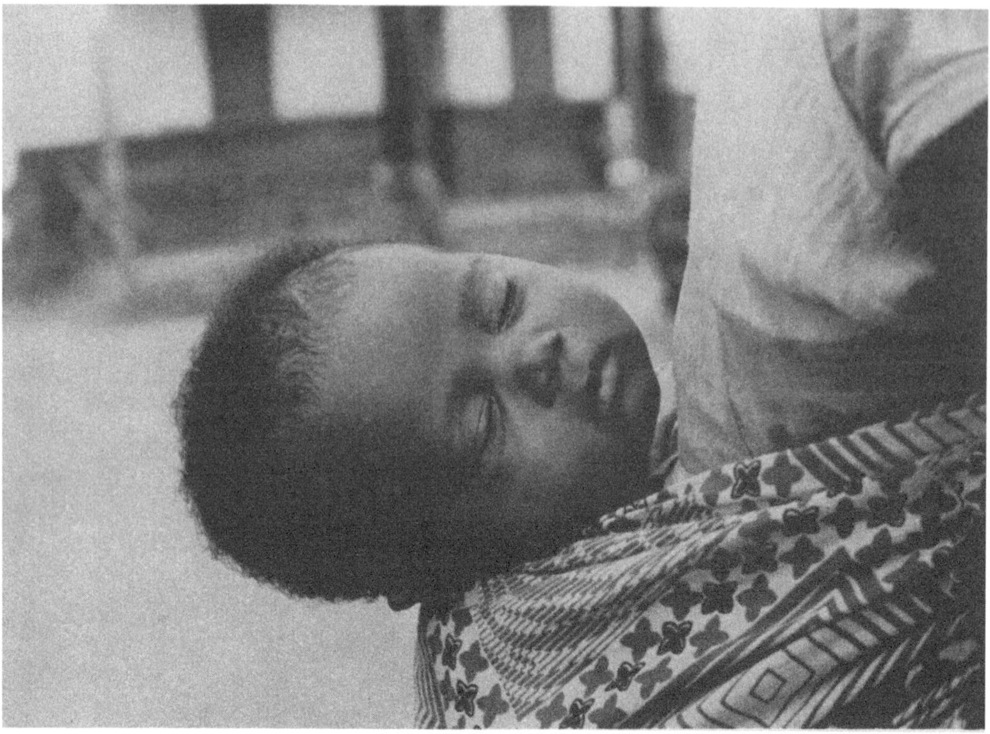

Infants being carried. 15. When very young infants are carried on the back, their limbs and shoulders are totally enclosed within the carrying-cloth to afford support to their necks. Taken in Tamale.

16. Baby, said to be eight months old, but still with its arms inside the cloth. Taken in Goviefe.

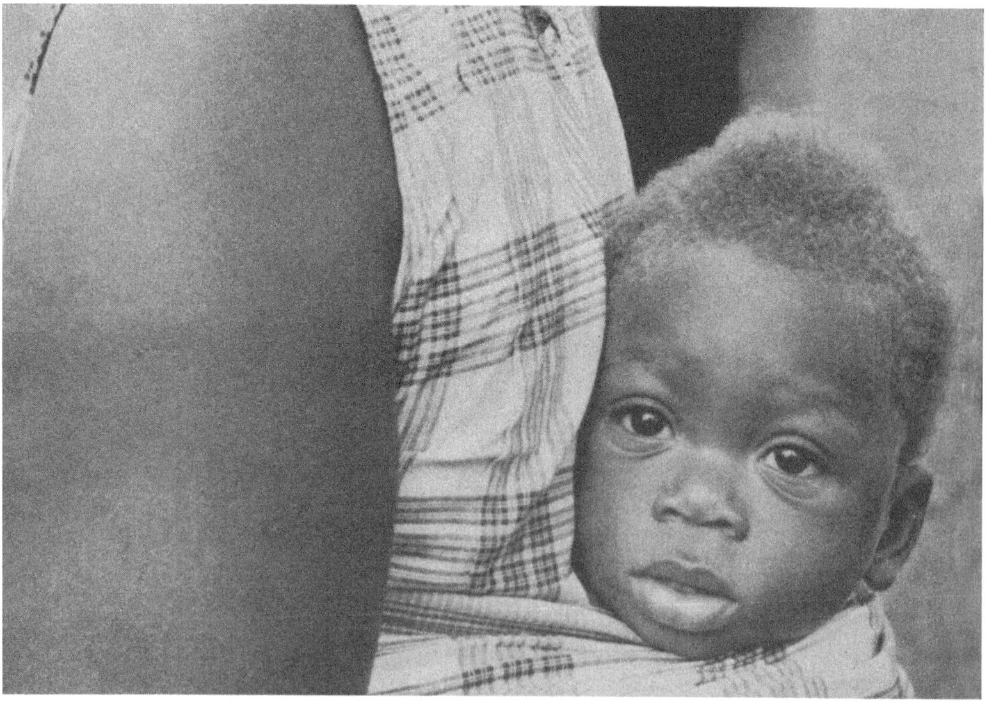

to feed, kola nut juice is smeared on the head to close it up. In BOSOFO (Asante) if the baby refuses to feed, the mother becomes worried, unless it is newly-born. The bystanders are driven away, the child is beaten and the breast pushed into its mouth. 'At other times when all things have been done to induce the child to feed and he does not, he is beaten and as he cries the breast is pushed into its mouth and he is forced to suck.' In BEREKUM (Brong) the child who refuses to feed is examined to see if it is ill. If there are any visible signs of illness, it is assumed to have stomach-ache and is given an enema. In WINNEBA (Efutu) if the baby refuses to feed, stomach-ache is suspected, and a purgative or an enema is given.

The general attitude of mothers towards nursing is one of pride and pleasure; pride from their status as mothers, pleasure from the act of breast-feeding as such. No concern is felt about the spoiling of the mother's figure, and the flabby breasts of the experienced mother command respect rather than pity. In BENIM (Asante) 'a young mother told me that she was so happy when she fed her baby that she wished she had nothing to do beside baby-feeding'. In JAKOBO (Asante) most of the young mothers 'enjoy nursing their babies tremendously'; though it was generally agreed that to have to get up to feed the child during the night was an inconvenience, leading to loss of sleep. Nursing, however, becomes a burden if husbands neglect the older children, and the mothers therefore have more work to do. In VAKPO (Ewe) 'as a rule every mother enjoys nursing her baby. The mother is happy to use feeding time for establishing close relationship with the baby. At the same time, she wants to see her baby grow up properly and so she does the nursing cheerfully. Some women dislike too much feeding in the night because that gives them sleepless nights; but all the same no mother disregards the call from a fretful child in the night. The breasts lengthen in size and look rather flat and flabby as the result of nursing and spoil the natural form of the mother, but she regards her new form with respect rather than with scorn.' In AYIKAI DOBORO (Ga) nursing is regarded by mothers as an enjoyable duty. 'They affirm that it gives them enough exercise in the practice of patience and love for mankind in general.' In KORDIABE (Shai) the mother's attitude towards nursing is 'business-like. She takes nursing as her bounden duty and she performs it with joy, because she regards her child as a highly valuable property.' Among the ISALAS 'the mother takes delight in feeding her child and enjoys the process. The thought of spoiling one's figure through child-bearing is never entertained by any Isala woman. Women without children are regarded as social outcasts.'

The ability to nurse one's child is in a few areas regarded as evidence of a virtuous life before marriage, and this attitude adds to the pride with which a mother feeds her child. Similarly, it leads to an attitude of scorn towards those mothers who have insufficient milk, and who are thought to be thus punished for their unchaste lives. On the other hand, lack of milk may be attributed to the breaking of a taboo during pregnancy, or, alternatively, to the good fortune of a woman, destined by fate to be childless, but for whom propitious circumstances led to motherhood. The usual remedy for insufficient milk is to drink plenty of palm-nut soup, which is believed to build up the mother's milk supply. In addition, her breasts may be massaged and smeared with shea butter or herbal preparations. The baby may be given supplementary bottles or, more usually, a nursing relative is asked to supplement its feeds. In TUTU (Akwapim) a woman with not enough milk is regarded as not a good mother, and she is described as a 'bad sheep'. She is given medicine and palm soup. If a disease is suspected, the breasts may be massaged or vaccinated. In DWINYAMA (Asante) the woman with insufficient milk becomes an object of pity, and she is helped by a nursing relative. She drinks herbal remedies, particularly one made from the root and bark of a tree which has long breast-like fruits. She also drinks a lot of soup. In CENTRAL ACCRA (Ga) the mother who has too little milk, chews corn with coconut and sugar, while shea butter is rubbed on her breasts, and everyone stands around singing and clapping their hands. This old custom is believed to increase the flow of milk. In CHRISTIANSBORG (Ga) a woman who has too little milk is regarded 'as an unfortunate being, one who has misbehaved, abused herself during pregnancy'. In TEMA (Ga) a woman with too little milk is regarded as one who was destined by faith to have no children, but due to some unusual circumstance has been blessed with offspring. In LARTEH KUBEASI (Guang) 'having insufficient milk is attributed to a defiled soul' and a medicine man is consulted. Among the ISALAS 'a mother who has too little or no milk in her breast is supposed to have wronged the gods during her period of pregnancy', and sacrifices and offerings are made in order to propitiate them.

In nearly every area studied, marital intercourse is restricted after the birth of a child. Intercourse with the mother is usually prohibited for three months, though in some cases, particularly in polygynous families, a period of six or nine months is allowed to elapse; in the Northern Territories, a period of two to three years is usual.[1] On the other hand, some couples resume intercourse after six weeks, or when the birth wounds have healed. One factor affecting the resumption of intercourse is the belief that a second pregnancy too soon after the birth of a child may adversely affect the child's development, and couples who find themselves in this situation may be condemned by their neighbours as greedy and unable to control themselves.[2] Intercourse is also believed in some areas to be bad for the nursing mother's milk, and thus indirectly to affect the child's health. In ABURI (Akwapim) 'illiterate parents believe that if marital intercourse takes place during the first six months of the child's life he does not grow to be strong and healthy'. Intercourse may affect the quality of the mother's milk and it is said that many children die as a result of this. Sometimes the baby is given artificial feeding. If such a thing happens, public opinion turns against the parents, especially the father; people say that he cannot control himself, that he he is a wicked and greedy person. The majority of parents refrain from marital intercourse during the nursing of the baby. In BOMPATA (Asante) three months after birth is the usual time when marital intercourse is resumed. There is a saying, that, when the baby is able to smile at people playing with it, its parents have resumed sexual intercourse. Polygynous husbands do not resume marital intercourse until after the child is weaned; that this arrangement is resented by the woman 'has been the cause of many family feuds'. Sexual intercourse before the end of the eighth week after birth is thought bad for health, though it is not tabooed. In APAM (Fante) marital intercourse is avoided

[1] The usual period of abstinence in the Northern Territories is that from birth until the child is weaned and old enough to walk; this is confirmed of the Tallensis by Fortes, (14) 167; of the Birifors, the Walas, the Kusasis and the Gurensis by Rattray, (32) 438, 454, 387 and 288-9; of the LoWiili by Goody, (19) 47. The reason usually given is that intercourse would affect the mother's milk and that, moreover, she needs to give all her attention to the young child.

[2] Confirmed of the Birifors, Walas and Gurensis by Rattray; (32) 438, 454 and 288-9.

during the first three months after birth. The first occasion is referred to as 'picking pepper'. 'It is so called because the pains experienced, they say, are just like putting pepper into the vulva. Despite this some mothers do it even after six weeks.' In AYIKAI DOBORO (Ga) marital intercourse is not allowed during the first three months after birth on account of vaginal sores, and because it is believed that sexual intercourse affects the milk. Most mothers resume marital intercourse after six months of nursing. Wives of polygynous husbands may wait until nine months have elapsed. In TEMA (Ga) marital intercourse is prohibited while the fontanelle is soft. In general, couples are recommended to refrain until the child is weaned, even if weaning is delayed until the child is two years old.

CHAPTER SIX

WEANING

> 'Children who have been weaned by force generally dislike their mothers and shun their company. They prefer staying with their elder sister to staying with their mothers in the house.'

THERE is no fixed age at which weaning takes place in Ghana, and practices vary widely, not only from place to place, but also from one mother to the next. Children may be weaned at any age from six months to three years or even older; the average age appears to be between one and two years old, except in the Northern Territories, where it is about three. When the child can walk is a widely accepted time for beginning weaning.[1] In ABURI (Akwapim) formerly a child was suckled until a new baby was born; nowadays children are weaned when the mother discovers she is pregnant, or when they are over one year of age. Older people attribute this hurry to a desire for the resumption of marital intercourse; in olden days mothers allowed their children to feed on breast milk till they were about three or four years. In TUTU (Akwapim) 'generally, weaning is effected at any time when the child is between one and a half and two years old, when the breast milk begins to fail. However, there are instances in which a four to five year old child is allowed to suck, even though there is almost no milk in the breast until the mother is pregnant again; also there are a very few cases in which the child voluntarily stops sucking when it is

[1] Christensen says that, in Elmina, it is not uncommon for a child to be breast-fed for two years; (5) 97. Fortes says that, among the Tallensis, weaning is usually accomplished by the time the child is three; (14) 188. Grant notes that, in Ayeduase, a village in Ashanti, there was a wide range in the age of weaning, with seven months the youngest and eight years the oldest she recorded; (20) 23. In Dome, a Ga village, she gives the average age of weaning as between sixteen and twenty-three months; (20) 44.

a year old.' In BANKO (Asante) mothers 'regard weaning as something unnatural, and say they think that children may be allowed to suck when they are well over two years. Few mothers will attempt to wean their children before they are two years or at least eighteen months old. Many mothers regard prolonged nursing as a sign of good-motherliness.' Some children are still sucking at nearly four years of age, especially ninth and tenth children, but it is generally believed that they will become babyish. In BOSOFO (Asante) 'generally, a mother does not start weaning the child until she becomes pregnant again'. In JAKOBO (Asante) children are allowed to suckle up to the age of three to four years. There is a belief that children get seriously ill and sometimes die if weaned too early. Some mothers begin to wean as soon as they are pregnant, others carry on to suckle both child and baby. In APAM (Fante) children are weaned when the mother becomes pregnant, as her milk is then said to be unfit. Among the KWAHUS children are weaned when the milk fails or when their mothers are pregnant. In VAKPO (Ewe) children are usually weaned at one year of age; otherwise when the mother becomes pregnant. In AYIKAI DOBORO (Ga) there is no fixed age when children are weaned; some children are weaned when their mother next conceives, others at two or three years of age. In TESHIE (Ga) there is no general rule as to when weaning should take place. Some mothers wean when they become pregnant, some when their milk is running out, others at their convenience. In APIREDE (Cherepon) 'generally a mother does not make any effort to wean a child until she becomes pregnant again'. Among the ISALAS 'weaning is a gradual process spread over a period of three years'.

Reasons for weaning are varied. It is widely believed that the milk of a pregnant mother is harmful for a child, and for this reason children may be weaned suddenly if the mother discovers that she has conceived. This would appear to be the most common reason for weaning.[1] On the other hand, cases are reported of infants being nursed during pregnancy, and even, occasionally, after the birth of the new baby. Other mothers wean their children when their milk begins to fail, or because

[1] Grant found that, in Ayeduase, Ashanti, the women say 'that the child is affected adversely by heat from the body of the pregnant mother or that the child's spirit is crushed by the unborn child'; (20) 23.

they want to go out to trade. In some cases, weaning may be delayed because it is believed that nursing prevents or hinders conception. There would seem to be a tendency for weaning to take place earlier among the educated classes, and this leads to occasional clashes of opinion between generations, and to accusations by grandmothers of their daughters' heartlessness. Last-born children tend to be weaned much later than their elder siblings, even though it may be thought that prolonged nursing makes the child sickly or babyish. In BENIM (Asante) there is no fixed time for weaning. Often a new pregnancy is the cause for it, since it is believed that if a child sucks from a pregnant mother it will become 'sickly and nasty to look at' as the breast is then filled with blood. Last-born children may be allowed to continue to feed at the breast for a long time. In BOMPATA (Asante) there are three reasons for weaning: some mothers wean when they are pregnant; some when they think their children have enough teeth to eat solids; 'and some when their milk begins to fail. If there is no new pregnancy, mothers are generally in no hurry to wean their babies.' In JAKOBO (Asante) children are allowed to suckle up to the age of three to four years, as there is a belief that children get seriously ill and sometimes die if weaned too early. Some mothers begin to wean as soon as they are pregnant, others carry on to suckle both child and baby. The former think that if they allow their children to suck while they are pregnant, the children will become sickly and susceptible to disease. Some people say that a long suckling period prevents them from growing fat. Among the DENKYERAS weaning is carried out at the mother's convenience, or when she becomes pregnant, since it is believed to be dangerous to her health if a pregnant woman suckles. In GBLEDE (Ewe) there is no fixed time for weaning. Children are weaned when they can walk, or when their mother becomes pregnant. In this last case it becomes an urgent matter as the breast milk of a pregnant woman is thought to be bad for children, and weaning is abrupt. In CHRISTIANSBORG (Ga) weaning depends upon the child's reactions. Sometimes nursing is carried on through pregnancy and cases occur of both newly-born infants and their siblings being nursed together. Nowadays, however, educated mothers are beginning to insist on earlier weaning, as a result of talks at the weighing centres, and this has led to a clash of opinion between them and the illiterate women. Generally, weaning is left as long as possible. In AGOMANYA (Krobo) when the child reaches out for some of the food it sees on the plate, it is said to be ready for weaning. In LARTEH KUBEASI (Guang) 'many of the women I interviewed said that they were not sure themselves of when and how a child should be weaned and so they seem to be changing their methods of weaning with each child in the family'.

Methods of weaning vary. Where a child is weaned because its mother has discovered that she is pregnant, the weaning is nearly always abrupt and often accompanied by such deterrents as the smearing of bitter herbs on the breasts, the adorning of them with cotton wool or feathers, threats of ghosts or monsters, or the pretence that the breasts contain a wild animal. Herbal nose-drops are widely used to disgust the child with breast-feeding. At other times, weaning tends to be gradual. Some mothers, having started to wean, may persist in the face of their children's resistance; others may give up the attempt.[1] In MAMPONG (Akwapim) bitter herbs, threats of ghosts and teasing are used as deterrents. In APA (Asante) bitter herbs are used and the child is dissuaded from sucking by threats of wild animals; 'a sheep will catch you if you suck'. In DWINYAMA (Asante) bitter herbs are used. An enema of a herbal mixture, which is said to make the milk unpalatable, is given to stubborn children. In APAM (Fante) bitter herbs are used, or dead crabs are tied to the breast. In GOVIEFE (Ewe) 'weaning is a hard time for the child. He cries and cries, and the more he cries the more solid food is forced down his throat and the more he is scolded. He becomes helpless and dejected. At night he cries much and sleeps but little as he struggles in vain for the breast. Food is got ready in the preceding evening, against the night's feeding. As the child still persists in getting access to the breast, the mother may tie a cloth over it. It is at a time like this that mothers try to disgust their children with the breast. The mother tries to tell him that the breast is smelling and should not even be touched. In the case of an older child he is told that there is a frightful thing in the milk, or that if he sucks it, his

[1] Fortes says that, among the Tallensis, weaning is usually very gradual, except if a mother becomes pregnant again 'through lack of self-control during the nursing period'. In such a case, weaning is sudden, but the mother does not need to resort to deterrents as, it is averred, a pregnant woman's milk disgusts a baby; (14) 188. According to Manoukian, among the Ewes weaning 'is usually somewhat abrupt'; (26) 42.

teeth will become rotten. Threats of seizure by bogy men, the man who circumcises, etc., are given. The mother may treat the breasts with bitter or smelling herbs or leaves. Some children, however, soon get used to the taste and are prepared to suck on, despite the application. The child is compelled, there being no way out of the inconvenience caused him by the forced weaning, with the passing of time, to leave the breasts and stick to the solid food.' In AYIKAI DOBORO (Ga) bitter roots are rubbed on the nipples during weaning, even though this is said to be ineffectual. The mother may try to frighten the child by telling him that a harmful creature lives in her breast. In extreme cases, the child who refuses to be weaned is sent to live with a sister or aunt. Among the ISALAS if a child continues to demand the breast at the age of three or over, bitter herbs are applied as a deterrent.

Pieces of bone or wood may be fastened to the wrists of infants for them to chew; these may act as comforters, though they are often intended to distract children from sucking their thumbs. The breast may be given occasionally to children who have been weaned, as a comforter; sometimes they are given their grandmothers' dried-up breasts to suck. There would appear to be little use of teething rings or objects, though in some cases children who look as though they are going to cut their upper teeth first, are given bones to rub on their lower gums in an effort to avert this bad omen. In JAISI (Asante) objects carved from thorny bark are given as comforters; smooth bones are used when the child is teething. To rub salt on the infant's lower gums during teething is said to give much relief. In KOMENDA (Fante) no teething objects are given; a child who persists in biting its mother's nipples while nursing is given a dose of gripe water. In GOVIEFE (Ewe) bones are tied to the child's wrist to act both as teething objects and as distractors from thumb-sucking. In TEMA (Ga) the newly-weaned child is allowed to suck at its grandmother's dried-up breast as a comforter. When the child begins to teethe, it is given some hard food such as raw yam or a piece of bone to gnaw, or a wooden knob is tied to its wrist. Among the ISALAS 'children are not given any particular things to suck; they suck anything they can lay hands on, for example, their own fingers or the fingers of the adult holding them, stones or any piece of wood within reach'.

In many areas it is thought that weaning may have an adverse effect on the child's health, and this belief may be accepted as a reason for postponing weaning if the first attempt meets with some resistance on the child's part. It is also recognized that weaning is accompanied by a change of the mother's attitude towards the child, who may enter upon a period of punishment or neglect.[1] In TUTU (Akwapim) 'mothers are aware of the fact that weaning is a very unpleasant thing for children and that during that time children become distressed and feel estranged from their mother's affection. Owing to the sudden change of diet the children are often attacked by diarrhoea.' In DWINYAMA (Asante) weaning completely changes the relationship between child and mother and opens the way for the use of force as well as reason. He is scolded for misbehaving and his efforts to attract attention may meet with indifference. Weaned children are expected to become cross and irritable. In JAKOBO (Asante) it is believed that early weaning, i.e. between one and two years of age, leads to serious illness and sometimes death. In VAKPO (Ewe) 'children who have been weaned by force generally dislike their mothers and shun their company. They prefer staying with their elder sister to staying with their mothers in the house.' In APIREDE (Cherepon) 'whatever method is used, all the mothers interviewed said weaning generally makes their children irritable and unhappy. Those children who are not healthy may become ill.'

The attitude towards thumb-sucking varies considerably. In some areas it may be permitted, even encouraged, while in others it is regarded as unlucky, and an omen of the death of a parent. In some villages, while the child is severely punished for sucking its thumb, it may be permitted to suck its middle finger; in other villages, it is thought best to suck all four fingers together. A common deterrent is for a number of cuts

[1] Field reports that, among the Gas, a special form of jealousy is recognized, which affects children when the next sibling is born, or even before. This jealousy results in the child's becoming thin, bad-tempered and greedy, and it is treated by sending the child to stay with an aunt or grandmother, who cossets and indulges it. The name the Gas give to this jealous condition is *kwashiorkor*, which is also the name under which physicians recognize a protein deficiency disease; (8) 165–6 and 177 (where the name given to the condition is *samioko*). Among the Tallensis, Fortes reports that 'one or two more thoughtful informants' attribute successive sibling rivalry to weaning; (14) 254–5. Grant notes that, in the two villages she studied, one near Kumasi and one near Accra, women were aware that children frequently sicken at or near the time of weaning. This was explained by the harmful effects of the pregnant mothers' contact with them; (20) 23 and 45.

to be made on the tip of the unlucky digit, and for the juice of crushed peppers to be rubbed in. With infants, attempts are made to distract them from thumb-sucking by tying pieces of wood or bone to their wrists. In TUTU (Akwapim) 'thumb-sucking is regarded by women as bad manners and is attributed to a child's desire for food, a habit which if not curbed in its early stages may develop into gluttony'. Children are threatened, beaten, or their thumbs are cut and pepper rubbed in for thumb-sucking. In BOSOFO (Asante) thumb-sucking is believed to have a bad effect on the child, though the exact harm done is not known. Children are told that they may bring about the death of their parents if they persist, and every endeavour is made to cure the child of the habit. In JAKOBO (Asante) thumb-sucking indicates hunger on the part of the child but it is tabooed, since it leads to the early death of the parents. Children are given pacifiers as a distraction. In BEREKUM (Brong) thumb-sucking is regarded as an omen of bad-luck; in olden days children who persisted in the habit were killed. Bad luck is attributed to thumb-sucking children until they are past the age of four. In GOVIEFE (Ewe) 'there is a deep-rooted belief that if a child is allowed to suck his thumb, his parents especially the mother will fall sick and may even die'. In CENTRAL ACCRA (Ga) thumb-sucking is favourably regarded since it provides an alternative comforter to the mother's breast. In TEMA (Ga) attitudes towards thumb-sucking vary; some parents do not mind, while others try to stop it. In the latter case, bitter or hot herbs are rubbed in, or the thumb is slightly cut or bandaged. In OTROWE (Adangme) 'the mothers and fathers feel uneasy and anxious about thumb-sucking, since it is believed to indicate the child's displeasure with the care it receives. Thumb-suckers are distracted with wooden or ivory toys.' Among the DAGABAS 'thumb-sucking is regarded with considerable misgiving and the child is discouraged from it by either rubbing pepper on the thumb, or by tying a bone to its wrist which it may suck'.

In all areas studied, solid foods are introduced into the child's diet before weaning. The most common first solid given is akasa, a pap made from corn. The baby is often forcibly fed if it refuses to take it. This is followed by mashed yam, mashed cassava and fufu. Meat may be given; if it is, it may be pre-chewed by the mother, though this is sometimes regarded as a dangerous practice, since evil habits may be passed on to the child through its mother's saliva. In APA (Asante) kenkey (rice, cooked and allowed to ferment slightly), and ampesi (cooked mashed yam) and raw yam are given; meat is added when the child begins to teethe. In BOMPATA (Asante) children are given pieces of yam, kenkey or plantain to nibble from about six months of age. It is forbidden to prevent children from eating what they find on the ground as to do so would cause the child's soul to depart, since it would believe that the parents want to starve it. First solids are given by hand; some mothers pre-chew harder foods but others argue that this practice spreads toothache. A spoon is used for soup. In DWINYAMA (Asante) akasa, porridge made from plantains and porridge made from cocoyam are given from about six months. Pre-chewing is regarded with abhorrence, as it is believed that evil habits can be transferred in the saliva. In SUPOWMU DUNKWA (Fante) akasa is given at four months or thereabout by hand or spoon. This is followed by rice and then fufu. In GOVIEFE (Ewe) akasa is the first food given. 'To feed the child, the mother sits down, her legs stretched forwards and the knees bent a little so that the lap slopes gently downwards. The baby is laid on the lap on its back with its head towards the mother's belly, tilted a bit to rest on, or just laid across the mother's left thigh. With the mother's cupped hand to its mouth, the semi-liquid food is poured into the mouth little by little. The baby of course does not like the taste of the food to begin with, and so cries and struggles, blowing bubbles through the food and refusing to swallow it. The mother therefore holds its nose for a few seconds at a time and, in trying to inhale the air through its mouth, it takes in the food bit by bit. This continues till the mother feels it has had enough. Its face and clothing which have become wet and soiled with bits of the food are cleaned. The mother holds it up, plays with it for a while and lets it supplement the food with a few minutes' breast-feeding. The remainder of the porridge is put back into the dish or calabash, covered up and kept away.' In CHRISTIANSBORG (Ga) solid foods such as yam, kenkey, plantains, cocoyam and dry bread are introduced into the child's diet from nine months. These solids are sometimes forced down the child's throat if he refuses them. Special liquid foods are not given, for to do so would be thought to be 'putting on airs and mimicking Europeans'. In AGOMANYA

(Krobo) porridge is introduced into the child's diet at about five or six months old; mashed yam at about ten months old. Children are fed by spoon and force is used if necessary. In APIREDE (Cherepon) soup and porridge are given from the third or fourth month; mashed yams and similar foods after the first teeth have appeared. When the child reaches for any kind of food, that is taken as a sign that he is ready for that particular food. Meat is often pre-chewed by the mother before being given. Among the DAGABAS solid foods are introduced during the years of weaning. Porridge is the first solid given; subsequently millet dough, yams, rice, beans and pears, which are always pre-chewed by the mother, are also given. Meat and fish are given when available but they are pre-chewed. Native beer is given to children as it is regarded as a good source of nourishment.

CHAPTER SEVEN

CHILDREN'S MEALS

> 'Many mothers take delight in seeing their children with protruding, shiny stomachs at the same time ridiculing them with being gluttonous.'

THE general pattern of feeding in Ghana is for young children to eat in groups, usually of one sex. Their meals may be given to them at the same time as, or at different times from, those of the adults. The children form circles round two common bowls, the boys squatting round theirs, the girls sitting on stools or boxes. The eldest child is responsible for discipline, for sharing out the meat or fish and for seeing that the chores are done, while the mother or any other nearby adult may check the children's eating manners.[1] Very young children are usually fed separately by their mothers, who may also reserve some food for the youngest members of the children's eating groups, in case they do not get enough from the common bowl.[2] When children are old enough to behave properly, they may join the adults of their own sex for meals. The age at which they do this varies; in some areas children eat with the adults from a young age, and in any case, where there are only a few children, they tend to eat with their parents for convenience' sake. In many areas, for a boy to be invited to eat with the men is regarded as a mark of honour. A very common saying is that boys are ready to eat with the men 'when they know how to wash their hands', that is, when they have mastered their eating manners.[3]

[1] I have used this term in preference to *table manners*, as tables are rarely used.

[2] See Plates 11 and 14.

[3] Christensen notes that, among the Fantis, fathers and sons usually have their meals together; (5) 98. According to Manoukian, Ewe boys continue to eat with their mothers and remain exclusively in their care 'at least until circumcision, and usually till about six or eight years of age'; (26) 42. According to Grant, in Ayeduase village, Ashanti, 'older children usually eat together, but a younger child may share their food. A favoured child may be served alone, and any child may

In TUTU (Akwapim) children under three eat with their mothers; thereafter they join the other children. In BOMPATA (Asante) as soon as they can manage by themselves, children eat with their siblings from a common dish, as it is believed that they eat more heartily when with other children. In some homes, food is reserved for those who get left out; in others not. Boys join their fathers for meals at about the age of ten or when they have learnt eating manners. In some families, however, boys do not join the men until they are eighteen or nineteen; the discipline is a strain on enjoyment. In BEREKUM (Brong) children of two to six eat together under the surveillance of nearby parents and under direct charge of the eldest. At six years of age, a child may join the adults of its own sex, provided it is believed that its eating manners are acceptable. In SUPOWMU DUNKWA (Fante) children are fed with the mother until they are ready to join their siblings. In VAKPO (Ewe) children of three or four years of age join their siblings for meals; the youngest child sometimes eats with the parents. In CENTRAL ACCRA (Ga) the child eats alone as soon as he can feed himself. After about six years of age, children eat together, sitting round the bowl in a circle; the boys form one group, the girls another. The oldest is responsible for the distribution of the meat or fish, which is always kept on a separate plate. A boy of outstanding character is keen to eat with the grown-ups. During the meals, he stands while the rest sit and he does not eat fish or meat in the soup unless he is invited to do so. It is a great privilege to be asked to eat with older people. In OTROWE (Adangme) children under three eat by themselves; thereafter 'generally, boys eat with their fathers and girls with their mothers'. Among the ISALAS 'children who are below three years of age feed with their mothers and after the age of three years all children in the family feed together from a common dish'.

have an occasional meal alone'; (20) 25. Among the Gas, according to Field, boys eat with their fathers in the men's compounds, to which the wives send the cooked food; (9) 60-1. Rattray notes that among the Gurensis, the head of the household 'eats alone with his small grandson or youngest son, never with his eldest son'; (32) 264. According to Goody, among the LoDagabas, the husband eats his daily meal on the roof of his house, together with his adolescent sons; the girls and younger children eat with their mothers; (18) 75. The Forteses say that, among the Tallensis, the husband eats with the youngest of his weaned sons, and any unmarried dependent brothers. His other sons form a separate group, and his wives and daughters form as many groups as there are separate kitchens; (15) 270-1; see also (14) 223.

In many areas, meal-times are irregular, and children may be given food at any time of the day if the mother is there. In those households where the parents are away at the farms for most of the day, the children left behind may cook their own meals, or eat food left over from breakfast or the night before.[1] The evening meal tends to be the most important of the day.[2] In ABURI (Akwapim) 'when some children tell their mothers that they are hungry, the mothers remark they eat too much and that is the end. They begin to cry but the mothers do not mind them at first. If it goes on for some time they are beaten or scolded.' In APA (Asante) when the parents go to the farm, they leave food ready prepared for the children to eat when they are hungry. In BOMPATA (Asante) 'it is very common to see little children aged between three and five whose parents have left them at home without any proper arrangements having been made for their feeding'. In DWINYAMA (Asante) children are fed when hungry. In KOFORIDUA (Asante) 'the question of children going hungry for many hours in the day is not one of food difficulties. In fact, there is always enough food in the house and to spare, because food and firewood are brought from the farm every Saturday for use the whole week. The reason is that the people of Koforidua have just one big meal of fufu between five and six p.m. when they return from the farm or from the market. Anything before this is the small food they buy from hawkers in penny-worths, or the ampesi if the mother has had time to prepare it.' In VAKPO (Ewe) children are fed at intervals but these are not fixed periods. The mother feeds the children three or four times a day when they are at home, but when they work on the farm there are two principal meals every day. In AGOMANYA (Krobo) meals are regular but children eat snacks in between. In APIREDE (Cherepon) children are fed when they are hungry. Among the ISALAS 'the child, in addition to the regular feeding hours of the adults in the family, is fed whenever it is hungry and expresses it. Parents make

[1] See Plate 13.

[2] Beckett says that, in Akokoaso, Akim, the main meal is the evening meal and irregularity in meal-times is the rule; (3) 28. Purcell notes that, in Akim, two meals are taken daily; at midday, and in the evening; (28) 2. According to Field, the Gas take three meals daily; one at eight or nine in the morning, another immediately after the midday sleep, sometimes not before three o'clock, and the evening meal at about eight p.m.; (9) 59. Lawson notes that, in a village on the Lower Volta, the main meal was taken in the evening, though sometimes food was also taken at midday; (24) 124.

provision for this by keeping food aside in case the child should ask for it.'

In all areas, for a child to refuse food arouses considerable anxiety in its mother, who suspects illness. A popular remedy is to give the child an enema of ground red peppers. Children may also be coaxed, threatened with bogy men or beaten in order to induce them to eat. In APA (Asante) 'if a child refuses his meal it means he is feverish and so red pepper and ginger are ground and pushed down the rectum to make the child warm and promote an appetite. This medicine is very hot and painful so children try to avoid it as much as possible by eating whatever is given them.' In BOMPATA (Asante) loss of appetite in a child causes its mother much anxiety; the child is coaxed to eat and promised delicacies such as meat. Some mothers feed unwilling children by force; this was a common practice some time ago. In JAISI (Asante) children who do not eat are threatened with bogy men and policemen, or if they are older, they are beaten. If illness is suspected, an enema is given. In KPANDU (Ewe) mothers are greatly worried if their children do not eat, and try to induce them to do so by promises, threats and stories of bogy men. An enema may also be given. In CHRISTIANSBORG (Ga) if children refuse solids, they are sometimes forced down their throats. It is believed that children are likely to refuse food after the birth of a sibling and a ceremony is performed to cure this condition. In TEMA (Ga) children are not normally forced to take food though mothers worry about it; 'How can a child grow if he eats very little?' If a child refuses to eat out of anger, the mother forces him to do so and smacks him if he is stubborn. Among the ISALAS children who refuse to eat or do not eat enough are given ground ginger and herbal rectal suppositories.

In most areas the attitude towards over-eating is permissive, and parents encourage their children, especially young children, to eat as much as they can. However, some parents are reported as deprecating extreme indulgence in food, and gluttons are sometimes mocked by their fellows. In TUTU (Akwapim) 'a mother will admire her child's over-feeding and will sometimes urge him to eat more than usual till his stomach bulges to capacity'. In DWINYAMA (Asante) over-eating is not allowed, and offenders are scolded and sometimes flogged; their food may be rationed and other children encouraged to mock them.

F

In APAM (Fante) 'many mothers take delight in seeing their children with protruding, shiny stomachs at the same time ridiculing them with being gluttonous'. In KPANDU (Ewe) 'over-eating is regarded as a mark of good health and parents are rather happy and laugh when anyone takes in much food and has a protruding belly as a result'. In KORDIABE (Shai) over-eating is believed to lead to inflammation of the stomach, and there is a recognized treatment with a special necklace and diet. Among the ISALAS 'over-eating is not encouraged by parents. If, however, the child does over-eat, a sweeping broom is passed over its stomach several times to relieve tension. It is held that by so doing some of the food is swept away.'

Among foods considered good for children, fufu, mashed yam and plantains are widely mentioned. On the other hand, fufu is often mentioned as a food that should not be given to very young children, and the belief that men and boys should not eat yesterday's fufu is widespread. Various fruits, such as mangoes, should also be avoided by young children, or eaten only in small quantities, and in some areas various foods are tabooed, according to the child's totem.[1] In BANKO (Asante) kenkey, porridge, boiled or roasted yam and plantains are considered specially good for weaned children of two or three years of age 'because they can be easily digested by the worm in the stomach'. In DWINYAMA (Asante) no food in particular is considered good for children. In KPANDU (Ewe) fufu and soup are foods considered specially good for children. Among the DAGABAS 'the only food considered especially good for children is porridge, at about the age of three or four years. The Dagabas regard pepper as a substance which possesses energy and consequently is essential for the proper physical development of the child. It is, in consequence, introduced intermittently by a finger thrust into the child's mouth in spite of its protest in the form of screams and yells.' In BOSOFO (Asante) too many oranges, mangoes or pawpaw causes diarrhoea in children; biscuits are believed to cause constipation. In KPANDU (Ewe) cassava is excluded from children's diets. In CENTRAL ACCRA (Ga) certain foods may be tabooed by the worshippers of tribal and other gods. In AGOMANYA (Krobo) male children are warned not to eat yesterday's fufu for breakfast 'as it weakens

[1] Fortes mentions various food taboos which the Tallensis must observe from infancy; (12) 38-9.

and renders them useless in sex relations'. Among the ISALAS children are not to eat the flesh of animals such as the lion or the leopard as 'it is considered that if a child should eat the flesh of these animals, it will remain small and weak all its life'.

Food is often used as a means of rewarding helpful children or punishing disobedient ones; the former are given delicacies, such as meat, fish or eggs, which the latter are denied.[1] Total deprivation of food as a means of punishment, however, is not often resorted to. In MAMPONG (Akwapim) disobedient children may be denied fish or meat. In BANKO (Asante) children who help their mothers with the household duties are rewarded with the choicest delicacies. Children may be punished for disobedience by being denied foods, though some mothers said they would feed them however badly they behave; 'If I do not feed my child, who is to do so?' In JAKOBO (Asante) 'generally speaking, children are not forced to eat foods they dislike'. Some mothers use the deprivation of food as a punishment for disobedience. In KPANDU (Ewe) 'whatever wrong a child may commit, he is given food as usual and to punish a child by not giving him food is unknown in the whole area', though he may be deprived of meat as such. In AYIKAI DOBORO (Ga) helpful children are given extra fish; disobedient children are denied any extras. Children are not forced to eat foods they dislike, though an attempt may be made to persuade them. In TESHIE (Ga) lazy rude children get little meat; helpful, pleasant children receive large portions. One case was quoted of a boy of eight who was punished by his father for refusing to fetch water for his mother, by being forbidden food for the next day. In WINNEBA (Efutu) children who are disobedient are denied delicacies, offered unpalatable foods or in serious cases denied food altogether. 'In the case of kenkey,[2] which is considered good but unpalatable, children are often coaxed to eat it by being promised rewards of toffee or other confectioneries.'

By the time they are three, the diet of children in Ghana is basically the same as that of the adults, except that they get much less fish, meat or eggs. These foods are shared out according to age, so that the major portion of such meat as reaches the children is kept by the oldest child for himself, and

[1] Field observes that, among the Gas, 'a rude, lazy boy can expect little or no meat; a helpful, pleasant, popular boy receives plenty. Girls are similarly treated'; (9) 61.

[2] A paste made from slightly fermented rice or corn.

younger children may get little or none.[1] In ABURI (Akwapim) children eat the same food as the adults; 'they are given some of the food prepared for adults because the mothers say that if they train their children in this way it will help them to be hardy to meet difficulties in future'. In BOMPATA (Asante) it is believed that children do not mind what they eat, and so they are given food which the adults have left or do not care for. Examples were given of kenkey which had been found to be bad being taken home for the children. In APAM (Fante) children eat the same food as their parents. In GBLEDE (Ewe) children over one year of age have the same diet as adults, though they get less meat; 'meat or fish when there is any in the soup, is shared directly in proportion to age, younger children invariably get less or practically none'. In AGOMANYA (Krobo) the diets are the same except that children get less meat and fish; such meat or fish as is given to the children is distributed by the oldest, who usually keeps the largest portion for himself. In LARTEH KUBEASI (Guang) there is little difference between a child's and an adult's diets.

Considerable importance is attached in all areas studied to good eating manners, and there is general agreement on what constitutes them. The most important rules are that hands should be washed before and after meals, that only the right hand should be used for eating,[2] that while doing so the left hand should not be placed on the ground (or the food will flow through it into the earth, and the body thereby be deprived of its nourishment), that small mouthfuls should be taken, which should not be eaten noisily, that the mouth should be kept closed while eating, and that singing and unnecessary talking should be avoided. Other rules are that children should wait to be given their portions of meat or fish,[3] that they should take care not to touch the nose with a finger while eating (which might lead to the death of a

[1] Details of the diets and their nutritional values of four households in Ayeduase, Ashanti, four households in Dome, near Accra, three households in Mampong, Akwapim and one household in Accra, are given by Grant in (20) *passim*. Lawson gives details of the diets of five households in Battor, Lower Volta, in (24) *passim*. She notes that the diets of schoolboys in these households were notably deficient in all food requirements except Vitamins A and C. This fact she attributes to their casual eating habits and the lack of adult supervision; (24) 128. The Forteses note the special provision made among the Tallensis for insuring that children have sufficient food, by reserving left-over porridge for their consumption; (15) 271.

[2] Rattray notes that the left hand is used for toilet purposes; (30) 13.

[3] Field notes that, among the Gas, boys eating with their fathers may not touch the meat or fish until an elder hands them a piece; (9) 61.

parent), and that care should be taken not to get the hand and fingers too messy while eating. It is the duty of the youngest child to wash up the bowl when the meal is finished.[1] Parents supervise their children's meals to see that these rules are learnt.[2] In TUTU (Akwapim) 'from a very early age children are taught how to behave well at meals'. They learn not to take too large mouthfuls, to chew their food well before swallowing it, not to spit out chewed food, not to make noises while eating and to keep their mouths shut while they are chewing. If the fourth finger touches the tip of the child's nose while he is eating, it may cause the mother's death. Talking while eating may lead to the death of the father. To eat quickly leads to constipation; singing at meals is a sign of ingratitude. Children should keep their hands and fingers tidy and not allow the food to run all over them. They should not place their left hand on the ground while they are eating, for the food will flow out of their bodies into the ground and they will not be properly nourished. They learn to wash their hands before and after eating. 'A child is discouraged from picking up bits of food that fall to the ground; if he does that he is held up to ridicule by his fellows with these words: "Pick up, pick up insects from the ground to eat". If in the course of eating, a portion of the food falls on to the ground, it is believed to have been offered and accepted by ghosts or spirits, and therefore more is added.' All children are expected to have learnt these manners before they reach the age of six. In BOSOFO (Asante) the child is taught not to use his left hand for eating, to wash his hands before eating, to eat small pieces and to chew them well, not to talk during meals, not to eat messily, and not to put the left hand on the ground while eating lest all the food flow through it into the ground. If he sings at meals his parents will die. If he eats in other children's homes, their mothers will withdraw the food they have given him from his stomach while he is asleep. In JAKOBO (Asante) children are taught to use the right

[1] Field says that, among the Gas, when eating stew it is not etiquette for a junior to have his hand in the bowl at the same time as a senior; 'only equals dip together'; (9) 61. Fortes notes that, among the Tallensis, equals sharing a bowl can start together and dip their hands in the bowl together, but when a child is eating with his parent, 'he will wait for his parent to begin first and to tell him to eat, and will wait for his parent to finish and leave the dish to be "cleaned out" by him'; (14) 197.

[2] Christensen says that, among the Fantis, fathers instruct their sons in the totem food taboos and in eating manners when they are taking meals together; (5) 98.

hand only, not to put all fingers in the mouth while eating fufu, to use two fingers and the thumb in cutting fufu, not to let the index finger touch the nose while eating fufu or the mother may not live for long, not to gulp food down nor make a mess, not to talk while eating, not to put chewed bones back into the soup nor to spit into it, and not to snatch at the meat but to wait until the oldest child serves it out, though some mothers in order to prevent quarrelling may themselves serve out the meat or fish, taking care to begin with the oldest child. The last child served, who is the youngest, is said to have 'swallowed Mother' and is responsible for washing up the bowls. In GOVIEFE (Ewe) while boys may squat to eat, the girls must sit. They are taught to wash their hands before meals, to take small morsels, to eat quietly, and not to talk during meals. In CHRISTIANSBORG (Ga) clean habits of eating with the hand are demonstrated by the child's mother or another adult, the child being made to eat with her for this purpose. Amongst the various rules is that the child should not gulp his food nor take too large morsels, and the adult stands over the children's meals to see that they behave correctly. Among the ISALAS 'children of about the same age feed together from a common dish placed on the ground before them and parents insist that they wash their hands before the meal. When the dish of food is placed before them, the younger ones in the group are taught to support the dish with their left hands while they eat so as to keep it from being pushed about. As the food gets gradually diminished, the senior children stop eating according to age and in the end the youngest of the group is left to finish off what is left in the dish. Any of them who feels he has not had enough food reports to the mother for more. Talking during meals is not encouraged by parents and children are hushed up when they do talk.'

CHAPTER EIGHT

TOILET TRAINING

> 'A child who is found putting its hands in faeces or eating them is given raw eggs to eat to pacify its soul.'

THE age at which toilet training is begun in Ghana varies considerably. In some households the child is trained from early infancy—within a month or two after birth; in others it is left until over a year old, and in the Northern Territories training may not begin until the child is two.[1] In several areas studied, it was reported that there is no fixed age at which training begins. In most of the remaining areas, toilet training was said to begin some time between three and nine months of age. In MAMPONG (Akwapim) toilet training begins from the first week of age. 'To be sure the child's bowels are free, the mother gives him an enema in the course of bathing.' From four months of age, the child is put on the pot, which is one of the gifts made by its father at the out-dooring ceremony. In BANKO (Asante) 'mothers think it is premature to give children toilet training until the fourth or even the sixth month'. In BOMPATA (Asante) by the time they are one year old, children are expected to indicate when they want to pass a motion, and they are then put on the pot, or on their mother's extended feet. In KOFORIDUA (Asante) 'there is complete disregard for toilet training during the pre-walking period'. In AYANZILI (Nzima) toilet training begins after the third month. In TESHIE (Ga) toilet training begins early, at times within a month or two after birth. At six months of age the baby is held over the pot, or on its mother's feet, while it defecates. This is done often during the day, and the child is awakened frequently at night. 'The child is subjected to

[1] Fortes says that, among the Tallensis, children are not expected to be house-clean until they can run about by themselves; (14) 189.

an intensive campaign at a very early period, at times within a month or two after birth, to bowel training. Zealous mothers often take a competitive pride in accomplishing the training as early as possible.' In APIREDE (Cherepon) 'a child's toilet training commences from the age of about a fortnight'. Among the DAGABAS children are not scolded for soiling or wetting their mats until they are four years old or older.

While in several towns some children are regularly placed on a pot as part of their training, the most common method followed is for the mother to watch the young child for signs that it is about to empty its bladder or bowels. When she sees such signs, she holds the child out in her hands, or, sitting down, balances it on her extended feet. To encourage it, she hisses or grunts. In the Northern Territories, children are expected to learn to defecate outside the compound, by following the example of their elder siblings and adults.[1] As they grow older, children are expected to indicate when they want to eliminate. This they are encouraged to do in a corner of the compound, or behind the house. This enables the mothers to examine the excreta for signs of ill-health. Round about the age of five, children are taken to the public latrines by a parent or elder sibling. In ABURI (Akwapim) from the earliest weeks a child is held out now and then by its mother. She watches it for signs that it wants to eliminate; if she thinks that it wants to urinate, she holds it out and encourages it to do so by hissing. If she thinks that it wants to evacuate its bowels, she places it on a small pot or on her extended feet, or over a rag (which must be washed and not thrown away, otherwise the child's spirit may become sad). In BOSOFO (Asante) from the first few weeks the child is held out by its mother whenever she suspects that it wants to urinate and encouraged to do so with hissing. After three months of age it is put on the pot in the morning, afternoon and evening, and three times during the night. In JAISI (Asante) children are placed on their mother's feet in the morning; in some homes they are potted. Older children defecate in the compound, and the mother sweeps it away. Older children also defecate behind the house. By the time they are four years of age they can be taken to the public latrine. It is

[1] Fortes observes that, among the Tallensis, children are not given direct toilet training, but as they grow older they may be rebuked for not following the example set by others; (14) 189 and (12) 26.

said that infants should not be kept on the pot for too long, or later on the child will delay over its motions and this is thought to be a bad practice. In BEREKUM (Brong) in literate homes the child is placed on a pot; in illiterate homes it is shown a corner of the compound (usually an obscure corner, in case the sanitary inspector sees). At four years of age the child is taught to go to the public latrine. In AYIKAI DOBORO (Ga) children are trained by being placed on the pot, or on their mothers' extended feet. 'Children from one to five always find the mother or any other adult in the household ready to hand to show them a place for elimination.' In WINNEBA (Efutu) children are potted from eighteen months of age; at five or six years of age they are trained to use the public latrine. Among the DAGABAS there is little direct training. Children learn to defecate outside the house by following their siblings during play.

In some areas it is thought that to show disgust at an infant's excreta may alarm the child's soul and lead to its death. For this reason, disgust should not be shown by anyone carrying a baby if it soils her clothes; instead this is regarded as a good omen, indicating that the soiled person will have a child herself. Similarly, if a baby, sitting on its mother's lap while the adults are at their meal, should eliminate into the food, at least a part of the contents of the dish should be eaten.[1] In APA (Asante) if the baby's faeces should happen to drop into the soup or fufu while it is sitting on its mother's lap during a meal, everyone, including the mother, should continue eating, otherwise the baby might die. If the mother's clothes are soiled by urine while she is carrying her child, it is believed that she will have many children, so mothers are pleased when this happens. In JAKOBO (Asante) any person who showed disgust at a child's excreta would be suspected of lacking affection for children. If an infant under four months of age should eliminate into its mother's food, she may remove the faeces, but she must eat the food, or the child will become ill. If the child is over four months of age, a token tasting of the soiled food will suffice. When a child soils the clothes of an adult carrying it, this is regarded as a sign of good luck; if the adult is childless, it is accepted as indicating that she will bear her own children in the near future.

[1] Fortes notes that, among the Tallensis, the infant's excretory processes arouse no embarrassment; (12) 38.

In VAKPO (Ewe) any sign of disgust towards the child's excreta is believed to displease its mother's soul, and to prevent her from having further children. In DOME (Ga) 'a child who is found putting its hands in faeces or eating them is given raw eggs to eat to pacify its soul'. Among the ISALAS 'a mother does not show disapproval at soiling and wetting the clothes by the child; she considers herself fortunate to have a child to wet or soil her clothes'.

The age by which toilet training is supposed to be completed varies from two to five years old.[1] In some areas it is thought that boys are easier to train than girls, while the reverse is argued in others. The age by which children are expected to eliminate privately varies from three to six or seven.[2] In JAKOBO (Asante) children over two years of age are not expected to wet the bed at night and may be beaten for doing so. Training is supposed to be completed by three to four years of age. In TESHIE (Ga) toilet training is supposed to be complete by the age at which the child can walk and talk; some mothers say by three years of age. Mothers take pride in their children completing their toilet training earlier than others. Among the ISALAS 'toilet training is supposed to be complete at the age of three years'. In ABURI (Akwapim) it is claimed that girls learn to control their bladders more quickly, while boys find it easier to control their bowels. In BOSOFO (Asante) girls are said to be toilet-trained earlier, some say because of their anatomy, others say because boys eat more. In SUPOWMU DUNKWA (Fante) 'when I asked the people in Dunkwa which sex learnt toilet manners quicker, the men insisted that the boys did so, while the women claimed the honour, and so I was unable to come to any impartial conclusion'. In GOVIEFE (Ewe) girls are easier to train, but 'bed-wetting after the age of about five years is commoner in girls than in boys'. In APIREDE (Chere-

[1] Fortes says that, by the age of three, most Tallensi children have learnt to run outside to defecate, though they are still apt to urinate indoors wherever they may happen to be; (14) 189.

[2] Rattray notes that, among the Ashantis, a father will teach his young son to go behind the wall of the hut to ease himself; (30) 12. Busia notes that, in Sekondi-Takoradi, the remoteness of the public latrines, and the inadequacy of private facilities, encourage insanitary habits, especially among children; (4) 8. Acquah notes that the average number of persons per latrine in those houses provided with a latrine in the municipality of Accra was eight at the time of her survey (1954), but there were nearly three times as many persons living in houses without latrines as living in those with them. There were 214 public latrines in Accra Urban Area for a residential population of 136,047 (in 1954); this gives an average of 682 persons per public latrine; (1) 58-9.

pon) there is said to be no difference. In LARTEH KUBEASI (Guang) 'many parents agree that girls on the whole stop bed-wetting at an earlier date than boys'.

The child who persists in wetting his bed after the age of five or so is subjected to a traditional punishment. Early in the morning he is pulled out of bed, wrapped in his wet mat, smeared with clay or rubbed with stinging nettles, led to the sea or river accompanied by a crowd of jeering children and thrown in. It is thought that if he succeeds in catching one of them on scrambling out, the habit of bed-wetting will be then passed on. This treatment, in one form or another, is widespread throughout the country.[1] In ABURI (Akwapim) the child over two years of age is scolded and beaten for soiling his bed. If this is unsuccessful, pepper and ginger suppositories are forced into his rectum. Children who continue to wet their beds over the age of three are suspected of having some disease, and medicines are applied. By the age of eight years, a persistent bed-wetter will be tied in his wet mat, his body rubbed with irritating nettles and mocked by his friends. In BANKO (Asante) 'under no circumstances do mothers scold or punish babies who are under two years for soiling or wetting'. After that age they may be scolded or beaten. If the habit persists until the child is four or five, he may be given the wet-mat treatment. In JAISI (Asante) children under one year of age are not punished for bed-wetting. After they have reached the age of five, persistent bed-wetters are wrapped with an irritating plant, or taken to the medicine man for examination. In SUPOWMU DUNKWA (Fante) a child who can talk is punished for bed-wetting. After the age of four, bed-wetters are scolded and beaten. If this is unsuccessful, the wet-mat treatment is tried. If this also does not succeed, ground ginger enemas are given. Finally recourse is had to the herbalist. In GOVIEFE (Ewe) 'it is believed that if a child is punished, especially if beaten for soiling the bed or his clothes, his soul is defiled. His body might swell up and this could be fatal.' For this reason parents usually restrict themselves to scolding the bed-wetter. In CENTRAL ACCRA (Ga) 'the mother of the child who wets his bed invites older children to the house while the bed-wetter is

[1] It is described by Rattray, who says that fathers of enuretic boys invite other boys to come and carry out the custom, known among the Ashantis as *bonsua bono*; (30) 12. Fortes relates an anecdote in which a Tallensi father forced his eight-year-old son to roll in the mat he had wetted; (14) 192-3.

still asleep. Water is sprinkled on him and as soon as he gets up, he is grasped by the older children. The child's face, hands and legs are besmeared with powdered white clay, ultra-marine blue and charcoal all mixed into one in different proportions. The wet mat is wrapped round the body and held in position at the waist with a string. He is then conducted to the seashore. Children follow him singing. He is jeered at and pushed along. At the beach two strong boys remove the mat, raise him up and throw him headlong into the sea. He is then brought to shore and his body scrubbed with sand. No attention is paid to him when he begins to cry. The process is repeated three times and on the third time, he is freed and asked to chase and catch anyone of his followers. He then transfers his wetting habits to anyone he may chance to catch. Children afterwards find it uneasy to move along with their playmates. Some children, realising they have wet their mats, leave the house before daybreak and in many cases will not go to school that day. The public punishment is repeated four or five times if the child continues to wet his bed but if he does not stop after the fifth time, a medicine man is consulted. Another means of stopping bed-wetting is the eating of the intestines of a cooked mangrove crab which is believed to have the power of strengthening the bladder. Parents who do not want to expose their children to public ridicule, flog or scold them at home privately. Sometimes bed-wetters are denied food in the evening.'

The quality and appearance of a child's faeces are widely regarded as important criteria of health, and most mothers examine their children's excreta regularly, or if they suspect illness. Various conditions of the stool are recognized as symptomatic of ill-health. Diarrhoea is generally thought to be more serious than constipation; the treatment for either tends to be an enema made from ground ginger or crushed red peppers, with the addition of various herbs.[1] In BANKO (Asante) children's faeces are examined from three years onwards; watery, shiny stools are an indication of ill-health. In DWINYAMA (Asante) attention is given to the quality rather than the quantity of a stool, which is examined for worms, for a different odour or a different colour from usual. The normal remedy is an enema or a purge. In GBLEDE (Ewe) one important function of

[1] Rattray notes that, among the Ashantis, the method of treating constipation is to put red peppers up the rectum; (30) 12.

the mother is 'to examine the faeces of the child and classify them, and then to decide whether she needs to prepare a drug from herbs or from roots for a remedy. The following are the major classifications: (a) when the faeces are white and sticky, resembling phlegm; perhaps a sign of diarrhoea; (b) when there are small objects in the faeces which resemble the pupae of a fly; (c) watery faeces (free bowels); (d) constipation; (e) when there are actual live worms in the faeces; (f) good faeces, light yellowish in colour with a tincture of brown. In addition to these, if the faeces have peculiar coloration like green, or when blood is discovered on them, the mother or the father becomes greatly concerned as these may indicate either gastric trouble or the presence of some sore in the passage. Surely the mother does not say, "this child has gastric trouble". The nature of the faeces suggests the medicine she should use. The need for examining the child's faeces accounts for the fact that most parents would rather have their children eliminate where they can see the faeces.' In AYKIAI DOBORO (Ga) mothers examine their children's faeces only when they are ill. In DOME (Ga) hard faeces are attributed to constipation and an enema is given. Slimy green faeces are thought to be a sign of stomach-ache from the child's staying out late at night when the dew is falling. Slimy yellow faeces are accepted as a sign of health. In LARTEH KUBEASI (Guang) 'parents become alarmed if the excreta is unusually coloured or is rather too offensive, little, watery, hard and crumbly, slimy, or contains traces of blood or a few worms. Medicine men are often consulted without delay.' Among the DAGABAS 'faeces are sometimes examined for illness such as diarrhoea and dysentery which is treated by the administration of hot shea butter and tobacco applied gently into the anus'.

Adults generally refrain from eliminating[1] in the presence of children, for fear that they might see, and subsequently comment on, their genitals. In public latrines, however, privacy is not always possible, and in some cases parents go with their young children to the latrines, and even converse together while defecating. In ABURI (Akwapim) adults avoid being seen by children when they are eliminating for fear they will see their

[1] The word 'elimination' in the reports has usually been taken to mean the evacuation of the bowels. To see a man urinating in the presence of women and children is no uncommon sight, though he usually turns his back to do so.

genital organs and subsequently refer to them abusively. In SUPOWMU DUNKWA (Fante) parents usually refrain, though the sight of an adult urinating at the roadside in the presence of children is not an uncommon sight. In CENTRAL ACCRA (Ga) parents eliminate privately in houses where there are private latrines; in public latrines, there is no privacy, though new ones are being built with provision for private elimination. In APIREDE (Cherepon) 'at first, the father may take the boy with him to the latrine in order that he may see that he is safe of the pit; it is not uncommon to see father and son on the latrine engaged in a conversation while each defecates'. In WINNEBA (Efutu) adults refrain from eliminating before children; 'apart from its being merely indecent, such a practice would also be a means of creating situations for infantile gossips'. Among the DAGABAS, adults refrain from performing eliminatory functions before children.

The attitude towards wind-breaking in children varies. In some areas it is accepted as evidence of good health, or regarded as a source of amusement; in others it is thought bad manners for a child to break wind in the presence of adults. It may also be regarded as a sign of ill-health, for which the usual treatment is a red pepper enema. A widespread custom which is followed when a child breaks wind at a meal, is for the bowl of food to be placed on its head while the other children eat from it.[1] In ABURI (Akwapim) children are scolded for breaking wind. If there is an unusually sharp odour, ill-health is suspected and the child is treated with a pepper suppository. In BOMPATA (Asante) wind-breaking is regarded as a sign of health, the louder the more amusing for all. Adults over twelve, however, are ashamed of being accused of breaking wind, and a case is reported of a man who committed suicide because he broke wind before his mother-in-law. Bad-smelling wind in children is a sign of ill-health, and they are given pepper and herbal enemas. In DWINYAMA (Asante) children sit on low stools when eating, so as to avoid squatting which leads to wind-breaking. After six or so, to break wind before adults is a

[1] Rattray says that Ashanti children are taught never to break wind in public. He records an instance in which a priestess broke wind while dancing before a chief, and had to be ritually purified. He notes that, if a number of Ashanti men are eating together and one breaks wind, the pot is placed on his head and the others eat from it. It they are all friends, however, they would conceal their laughter for fear that he go and hang himself; (30) 373.

serious offence, for which the child is flogged. At meals a child who breaks wind has the pot placed on his head and everyone eats from it. Formerly, to break wind before a chief was a capital offence; nowadays a heavy fine is imposed and purification by the slaughter of a sheep is carried out. In KOMENDA (Fante) 'wind-breaking by young children is highly appreciated by adults who consider it as a very good exercise which promotes the expansion of the child's lungs and bowels. Wind-breaking, according to parents, is greatly recommended by Europeans to be exercised freely not only by children but adults as well for health reasons.' In GOVIEFE (Ewe) children are expected not to break wind noisily over four years of age, but 'on no account must an adult accuse a child falsely for having broken wind. It is believed that his spirit will take leave of his body if this happens.' If children break wind during meals, the eating bowl is placed on their heads while the other children eat from it. In APIREDE (Cherepon) wind-breaking in children is not regarded as a serious matter, and the parents may be amused at it. If it is persistent, however, the child may be regarded as ill and treated accordingly. Among the DAGABAS no significance is attached to wind-breaking.

Hiccups may be regarded as good for the growing child, or as a sign of ill-health. They are treated by placing a twig, straw or piece of cloth on the young child's head. Older children are told to drink water, often in a specified number of sips. In TUTU (Akwapim) young children who have hiccups are cured by having a stick put in their hair; older children take nine sips of water. In BANKO (Asante) hiccups in very young children of two to four months are regarded as beneficial and believed to make the child fat. In older children, hiccups may be harmful, and a herbalist may be consulted if they persist. It is believed that adults, if they are ill, may die from an attack of hiccups. In SUPOWMU DUNKWA (Fante) the cure for hiccups in infants is to put a piece of thread from a napkin on the baby's head. In adults, hiccups are considered dangerous and may portend death in sick people. In GBLEDE (Ewe) 'hiccups are regarded locally as a sign of the child's growth'. The treatment is to give the child sips of water. In AYIKAI DOBORO (Ga) children of one year and over who have hiccups are given water to drink. In infants hiccups are believed to help the expansion of the chest cavity; to cure it, a small piece of white cloth is placed on the baby's head. In AGOMANYA (Krobo) hiccups are regarded with grave concern. The treatment is to place a piece of wet rag or a sliver of broom-stick on the child's head; another treatment is to drink seven sips of water. In APIREDE (Cherepon) hiccups in children are treated by putting a stick or piece of rag in the child's hair, or by giving it seven sips of water.

In most areas, belching in children is regarded as a sign of having eaten sufficient, and is socially accepted. In TUTU (Akwapim) children are encouraged to belch at meals 'because most of the women whom I consulted agreed that it indicates that a child has eaten enough food and this gives mothers satisfaction'. In BANKO (Asante) belching is thought unnatural and undesirable and it is held to be rude to belch in public. In children, to do so indicates stomach trouble, which is treated with enemas. In BEREKUM (Brong) parents are happy to have their children belch, which is regarded as a sign of satisfaction. In TESHIE (Ga) if an infant belches while it is being nursed, its mother does not continue feeding it, as it might lead to her breast becoming swollen. Formerly belching in young children was taken as a sign of satisfaction, and a child who did so was not allowed to eat any more; nowadays the mother asks if it has had enough. In LARTEH KUBEASI (Guang) belching 'is regarded as the child's way of paying compliments to the farmer, who in most cases happens to be his own father'. Among the DAGABAS no significance is attached to belching.

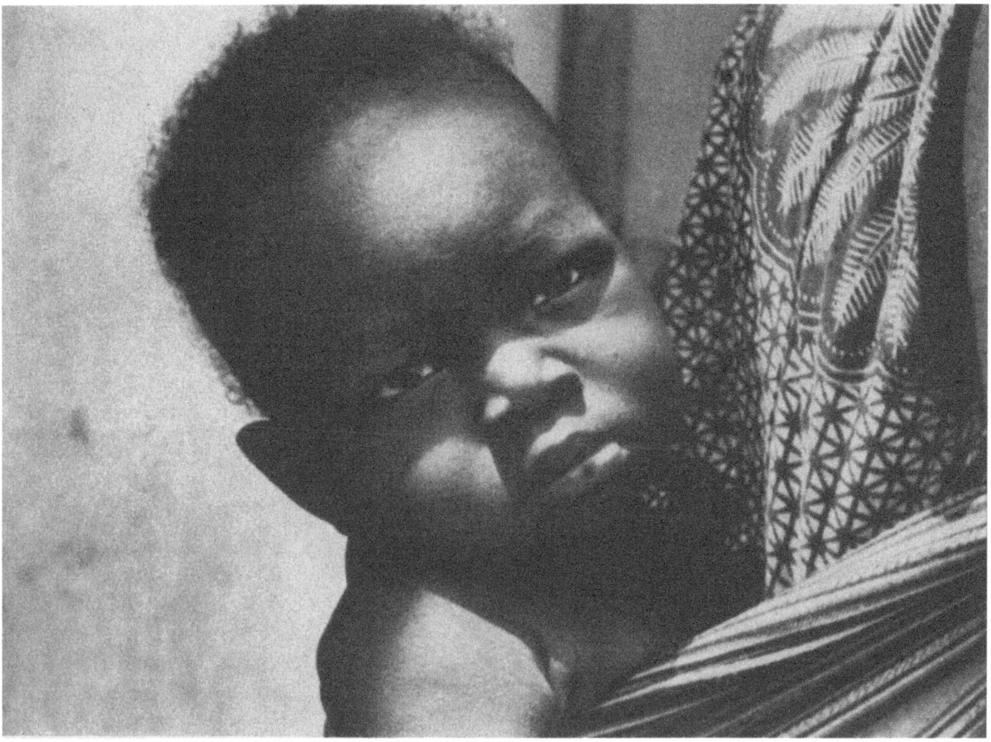

Infants being carried. 17. This child is being carried with its arms free of the carrying-cloth. Age given by the mother as four months. Taken in Vakpo.

18. Child of four months being carried with one arm free of the carrying-cloth (the right arm). Taken in Tamale.

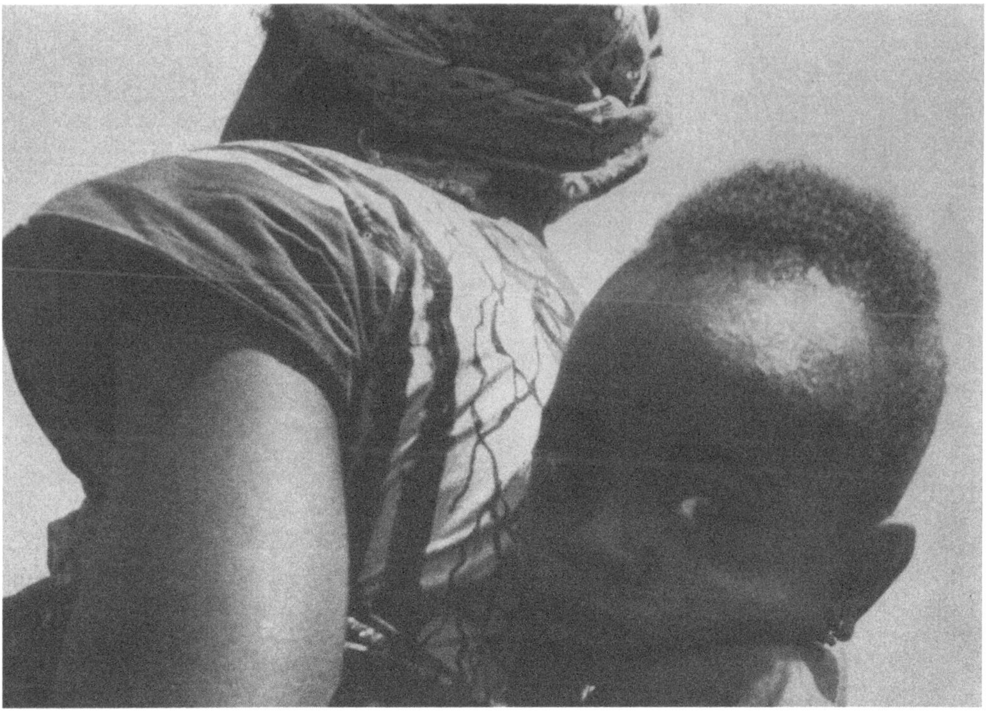

Infants being carried. 19. In the Northern Territories, where women do not usually wear cover-cloths or carrying-cloths, the baby may be carried in a small rush basket, which is either slung from the shoulder by a strap, or carried on the head. Taken on the road between Wa and Bole

20. Here is the baby, still asleep in its basket, which the young mother put on the ground to allow a photograph to be taken.

Infants being carried. 21. A baby being carried in a sling in the Northern Territories. Taken on the road between Navrongo and Bawku.

22. Young baby asleep on its mother's back. Taken in Apam.

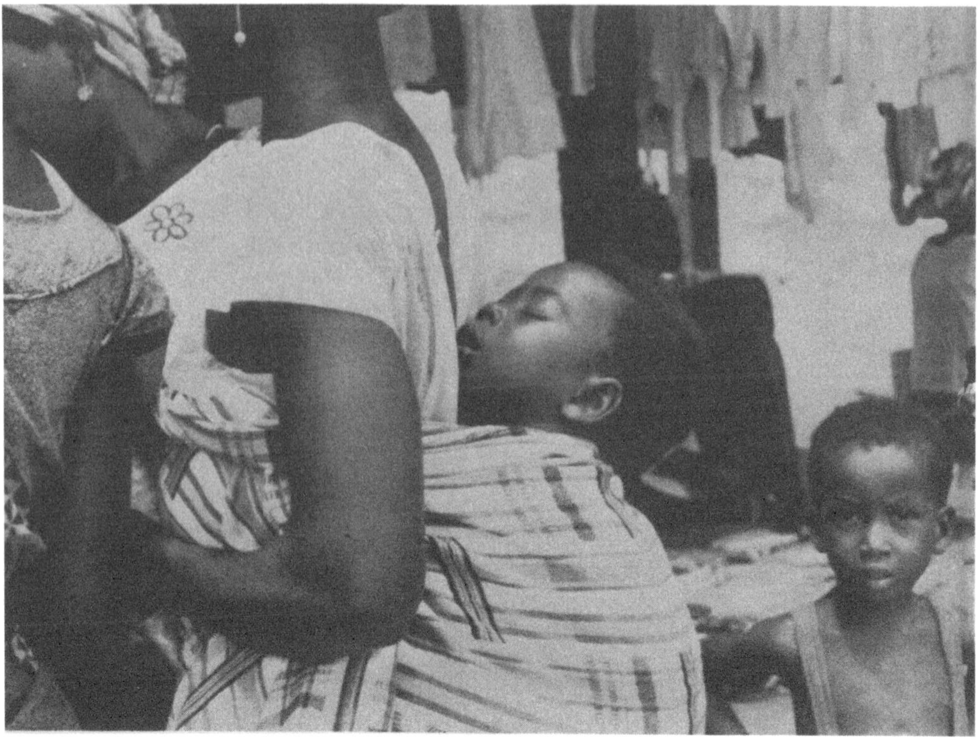

Infants being carried. 23. Infants on the back may accompany their mothers wherever they go. Here a baby sleeps peacefully while its mother examines cloths in the market. Taken in Vakpo.

24. This little girl on her mother's back seems totally uninterested in the argument which her mother is carrying on. Taken on the beach at Ahenboboi, near Cape Coast.

CHAPTER NINE

MOTOR DEVELOPMENT

> 'The proper way to crawl in Apa is on all fours, and a baby who shuffles forward on one leg is prevented from doing so by having big beads tied round its knee, so that it may feel pains when it crawls in the wrong way.'

SWADDLING clothes are not used in Ghana, and the only restrictions on the exercise of an infant's limbs are those deriving from the cloth by which it is tied to its mother's back. There is a widespread belief, however, that during the first three months of life, a child's neck may not be strong enough to support its head unaided, and for this reason its arms and shoulders are kept inside the carrying cloth and only the upper part of its head allowed to protrude.[1] After the age of three months, it is carried on the back with first one, and then both arms free of the carrying cloth.[2] In TUTU (Akwapim) for the first two to six months, babies are bound tightly on their mothers' backs to prevent strain on their necks. Girls are allowed more freedom of arms at three months, boys not until four months; 'the reason for allowing such a difference is that a boy is restless and his backbone is more delicate and less developed than that of the girl'. In JAKOBO (Asante) after a week the child is carried on its mother's back, and its limbs are tied down by the cover-cloth. After three months, its mother leaves first one hand, and then both hands free. It is thought that this support is necessary for its head and neck. In BEREKUM (Brong) very young babies are carried on the mother's back with their limbs confined. It is said that when the mother allows her baby's arms to hang free of the cover-cloth, this is a sign to her husband that she is

[1] See Plates 15, 16 and 22.
[2] See Plates 17 and 18.

ready to resume sexual intercourse. In TESHIE (Ga) a very young baby is carefully wrapped in the cloth by which it is carried on its mother's back; care is taken to see that this cloth encloses the whole of the baby's body, since it is believed that, as the baby is very fragile, its delicate parts must be held in place. In APIREDE (Cherepon) for the first three months the baby's arms and neck are enclosed within the cover-cloth; after that its arms are allowed to be outside. It is thought that this support is necessary for the child's neck. Among the ISALAS 'little or no clothes are worn during the early years of the child's life and the child is free to develop unrestricted by clothing of any kind'.

A period of time is usually allowed to elapse before new-born babies are carried on the back; this period varies from one week to six. Thereafter, very young children are carried about a great deal, and most infants spend a large proportion of the day on the backs of their mothers, elder sisters or other female friends and relatives.[1] Children under seven years of age are not as a rule encouraged to carry very young babies.[2] As soon as they can walk steadily, children cease to spend so much time on their mothers' backs, though they may still be carried to lull them to sleep, as a means of pacifying them or if the mother is going from place to place. Children may be occasionally carried on their mothers' backs until they are two or three years old, or even older; they are usually displaced by the arrival of a new baby.[3] A child may be carried by its father (in his arms, or on his shoulders) if the mother is very busy, or in the evening when he has returned home from work. In TUTU (Akwapim) the young child is carried all day by its mother or elder sister. Sometimes it is laid down to sleep. It may occasionally be carried by its father. By the age of six months, the child is carried less on the back. By nine months, children are carried on their mothers' backs only when they go to fetch water or to the farm. In BOSOFO (Asante) the young child is carried on the mother's back when she is going out, or to the farm, and at home when there is no elder sibling to sit beside it. The baby is also carried by its grandmother, aunts, elder sisters and sometimes

[1] In some tribes in the Northern Territories, children are carried on the hip, or in a sling, or they are placed in a basket and carried on the head. Rattray notes that the Lobers carry their children in cradles slung over their shoulders; (32) 438. See Plates 19, 20 and 21.

[2] See Plates 91-96.

[3] Christensen says that Fanti children, till about the age of three, spend much of their time on their mothers' backs; (5) 62. See Plates 23-6.

father. In JAISI (Asante) babies are left on the mat for long periods up to the time they are three months; thereafter they are carried by their mothers, siblings and other relatives. In BEREKUM (Brong) the child is carried by its mother and by other adults, especially when it is not well; when it is well it is often carried by its elder sister when the mother is busy or working. The father sometimes carries the child if the mother has a heavy load. At the farm the elder sister sits under a shady tree and looks after the baby while the mother works. In AYANZILI (Nzima) 'from the sixth month onwards, if the child is healthy, people from all corners of the village start to carry it about. It is taken from the first carrier by the second, third and so on and so forth, until the tenth or twelfth person, finding it crying without stopping, takes it to the mother; the father sometimes carries it in the evenings.' Among the KWAHUS the baby spends most of its daily life on its mother's back. In GOVIEFE (Ewe) 'the baby spends most of his time at the back of his mother, or grandmother, or aunt or sister, or house-maid, or any other female relative that happens to visit the house'. In DOME (Ga) the young child spends most of its time on its mother's back during the day. It is put down when it is asleep or when the mother is tired. Other adult relatives assist with carrying the baby when the mother is not at home or engaged in strenuous work. In LARTEH KUBEASI (Guang) the baby is carried about by either parent, by siblings, by the house-maid or by its grandmother. Children are carried on the backs of adults at different times until they are about three. Among the DAGABAS an infant is carried on the head in a basket made of reeds, or is carried by the mother on one side by her arm.[1] Children who have outgrown their baskets are carried at the side or at the back if the mother has a cloth.

The attitude of parents in Ghana towards their children's motor development is almost universally one of interest and encouragement. As soon as the child shows signs of trying to sit, he is encouraged to do so, by being placed in an upturned stool, or by being supported with boxes and cushions. An elder sibling or other child may sit behind him during his first attempts, and it is widely believed that if the elder child was himself an early walker, this will have a favourable effect on the new learner's development. Children are said normally to

[1] See Plates 19 and 20.

learn to sit at three to five months of age. Children are also encouraged in their efforts to crawl, which they are said to learn to do at about seven to nine months of age. Toys and other objects are placed on the ground in front of the infant, but out of reach; as he makes his way toward them, so they are moved further on.[1] In ABURI (Akwapim) boys are taught to sit at two months old, girls at three; pillows, chairs and other objects are used as supports for the child when it begins. 'It is believed that the more often the child is made to sit on the ground the quicker he learns to sit up. As soon as he sits up he is encouraged to crawl which he should be able to do on the sixth or eighth month. An attractive object is placed away from him. If the child shows interest, the grown-up tells him, "Come for it". The child stretches his hands and tries to reach it, screaming at the same time. The older person utters words of encouragement saying, "Yes, it is not very far, try hard". By stretching the hands and bending forward the child moves slowly towards the object. When he is about to reach it it is moved away from him. This goes on till the child becomes tired, begins to cry and is picked up.' In APA (Asante) children learn to sit at three to four months old; sometimes they are supported by an older child in doing so. The child is encouraged to crawl by its mother who stands in front of the crying child and moves back; 'sometimes, when the baby is crying, the mother takes no notice of it but rather goes to stand some yards in front of it, to call it; and the baby in its anxious state to reach the mother tries to move to reach her. As the baby moves forward the mother moves backwards to get the baby to have ample chance for practice. The proper way to crawl in Apa is on all fours, and a baby who shuffles forward on one leg is prevented from doing so by having big beads tied round its knee, so that it may feel pains when it crawls in the wrong way.' In BOSOFO (Asante) girls are made to sit for the first time at three months old, boys at four months. They are supported by their siblings, by cushions, or by being placed in an inverted chair. Children are encouraged to crawl by objects placed in front of them. 'Parents become interested in these achievements, and those whose children are not able to do that at this age get worried.' In APAM (Fante) children learn

[1] Among some tribes of the Northern Territories, special importance is attached to the occasion on which the infant crawls out of the compound for the first time; see Rattray (32) 133-4.

to sit from four months onwards; pillows are used to support it when it begins. Crawling is learnt between six and eight months of age, and the child is encouraged to do so by its parents, who place objects on the floor in front of it. In GOVIEFE (Ewe) 'it is considered a bad omen if a child begins teething before being able to sit alone'; the child is therefore taught to sit from four months of age, by the use of supports. It learns to crawl by the inducement of having objects placed out of reach in front of it. In CENTRAL ACCRA (Ga) when the child is seen making attempts to sit up, piles of cloths and other objects are used to support it in a sitting position. This usually takes place between the fourth and the seventh month. After it has learnt to sit, it is encouraged to crawl; objects are placed on the floor just out of its reach, and as it moves towards them so they are moved further still. 'Shouts of praise and approval are given as soon as the child touches the object.' In OTROWE (Adangme) the child learns to sit at four or five months old; 'between the sixth and the seventh month, the child is encouraged to crawl', by objects being placed in front of it out of reach. In WINNEBA (Efutu) the child begins to sit at about five months of age, when it is supported by cushions or by siblings. It begins to crawl at six or seven months, and is encouraged to do so by the placing of objects out of reach in front of it. Among the ISALAS 'learning to crawl is encouraged by siblings and mothers' sisters who carry the child outside the house for play. The mother's sister allows the child to sit and she begins to walk on all fours away from it. The child looks at her and also tries to imitate what the mother's sister is doing. The child is not forced into doing what the mother's sister does but by doing it over and over again in front of the child it soon begins to do so also.'

Parents show considerable interest in their children's efforts to walk, and begin to worry if they do not succeed in doing so by what is regarded as the normal age. Wooden three-wheeled walking frames are provided in many households; children may also be encouraged to walk by holding on to an upright stick for support, which is then moved along, or by being led or pulled along by the hands.[1] The age at which children are expected to have learnt to walk in most areas is between twelve and fourteen months.[2] Children who walk early are rewarded

[1] See Plates 27 and 28.

[2] According to Fortes, the average age by which Tallensi children have learnt to walk is two years; (12) 23.

with gifts; a boiled egg is a traditional reward in many places. Late walkers are given a good deal of attention. A walking frame is provided if it has not already been in use; the child's legs and joints are massaged with herbs; irritating enemas and suppositories may be given. Other forms of treatment which are said to have died out in some places, and which are still practised in others, are for the child to be tied into wooden splints and stood against a wall, or to be buried up to the thighs in the sand for a few hours, or to have a piece of thorn bush tied to its buttocks which pricks him when he tries to sit down. If these practices fail, a medicine man may be consulted.[1] In ABURI (Akwapim) the child learns to walk at about one year of age. 'If after one year he makes no attempt to walk then he is considered a lazy child.' His joints are vigorously massaged. Adults encourage him to walk by holding his hands and pulling him along. 'If the child shows reluctance he is dragged along till the older person feels he is tired. He is then left alone weeping.' A walking frame may be provided. Another treatment for late walkers is the insertion of medicine into the rectum which irritates him when he sits down, thereby forcing him to stand up again. In APA (Asante) children usually stand at eight months and they are encouraged to walk by applause and by being led along by an adult, or by being given a walking frame. Slow walkers are given rectal suppositories, two every morning; the witch-doctor is consulted, and the child is vaccinated in its joints, and sacrifices are made. In BOMPATA (Asante) some individual differences of development are allowed for in learning to walk, which are attributed to heredity, and to certain practices during pregnancy; for example, laziness during pregnancy on the mother's part may cause the child to be a late walker. Alternatively, late walking may be attributed to weakness, or to witchcraft. 'Nearly every elderly woman interviewed' knew of a herbal preparation, consisting of ground peppers and other herbs, to be used as a rectal suppository for causes of late walking. If late walking is attributed to laziness on the child's part, pieces of thorny shrubs may be tied to the child's knees and buttocks, so that it is pricked when it sits down. This is a well-known treatment, though not popular. If such home remedies fail, a medicine man is consulted. Early walkers are

[1] Fortes says that, among the Tallensis, parents do not worry if their children are backward in acquiring motor skills; (12) 25.

praised and encouraged, and rewarded with eggs. In KOFORIDUA (Asante) children are discouraged from walking early. 'The belief is that children who walk before their normal period of doing so, die early, for they want to perform their duties on here quickly and pass away into the next world.' Once the normal time for walking is past, however, the child's legs may be tied in splints, pounded herbs may be rubbed on its legs, and it may be given pepper and herbal suppositories. Among the DENKYERAS the child is taught to walk with the use of a walking frame, or by being held on its feet by adults; 'it is thought that without practice of this kind the child will become lazy and be unable to walk even when fairly big'. Slow walkers are given an enema. In GOVIEFE (Ewe) if the child has not begun to walk by the time he is about a year old 'the mother has begun to get worried; she wonders whether he is not going to walk. She finds ways and means of making him walk as early as possible. She feels his leg bones to see whether there is something wrong with them. She may accuse the child of laziness and cowardice. She suspects that the muscles at the back of his knees are weak and so in bathing the child she pays particular attention to these muscles and the legs, bending and stretching the knees and the ankles several times, pressing them with a hot towel and embrocating them freely with shea nut oil. If this treatment fails to yield the expected result, incisions are made on the muscles at the back of the knees and specially prepared medicine, charred and ground into powder, is rubbed hard into the cuts to ginger the muscle up to activity. The child grins with pain. This treatment may be repeated several times. As this treatment also fails to make the child walk, the mother again suspects the possibility of bowel sores or a kind of phlegmy matter in his waist. Special hot herbs are syringed into his rectum. This is repeated from time to time. The child feels much pain. The next thing the mother does is to try and pull the child along on his feet, but this too cannot be of any help. The last attempt made is to get him a wooden tricycle to push along. By this time the child may have reached the stage in his development when he can walk. And so, incidentally, after pushing the tricycle along for some time, the child may begin to walk clumsily at first, its feet wide apart. Everybody becomes very glad and pleased when the baby begins to walk by the fifteenth month or so. He is rewarded for walking early. He gets gifts of pennies and halfpennies from his parents, his grandmothers, aunts, as well as from his parents' friends and acquaintances. These coins, together with a few cowry-shells, are tied on strings and used as anklets for the child. When he walks, the coins and the shells jingle and jingle and the sound pleases him so much so that he seems to feel like walking all the time. He is praised by everybody interested in him. Some mothers give the child eggs as a reward; others may give him chicken broth and food.' In DOME (Ga) 'anxious adults help the child to walk as soon as it shows signs of standing in an upright position'. It is believed that the child will walk earlier if it is helped. Some parents provide a walking frame for their children. The average age for walking is at one year old, but any age between eight and eighteen months is usual. As soon as their children can walk, parents reward them with boiled eggs. In AGOMANYA (Krobo) the child learns to walk at about thirteen or fourteen months of age. If it reaches eighteen months and has not yet learnt to do so, a piece of its mother's loin-cloth is tied round its knee, or it may be given a special enema. Some late walkers, however, are left to develop on their own. In APIREDE (Cherepon) children learn to walk between eight and fourteen months of age. It is believed that walking too early, before eight months, causes long-leggedness. A special enema is used for late walkers. A walking stick, or a frame may be provided; 'there is much belief in this wheel as an effective aid for teaching the child to walk'. Among the ISALAS 'children are not rewarded for walking early. In fact, a mother is rebuked by the old ladies in the family if she encourages her child to walk earlier than a year old. The old ladies tell her she is impatient about sexual intercourse and that is why she wishes her child to walk so soon.'

In most households there is very little restriction on the movement of young children within the house and compound, apart from the area round the fire and cooking pots. Children are often warned away from hot or dangerous things by the mother's pretending to have burnt or cut herself, or by their being held near enough to the fire to feel the heat, or even by their being burnt slightly. An additional factor which may lead the mother to take special care of her child in this way is that she may be required to pay a pacification fee to her husband if the child is badly burnt or harmed through her neglect. In DWINYAMA (Asante) the child is allowed free access to all parts

Infants being carried. 25. From about the age of three or four months, infants are carried on their mothers' backs with one or both arms free of the carrying-cloth. Taken in Bolgatanga market.

26. Taken in Christiansborg.

Children learning to walk. 27. This toddler, said by the mother to be fourteen months old, was being encouraged to walk by being held by the hands. On the photographer's approach, however, he ran to clutch his mother's skirts. Taken in Winneba.

28. This eleven-month-old child was being encouraged to walk by the two women, but they abandoned the attempt as soon as the camera was produced. Taken in Goviefe.

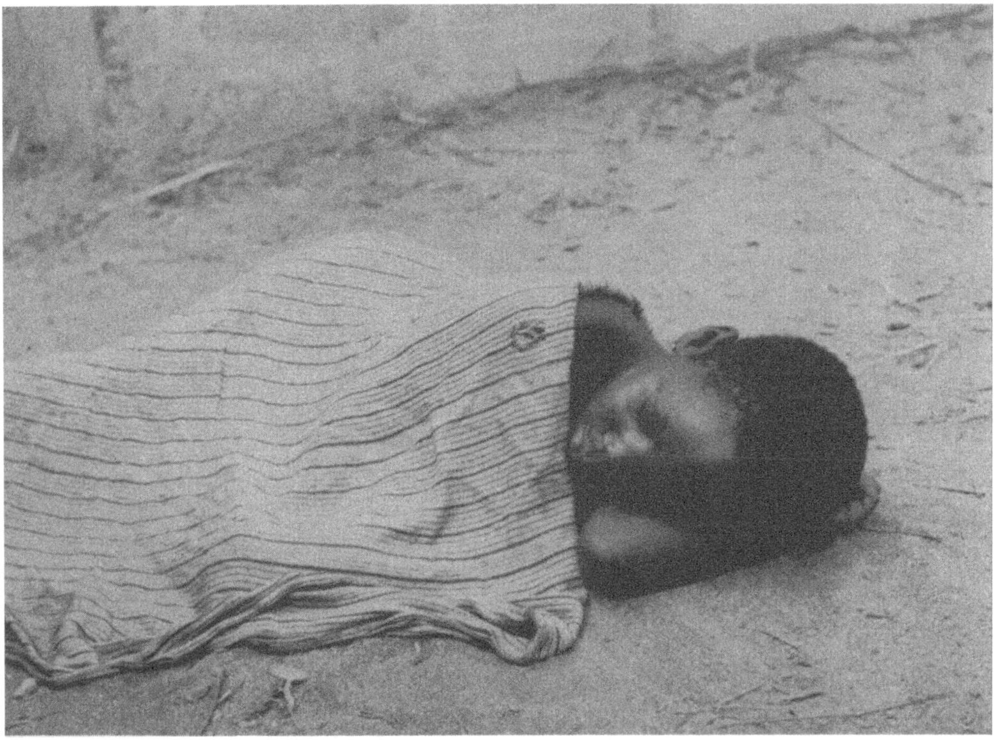

Children asleep during the day. 29. Children lie down and sleep during the day whenever they feel tired. Taken at Ahenboboi, near Cape Coast.

30. The children at the corner are intent on the photographer. Taken at Christiansborg.

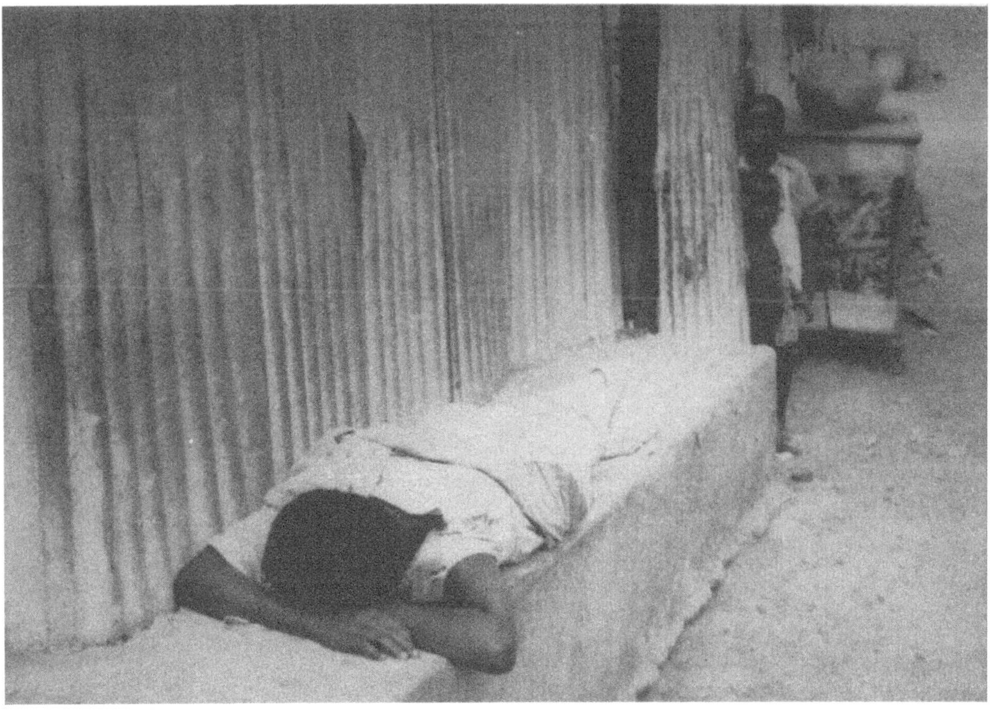

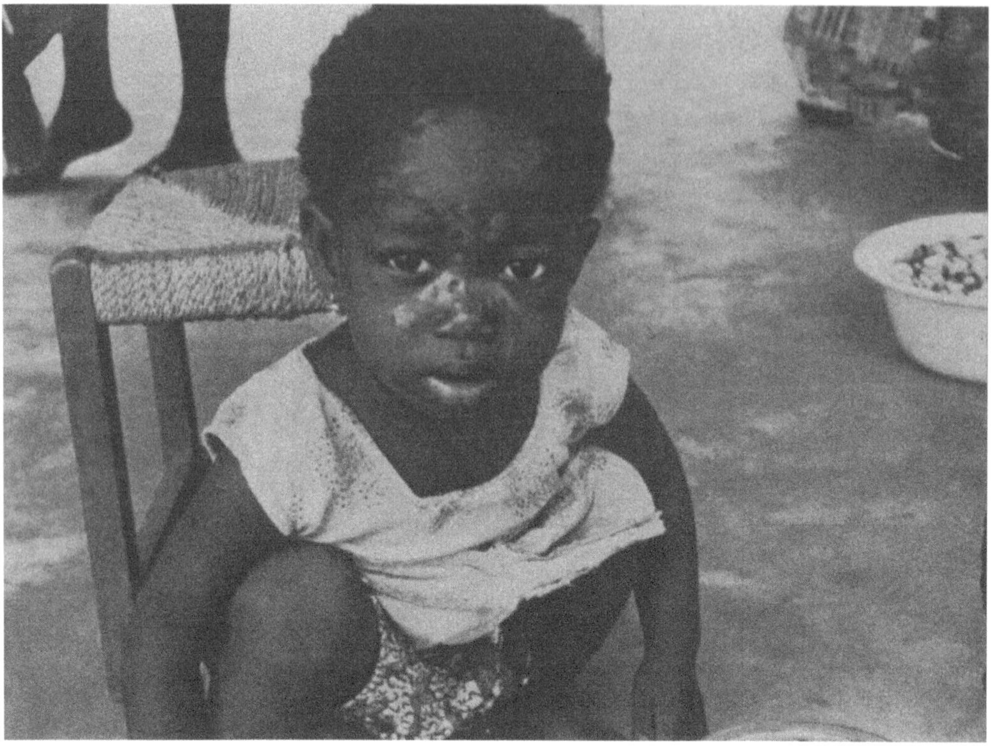

Children's health. 31. Open sores on children's skin are often left untended. This little girl was photographed in Vakpo market.

32. Taken in Winneba.

of the house, but it is watched by adults and elder siblings. In APAM (Fante) 'as soon as the baby learns to crawl, it is at complete liberty to move anywhere inside the house except near the fire'. In GBLEDE (Ewe) the young child is allowed to wander freely in the house except near the fire-place. In DOME (Ga) children are allowed full freedom of movement. They are encouraged to play outside, since 'parents do not want to be disturbed; that is the reason why they send them to play outside the house'. In LARTEH KUBEASI (Guang) there are no limits for the child inside the house except the fire and the cooking pots.

Young children are not allowed to wander outside the compound unaccompanied and various threats of bogy men, monsters, ghosts, policemen, white men, wild animals and lorries are widely used to keep them inside. Such stories of dwarves, cannibals, monsters and the like are also regarded as ways of keeping the children safely at home while the parents are away at the farm. In TUTU (Akwapim) 'to keep them from playing about the street, their mothers tell them frightening stories about madmen who will catch hold of them and cut their heads, or policemen who will put them into their long bags until they suffocate and die'. It is to be noticed that Tutu is on the main Accra road and there is a constant stream of traffic. For this reason parents are very anxious to prevent their children from going on the road, and stories of dwarves, and fairies who live in the bush underneath mango trees, and who catch and eat children, may be told. In JAISI (Asante) children who wander outside are threatened with lorries, or with doctors who will cut off their penises. Younger children are threatened with ghosts, bogy men and bearded cannibals in the bush. In JAKOBO (Asante) the mother is responsible to the father for the child's welfare, and should the child burn or cut itself, the mother must pay her husband a pacification fee of a fowl, eggs, or yam, and even a sheep if the child is seriously hurt. Children are not allowed outside the compound before they are five, and they are threatened with cows, or with 'men who cut off hearts', if they do so. Persistent wanderers have pepper pushed up the rectum. After the age of six, children are allowed to play freely outside, though they must come home to the evening meal. In GOVIEFE (Ewe) children are kept from fire by the mother pretending to be burnt, or alternatively by putting the child near enough to the fire to feel its heat. Threats of Hausa men, or a monster called *Sasabonsam*, are used to prevent children from wandering off. In CENTRAL ACCRA (Ga) 'a child who persistently walks to dangerous places is told stories of frightful people. He is told the man will come and circumcise him if he frequents dangerous places, or a white man will come for him, or a masked man will carry him away.' If the child persists, he may be frightened by elder children wearing masks. In TESHIE (Ga) parents do not bother to tell their children not to wander off, since there are very infrequent lorries on the roads, and there is no danger of the child's being lost since all the children are known by everyone. In WINNEBA (Efutu) children are kept from touching hot or sharp things by shouts from nearby adults. Children are frightened with stories of monsters to prevent them from wandering off. 'The stories that are told to frighten children are generally invented and some of them are as follows: (i) There are certain bad spirits in the universe who go about looking for children who do not stay at home, and whenever they come across them they mark them in a certain way. Then at night, when all is dark and everybody is asleep, they come stealthily home and take them away without their mothers seeing them. And far away in their dark horrible homes they keep them for ever as servants. (ii) A wicked old man called *Sasabonsam* (the devil) has a very big stick, and with this big stick which can break everything into pieces, he knocks off the heads of all young children who stray from their home. (iii) Some fearful men with a big knife-marks all over their faces go about morning and evening with old cocoa bags and when they see any bad boy or girl who roams about in the street or gives too much trouble to his parents, they throw him or her into their bag, and carry him or her off to be killed for their food. (iv) If a child does not pay heed to his mother's words and he walks about in the town, he may get lost for ever and will never see his father and mother and sister and brother again. (v) Children who do not stay quietly at home with their parents ultimately lose their navels and cease to be human.' Among the DAGABAS 'over-cautious mothers show alarm and relate dreadful stories to their children when they wander away from their homes; they speak of frightful animals and persons who may carry them away if they wander far from their homes'.

Generally, for children to sit still for any length of time on their own accord is regarded as a sign of illness.[1] They are expected to sit still and keep quiet when there are visitors, however, or when in the presence of elders. In MAMPONG (Akwapim) quiet children are praised; over-active children are sometimes thought to be bewitched. In BOMPATA (Asante) while children are not expected to sit still all the time, they are discouraged from dangerous play and punished for hurting themselves. A child who is invited by another to go and play with a ball, replies: 'Let me go and see if Mummy is not at home, for if she sees me playing and I hurt myself, she will push red pepper into my anus'. In BEREKUM (Brong) sitting still in children is attributed to illness or to hunger. In GBLEDE (Ewe) sitting still is taken as an indication of illness in children. In KORDIABE (Shai) 'in some cases some children are observed to be sitting still when they are hungry or when they are feeling homesick, for instance, the mother has left home for a long time and there is no sign of her coming'. In LARTEH KUBEASI (Guang) the attitude towards children's sitting still varies; some expect them to do so, others do not.

[1] Fortes says, however, that a Tallensi child of twelve to eighteen months may be left to sit still by itself for half an hour or longer without any diversion, while the mother is busy; (12) 24.

CHAPTER TEN

SLEEP

> 'Ghosts and weird stories of bogy men and the darkness are used to frighten children to sleep. This sometimes results in nightmares during which the children shout.'

THERE is little idea of a fixed bedtime for children in Ghana.[1] Very young children sleep on and off during the day while on their mothers' backs, and only 'go to bed' when their mothers do so. Children who sit round listening to Ananse stories[2] may fall asleep by the side of their parents; they are picked up and taken into their bedrooms when the parents themselves retire. On moonlit nights the older children play games, often until midnight. In ABURI (Akwapim) there are no fixed hours for children's sleep. In TUTU (Akwapim) six-year-olds are allowed to play up until eight o'clock, especially on moonlit nights. In DWINYAMA (Asante) younger children are expected to be asleep by eight o'clock. Babies are allowed to sleep when they like and are petted when awake. In JAISI (Asante) mothers try to get their children to bed early, as it is believed that insufficient sleep makes a child weak. In GOVIEFE (Ewe) 'on the whole children do not go to bed regularly or early enough. In some cases they are not to blame for this undesirable state of affairs. Domestic, social and farming practices affect the regularity or otherwise of the family mealtimes. Some of the farms are up on the hill-tops or sides and one has to go far into the plains to get a fertile area for one's farm. Then again, during the Harmattan[3] water becomes scarce. Women have to rise very early to go and fetch water and by the time they have gone twice it is already broad

[1] See Plates 29 and 30.
[2] See page 192 below.
[3] The dry season.

daylight. By the time a woman has finished with her domestic tasks and followed her husband to the farm the sun is already high up in the heavens. Before she returns home it is already dusk and so the evening meal is late. Before this time the children have begun dozing outside. Then, on moonlit nights the children are usually too much absorbed in their plays, story and riddle telling, singing, etc., to bother to sleep early or regularly. Also, during funerals, wake-keeping or other festivals, children enjoy the adult activities and stay out far into the night. Even if a child would like to go to bed early there might be strangers in the room conversing and so he might be compelled to wait. Then at night, they may be raised several times to urinate. They are also up at dawn, especially during the dry season, to accompany their mothers to the riverside. And so though the people realize the importance of good sufficient sleep for children, yet there are so many practices that affect the regularity and sufficiency of children's sleep.' In CHRISTIANSBORG (Ga) children's sleeping hours are generally fairly well regulated. All children under six are expected to be asleep by about eight p.m., but in certain areas, children who live near drinking bars, cinemas, and other night-spots may not sleep through the noise and go out, despite the threats of bogy men. Children of four to six years old who sleep during the afternoon are believed to grow up lazy adults, so this practice is not encouraged. In DOME (Ga) children's sleeping hours are not regulated, and they go to bed when they feel sleepy. They lie down to sleep anywhere, often near the adults who are telling stories. 'They do not go direct to their beds, but they lie down to sleep at any place in the house usually near a group of members of the household who are telling stories. The parents carry the younger ones to their beds when they themselves are ready to go to bed. They wake up the older ones to go to bed. Then each one is covered with a sleeping cloth.' Among the ISALAS 'the time for sleep is not regular, since parents go to sleep at any time they feel like sleeping. Children are at liberty to go to sleep earlier if they wish to do so, but they must all go to bed when the last adult retires to go to bed.'

Despite the uncertainty and irregularity of time for going to bed, once they are there, parents tend to be strict with younger children about going to sleep. To induce a child to sleep, various threats and stories of bogy men and monsters, often of a very elaborate kind involving the assistance of other adults as disguised ogres, are widely used. Children may also be lulled and sung to sleep, or beaten, promised delicacies or threatened with their denial. The customary method of settling an infant to sleep is to give it the breast. In TUTU (Akwapim) 'at two years old if a child does not want to go to sleep, he is first of all induced by his mother, sometimes with promises of food, dresses, playthings or anything the child likes most. If inducement fails she begins to threaten him with stories of bogy men, policemen, mad dogs, men and the tree-bear, and if this does not still send him to sleep he is beaten, and this invariably succeeds.' Children of six do not sleep during the day and are allowed to go to sleep when they wish. 'Dreams and nightmares sometimes disturb the sleep of many children between four and ten years old.' In JAISI (Asante) babies are crooned, sung, rocked and suckled to sleep; 'nearly all the mothers in Jaisi say that courting the baby's nap is the greatest task of the day'. For older children promises of food, beatings, pretended fear of wild animals, threats of policemen, bogy men, sanitary inspectors, and Mohammedans who will circumcise them, are used to send them to sleep. In JAKOBO (Asante) nothing is done to send children to sleep; there is a saying that eating and sleeping are never forced on a child. Babies, however, may be coaxed and petted to sleep. Children are allowed to play at all hours, though some children who play late in the streets and have to be fetched home may be smacked. Children who play late on moonlit nights often sleep during the afternoon. In GOVIEFE (Ewe) 'the usual threats of bogy men, juju-men, dead hyaenas, Hausa men, and executioners are used. The mother may pretend to call a Hausa man to "Come and carry away a child who does not want to go to bed". She pretends the Hausa man has responded by using another tone of her voice. She may arrange with somebody, say the father, to give the response, to growl, strike the fence and utter strange, fearful sounds. Or the mother may ask his father to call a dead hyaena to come and catch him. While the father calls out, or pretends to go out to call the monster, the child, sorely terrified, clings fast to his mother, sobbing. The mother tells him to close his eyes or cover them with his cloth and keep quiet so that the dead beast might not hear or see him, and that he also might not see it. While the father still calls out, or pretends to leave the house, the mother pretends to plead on the child's behalf for mercy and asks her husband to stop, as "Kofi has closed his eyes and has promised to go to bed immediately". The father pretends to insist on calling the dead beast till the child worries the mother to take him to bed. The other children in the house may also help, as pre-arranged, by pretending to run to their bedroom for fear the dead hyaena might seize them too. Stories of bogy men are also told and advantage is taken of the fearful shrieks and cries of nocturnal birds and animals, such as owls, bats and monkeys, to warn him away to his bed. If a flash of light is seen the child is told it is a witch shining in the dark going out to search for children who do not want to sleep and suck their blood. He is told to run quickly to bed.' In KORDIABE (Shai) babies are lulled to sleep. 'When a child does not want to sleep he is often threatened. Then he would run to his bed and cover himself up with his cloth. The mother would ask someone to go outside the house to make strange sounds, usually imitating sounds of animals. Then she would say: "Ah! the beast is coming". Then she would say: "Come and sleep quickly so that it might not come and catch you". Sometimes as a result of this many children become terribly afraid and they fear to sleep alone; they prefer to sleep by their mothers. They are allowed to do so and are carried to their beds when they are asleep. A woman remarked how one night her little daughter about four years old was threatened to cause her to sleep. She said that she became so affected that for almost a year she was afraid to sleep alone.' Among the DAGABAS if an infant does not want to sleep, 'the mother induces it to do so by giving it her breast to suckle, or by seeing to it and rocking it'. If children refuse to sleep, mothers may resort to threats and stories of bogy men and wild animals. 'A mother may be heard to say, "If you do not sleep, I shall slaughter you", or "I shall throw you to the hyaena which is standing behind the house". She would then imitate the howling of a hyaena, "Humm, humm, so-and-so says it will not sleep, therefore come and take it away." The child becomes emotional and as it screams, the mother says, "If you do not wish the hyaena to take you away, then you should sleep". As the child closes its eyes to sleep, the mother shouts to the hyaena to go away.'

For fear of evil spirits, which are believed to be abroad at night, children are rarely allowed to sleep by themselves, and the younger ones usually share their parents' bedrooms; the baby sleeping in the same bed as the mother (unless she is pregnant, when her excessive body-warmth is believed to be harmful), the rest sharing sleeping mats on the floor. Older children may be put in another bedroom. The sexes are not usually separated before puberty, and even after puberty the separation may consist simply of their sleeping at different ends of the same room. In some areas, however, once the boys are old enough to work with their father (which may be from as young as seven years old), they sleep in the men's compound, leaving the girls and infants to share the mother's room.[1] In ABURI (Akwapim) babies sleep with their mothers on the same mat until the latter are pregnant again; thereafter the mothers sleep alone, as the heat of a pregnant woman is believed to be bad for children. Children under sixteen sleep with one another, boys and girls in separate rooms; if the number of rooms is limited, the girls sleep in the parents' bedroom. 'All the parents say that marital intercourse should not be carried on while the children are not asleep, but some children pretend to be sleeping in order to witness what their parents are doing.' Except in very few cases, children have to share their sleeping mats with one another. In DWINYAMA (Asante) the child sleeps in its mother's bed until it is fully weaned, which in some cases may be until it is seven years old. If the parents live together, the children may sleep in their bedroom; in some cases with girls until they marry. Children are not allowed to sleep by themselves as it is believed that evil spirits may harm them. Children always share sleeping mats with others. In JAKOBO (Asante) polygynous wives leave their children at home when they go off to their husbands' houses. Older boys sleep in a separate room, while girls sleep in the mother's bedroom with the babies. People do not sleep in the same room because there is not enough space, but because 'sleeping together in a room tightens the thread of kinship in a family'. Moreover, the baby's wants are more easily attended to.

[1] Rattray says that, in Ashanti, a male child sleeps with his father as soon as he is weaned; (30) 12. Christensen notes that, among the Fantis, 'sleeping arrangements often place a young child in a situation to observe coitus between its parents or other adults'; (5) 99. Field notes that, among the Gas, boys spread their mats on the floor of their parents' room during wet weather, their parents occupying the bed; (9) 9. Fortes says that, among the Tallensis, children sleep in their mothers' rooms until about seven or eight, when boys share another room; girls may remain in their mothers' rooms until puberty. When a woman's husband comes to her bedroom, children over the age of three are sent to another room; (14) 60-3 and 193-4. Goody says that, among the LoWiili, unmarried children sleep in their mothers' rooms; (19) 39.

Children's health. 33. Umbilical hernias are a very common sight in Ghana. Taken in Kpandu.

34. Boy with a pronounced umbilical hernia in Apam.

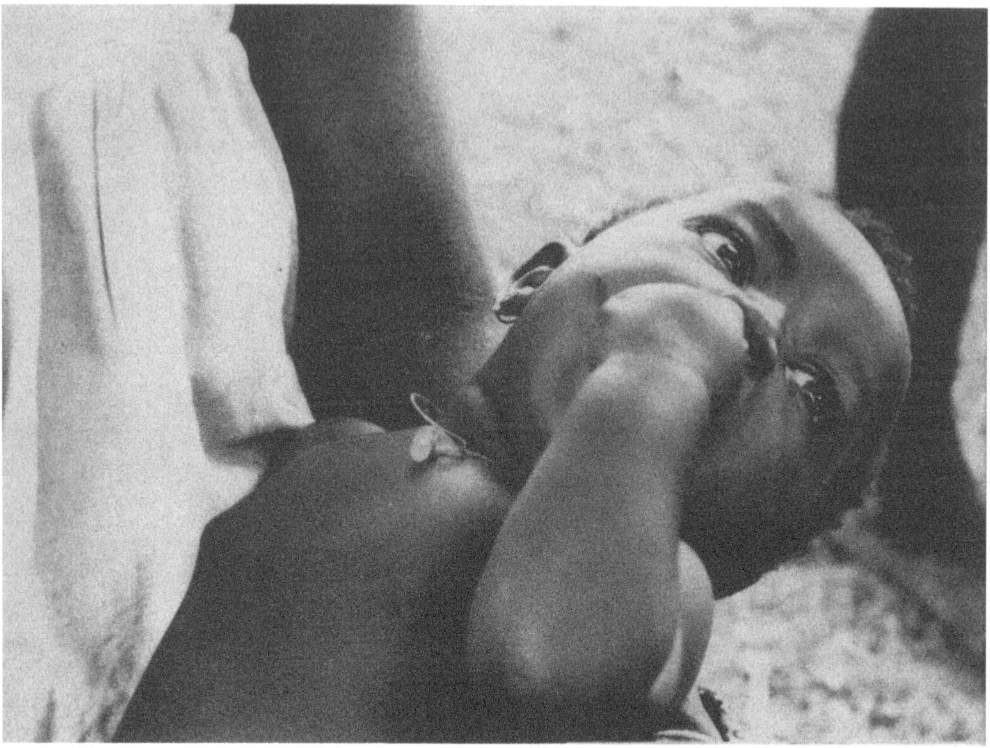

Children's health. 35. A baby of six months wearing a small coloured stone as a charm against fevers. Taken in Winneba.

36. A Lobi child of the Northern Territories with an array of amulets and charms round its neck. Notice the woman's lip ornaments. Taken on the road between Wa and Bole.

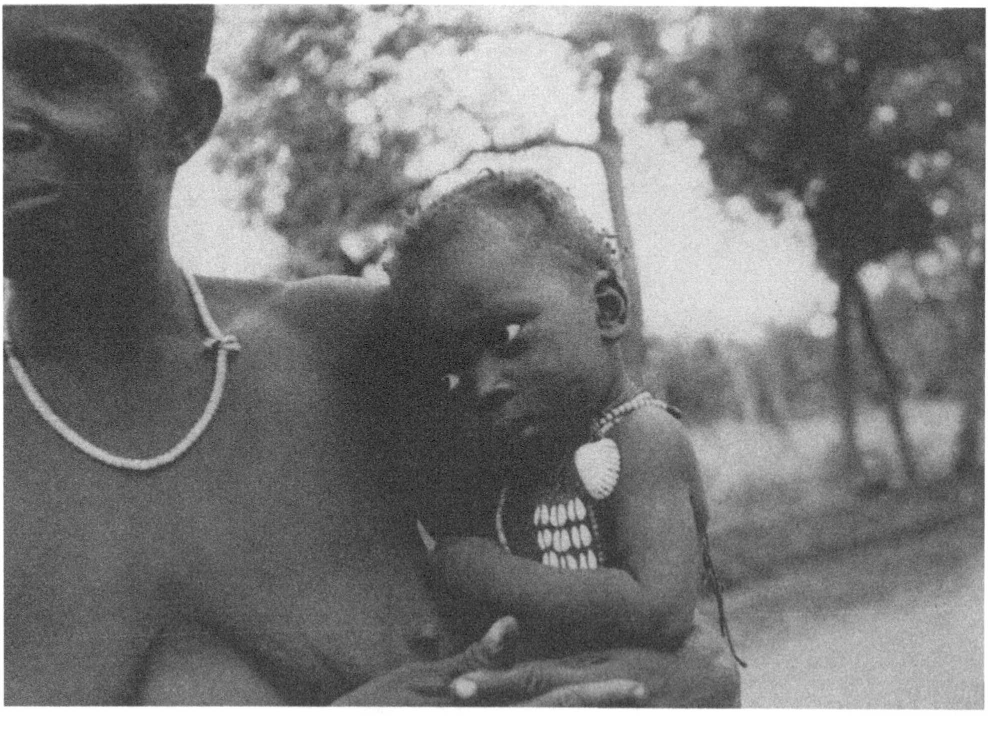

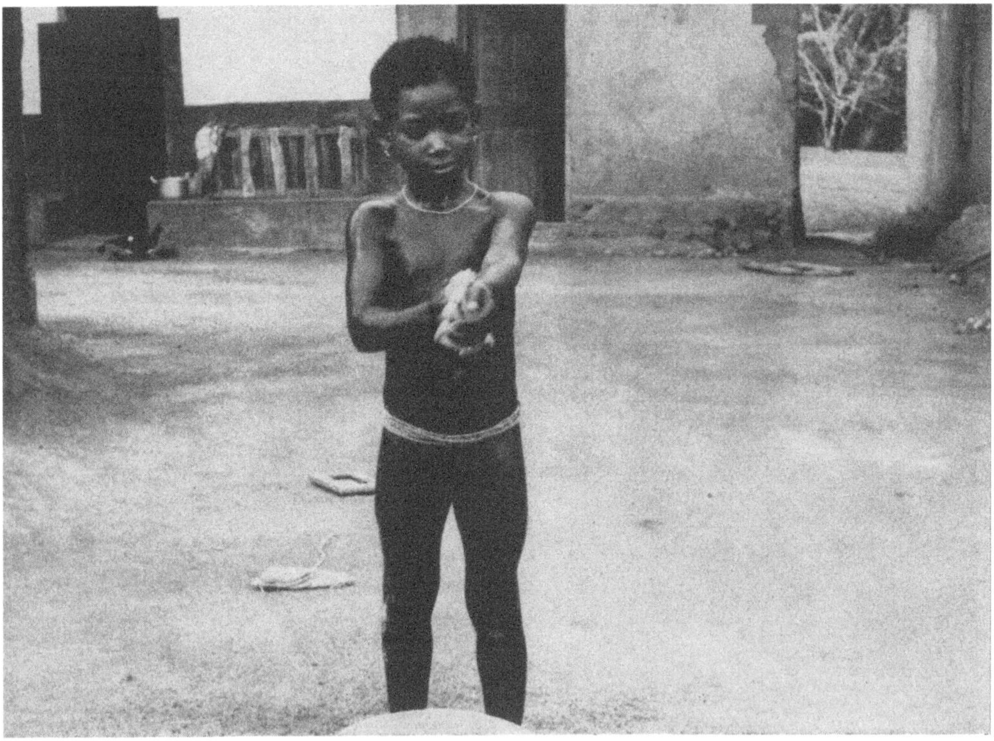

Children bathing. 37. A girl taking an early morning bath in an Ashanti village.

38. This six-month-old baby has been left to play in the water after being given a bath. Taken in Gblede.

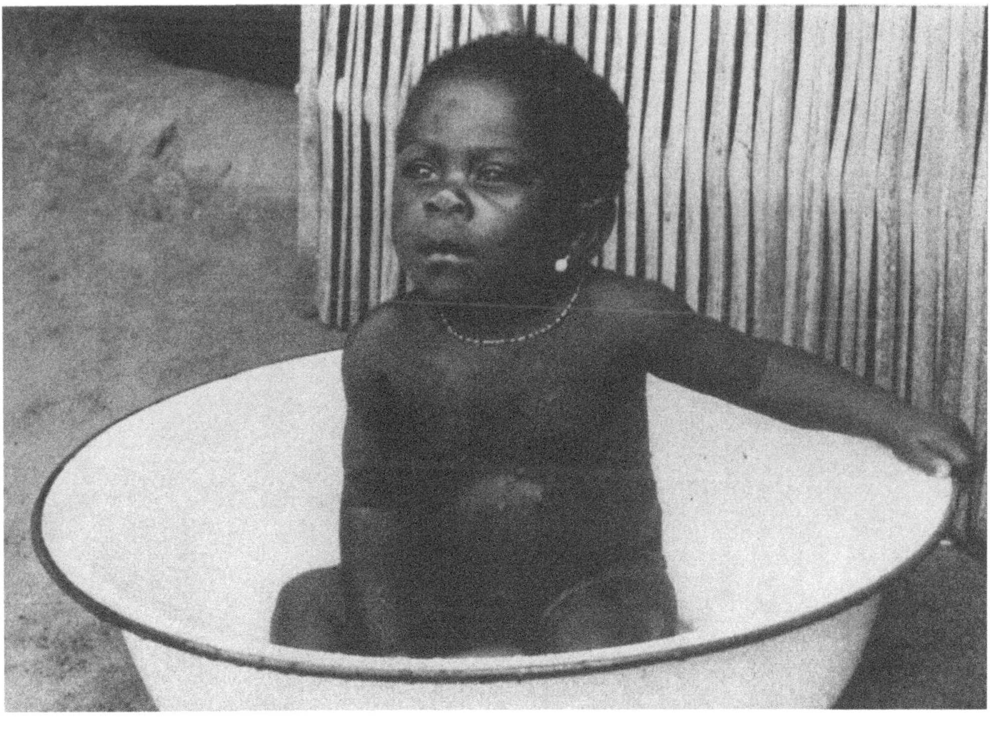

Children bathing. 39. Young boy about to soap himself. Notice discarded cloth in background, and wooden board to stand on. He is using a bunch of palm fibres as a sponge and a large piece of washing soap. Taken in Bosofo.

40. Two boys washing themselves in James Town, Accra. Notice the elder sister nearby, supervising.

Two or three children usually share a sleeping mat. Among the DENKYERAS the baby sleeps with its mother until it is weaned, it sleeps in the parents' bedroom until it is five, and thereafter with its siblings, the sexes separated on either side of the room. In KPANDU (Ewe) the youngest child sleeps in its mother's bed. 'When a husband and a wife sleep, no child sleeps between them. It is said that if a child sleeps between, and marital intercourse takes place, the fact that the man passes over the child to mate causes the child to be sick and it may eventually die.' Children stay in their parents' bedroom till they reach the age of twelve. In CHRISTIANSBORG (Ga) up to the age of six, children sleep in their parents' bedrooms; thereafter they sleep with their siblings, if there are enough rooms. The girls sleep on one side of the room, the boys on the other. In AGOMANYA (Krobo) children up to four years old sleep with their mother; the youngest in her bed. The rest of the children sleep together in the hall; adolescent boys and girls are separated. In WINNEBA (Efutu) young children sleep with their parents; thereafter with other children. 'Their belief is that ghosts visit their homes at night when they are asleep, and any child who sleeps alone will have the misfortune of being handled or dragged along by them. Also that some ghosts are cruel to the extent of sitting on the heads of children who are found lying by themselves and find amusement in suffocating them.' Children over five may sleep with other children of the same sex, though not necessarily with siblings. Children usually share sleeping mats.

CHAPTER ELEVEN

CHILDREN'S HEALTH

> 'Though there is a widespread belief in witchcraft and juju-men, and the constant consultation of fetish, also of wearing of amulets, every parent is aware that to ensure good health in themselves and their children, certain rules of health must be observed.'

WHILE such things as wetness, cold, over-eating and the neglect of sores are recognized by parents in Ghana to lead to ill health, yet the main cause that is thought to underlie disease is witchcraft. Stomach-ache, convulsions, infectious diseases are all thought to proceed from the activities of evil spirits, either through the agency of sorcerers, or on account of a failure to keep taboos. Even where the natural aetiology of a disease is recognized, the original precipitating cause is thought to be supernatural. In some areas, adultery on the part of either parent is thought, under certain circumstances, to lead to the illness or even the death of a child. In APA (Asante) 'mothers have got the idea that the underlying causes of their babies' ill health are stomach disorders in most cases'. Other suspected causes of ill health are staying in wet clothes and too much exposure to the sun. Convulsions in infants are attributed to evil spirits. The breaking of taboos is another cause of illness; 'Do not cut your finger-nails at night, or you will die at an early age. Do not pretend to pound fufu in the mortar when there is nothing in it, or else your mother's breast gets swollen. If you leave the pestle in the mortar without cleaning it after beating fufu with it, you will develop a stiff back. Do not tell stories during the day, otherwise you will develop elephantiasis. If you sing or talk at meals, your father will die. Cover the navel while a corpse is being taken to the cemetery, else your navel will decay. If you catch flies, you will suffer from a stomach-ache.' In BANKO whooping-cough is attributed to the influence of witches. The infectious nature of this disease, and of measles, is recognized, however. *Kwashiorkor* is attributed to the effects of weaning and the mother's new pregnancy. Diarrhoea is attributed to devils. Every child is expected to get yaws. In JAKOBO (Asante) wetness is considered a great danger to health, and children are not allowed to run about in the rain. Dirt is not considered dangerous, and children are allowed to eat food picked off the ground, as it is believed that this promotes strength. In BEREKUM (Brong) certain illnesses, such as yaws, are believed necessary to proper development in children; worms are believed to help digestion and they are not removed. 'The old ladies attribute most of the illness which attacks the young girls to the bad care and negligence of the genitals.' Among the DENKYERAS 'almost invariably diseases affecting young children are attributed to witchcraft and malign spirits'. In KPANDU (Ewe) 'among the chief dangers to the health of the young child are, according to magnitude, marital intercourse during nursing, witches sucking the blood of the child, charms by enemies, stomach disorders, wetness and colds and fever. Anyone seen rubbing or pressing the baby's head is suspected of trying to harm him and if the child feels ill within those days, the fellow is said to have charmed him.' In CHRISTIANSBORG (Ga) wetness, dirt and over-exertion are thought to be the chief causes of ill health. In KORDIABE (Shai) dirt, too much exposure to the sun, over-exertion and witchcraft are thought to be the main causes of ill health in children. In APIREDE (Cherepon) 'witchcraft is considered the greatest cause of illness in children and there is scarcely any person, Christian or pagan, who does not believe the diagnosis of the witch-doctor. Thus, if a child is burnt or scalded, parents are made to believe that it was a witch that pushed him into the fire or liquid. If he cries at midnight because he is suffering from stomach-ache, it is also believed that it is a witch or bad spirit. Juju-men are also strongly believed to possess the power of giving illness to the child. Every illness or disease and every accident that occurs in the child's life is supposed to be the evil practice of sorcery. Though there is a widespread belief in witchcraft and juju-men, and the constant consultation of fetish, also of wearing of amulets, every parent is aware that to ensure good health in themselves and their children, certain rules of health must be observed. They know, for example, that over-feeding may cause stomach-ache, that too much eating fruit may cause diarrhoea, that wetness may make the child catch a chill, that neglect of teeth may lead to decay or toothache.'

Hence, precautions against ill health are both magical and natural. Wet clothing is changed, children are prevented from taking part in too strenuous exercises, especially in the midday sun, and nearly all children are vaccinated with a local herb against convulsions. At the same time, they are often provided with charms or amulets,[1] and care is taken to ensure that they do not violate tribal or family taboos.[2] In BENIM (Asante) great importance is attached to the harmony between the child's spirit and that of his father, so that the mother is careful to keep her husband's *ntoro* taboos. Oil is smeared on the baby's chest to keep its muscles supple. In JAKOBO (Asante) the main precaution taken by parents is to give their children a herbal enema every so often; at other times, pepper and ground ginger suppositories are pushed into the child's rectum to safeguard its health. Older children are given a boiled herbal drink from time to time. In APAM (Fante) the child is given a copper ring to offset the effects of lightning. In DOME (Ga) children are taught to avoid certain foods, and not to take part in too strenuous activities. Some parents buy mosquito nets for their babies, although they do not use them themselves. In OTROWE (Adangme) 'most of the parents rely on the juju-man to safeguard the child's health'. Children are vaccinated against ill health and provided with amulets. 'Christians refrain from wearing the talisman but indulge in the sacrifices and the using of the black powder.'

Considerable importance is attached to personal cleanliness in most parts of Ghana, and most children are required to have at least one bath a day.[3] With young children, this may be two or even three baths a day, and these are often thought to be so important

[1] See Plates 35 and 36.

[2] In many instances the two kinds of precaution are mixed. For example, Fortes notes that, among the Tallensis, infants are given a daily drink, with or without an infusion of herbs, which is both hygienic and magical, the composition of which is prescribed by the children's spirit guardians; (14) 189.

[3] See Plates 37-40. Fortes says that Tallensi parents attach great importance to a daily bath in near-boiling water for young infants. The purpose of this appears to be both hygienic and magical; (14) 166-7. With adults and older children, however, bodily cleanliness as such 'is the least of the virtues'; (14) 187.

that they are undertaken, or at least supervised, by the mother or grandmother.[1] Care of the teeth is also held to be of importance, and children are expected to use a chewing-stick or chewing-sponge before breakfast.[2] In many areas it is regarded as bad manners for a child to use a chewing-stick or sponge before its elders.[3] In APA (Asante) the child is taught to wash its face the first thing in the morning and is beaten for not doing so, as it is thought to bring bad luck during the day. Children are never given food until their teeth have been cleaned; to make a mixture for cleaning the teeth, plantain stalks are pulped and mixed with charcoal, pepper and salt. In DWINYAMA (Asante) children are taught to bathe themselves at least once a day, and are scolded for being dirty, which is said to lead to skin diseases. Among the DENKYERAS regular bathing of children is a most important condition of health, and they are bathed thrice daily until they are weaned, and thereafter twice daily. How to wash thoroughly is part of the child's training. In CHRISTIANSBORG (Ga) great importance is attached to bathing. As soon as the child is one year old, its face is washed and its teeth cleaned daily. No food is given until the child has washed its face. When the child is still an infant, the grandmother undertakes its daily bathing at first, so that the young mother may learn how to carry out this important function. Children are allowed to bathe themselves from about four years old, but the main bath of the day is still given by the grandmother or mother, and this continues occasionally even up until puberty. Great importance is attached to the care of the teeth, and the mother teaches the child how to use a chewing-sponge. Some few parents add tooth-paste. One of the most disgraceful comments on children is to accuse them of bad breath. In OTROWE (Adangme) 'the child is given some chewing-sponge every morning and is taught how to clean the teeth, but parents are not strict about this habit'. In WINNEBA (Efutu) very young children are bathed three times, others morning and night. 'Great attention is paid to the personal cleanliness of children.'

Sick children are treated with great care, and the nursing of

[1] Rattray records an Ashanti mother as saying to him: 'I will watch my daughter's health . . . I teach her . . . how to wash her body; remove sleep from her eyes; soap herself from the head downwards and bathe two or three times a day'; (30) 16.

[2] See Plate 61.

[3] Rattray notes that an Ashanti child is taught not to use a chewing-stick in the presence of its elders; (30) 13.

them is regarded as an important task within the family.[1] They are put to bed, bathed and massaged, and various household remedies are applied.[2] A favourite remedy for any kind of internal disorder is the application of ground pepper or ginger enemas, the heat of which is believed to be very beneficial. As illness is generally attributed to supernatural causes, both fetish priests and medicine men may be consulted in addition to the local herbalist. In any case, most local practitioners include both herbal and magical prescriptions in their treatments. Sick children are taken to the hospital usually only as a last resort, though attitudes towards European medicine are said to be changing in some areas. It is sometimes thought that a European-trained private practitioner's medicine must be better than that given by the State hospital because it costs more. In BANKO (Asante) sick children are not allowed to sleep. 'When a baby is ill, e.g. when he has fever or a headache, it is thought inadvisable to make the child sleep too much; this will render him weaker still.' Sick children are taken to the local clinic only after native medicines have proved unsuccessful 'Usually, the little children's small ailments like cuts or sores, headaches, coughs are neglected until the mother begins to notice that the illness is becoming worse and worse.' In JAKOBO (Asante) the sick child is tenderly cared for and indulged. It is washed and massaged, and ginger is pushed up its rectum, as the heat is believed to give health. If the child's condition is serious, a native doctor is called in. If he fails to cure the symptoms, the child may be sent to hospital; this is usually done against the medicine man's advice. In GOVIEFE (Ewe) 'the sick child is well cared for. His bath is thorough; the head is massaged with hot water and oil; soft soap and sponge are always used. The joints are given much attention. The limbs are bent up and down, sideways and backwards, and given a thorough "beating" with a hot towel. The genitals are well bathed and hot water is jetted into the anus and the vagina. The mother does away with heavy work and devotes

[1] Field notes that, among the Gas, 'when a child is sick its father's mother has a right to take it into her house to treat it, but children die so easily that any grandmother is usually only too glad to shelve responsibility and willingly leaves the child and its mother in the other grandmother's compound'; (9) 28. Among the Tallensis, according to Fortes, the illness of a child causes considerable anxiety to its parents, so much so that the mother may refuse to eat. It is the father's duty to send for and pay the diviner who treats the child; (14) 167 and 138.

[2] Field observes that, among the Gas, many ordinary people 'have a great knowledge of the ordinary pharmaceutical properties of herbs'; (8) 130.

much time to looking after the child, comforting and inducing him tenderly to eat, lie down or ease himself and encouraging him that he will soon get well again. Any kind of food he feels like eating is given to him unless it is too sweet or the herbalist forbids him to eat it. Any time he asks to be carried, he is obliged immediately. In a word the sick child is treated with love, sympathy, indulgence, and is given first attention in the life of the family as a whole.' In KORDIABE (Shai) the sick child is given herbal treatments and its parents undertake the pacification of evil spirits or of the child's soul. Among the DAGABAS, *muni*, a disease which begins with a sore in the anus, is treated with lukewarm water and an application of pounded ginger into the rectum. Chicken-pox is treated by rubbing warm ashes over the body to overcome irritation and by giving a purgative to keep the bowels open. 'In an attack of cold, the child is massaged with warm water followed by oiling of shea butter.'

CHAPTER TWELVE

EARLY SEXUAL EXPERIENCES

> 'Children of opposite sexes play at husband and wife and sleep together on the same mat. When children are caught at such practices, the male child is given a good beating and never allowed to remain with the females alone anywhere in the compound. The female child is treated rather cruelly by the mother. She grinds pepper and applies it to the child's vagina. The other children in the family ridicule the unfortunate pair and the treatment becomes a warning to the other boys and girls against similar practices.'

VERY young babies are fondled and caressed by everyone in the house in most parts of Ghana.[1] They cease to be the centre of interest as soon as a new baby is born and, apart from being embraced by the mother on her return home, a Ghanaian child has very few physical contacts with its parents or other adults after its first year. In some areas the sexual organs are avoided when an infant is fondled; in others they are stimulated. Kissing is rare in some villages, and children are not required to kiss others. Restrictions on those allowed to caress young children include very old people, great-grandmothers and, widely, those suspected of being witches. In ABURI (Akwapim) 'everybody is fond of a new-born baby so a great deal of affection is shown him'. Children over two are not kissed as their mouths may not be clean. In DWINYAMA (Asante) 'people generally are fond of babies and lavish upon them various demonstrations of affection'. Parents, relatives, friends and neighbours will all stroke and

1 Fortes notes the abrupt transition from rough handling to fondling with infants among the Tallensis; (12) 36.

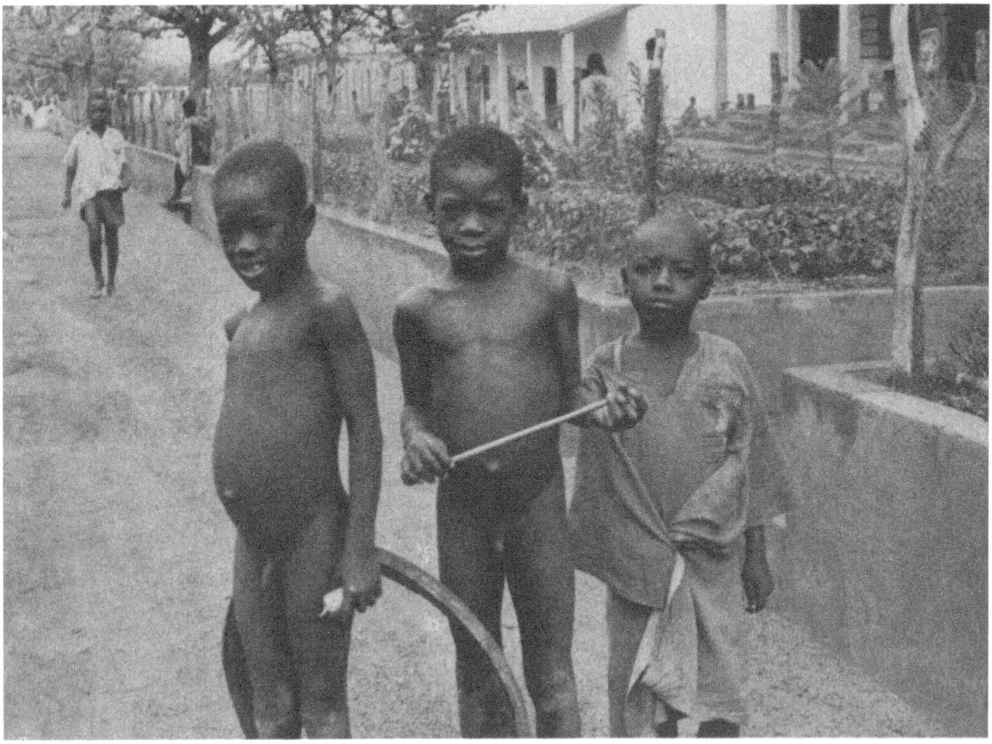

Circumcision. 41. Circumcised and uncircumcised children playing together. Taken in Wa.

42. An uncircumcised boy in Tamale.

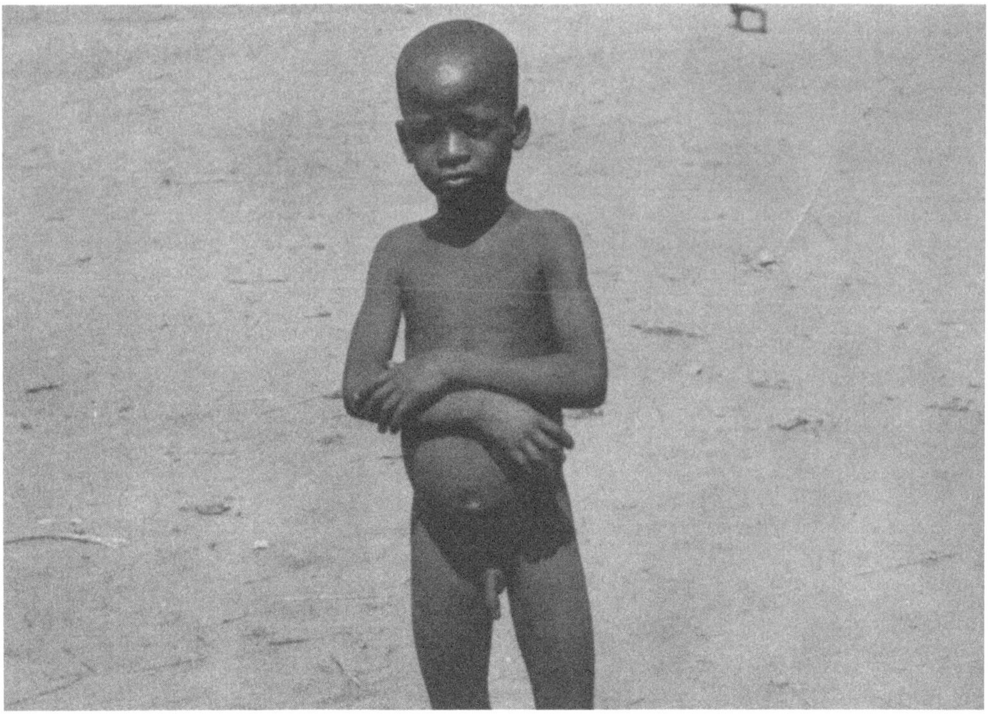

Modesty in children. 43. Although this little girl is not wearing a pad to cover her genitals, she does not appear to be showing any overt signs of modesty. Her age was given as six. Taken outside a compound in Tamale.

44. This girl, estimated at about fourteen years old, does not appear to be embarrassed at being seen or photographed with her breasts bare. Taken in Winneba.

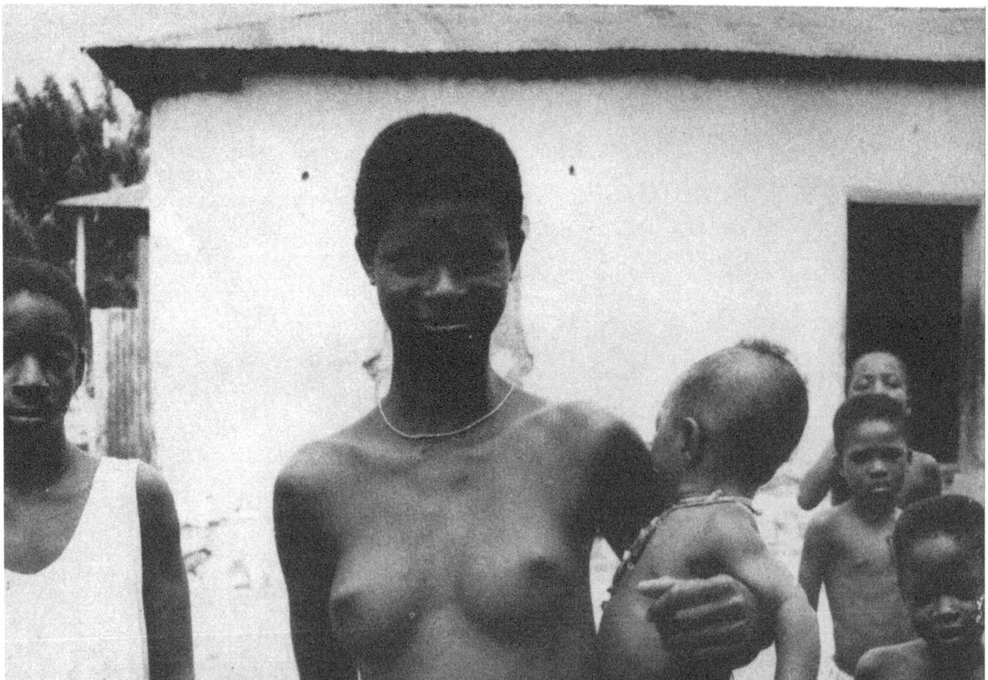

Modesty in children. 45. This girl, estimated at about seven years old, is showing signs of embarrassment at being photographed in the streets without her pad. Taken in James Town, Accra.

46. This little girl, estimated to be about seven years old, appears to be displaying modesty at being photographed wearing only waist beads and a pad. After the photograph was taken, she covered her genitals with her hands, and then stood watching the photographer for some time. Taken in Kpandu.

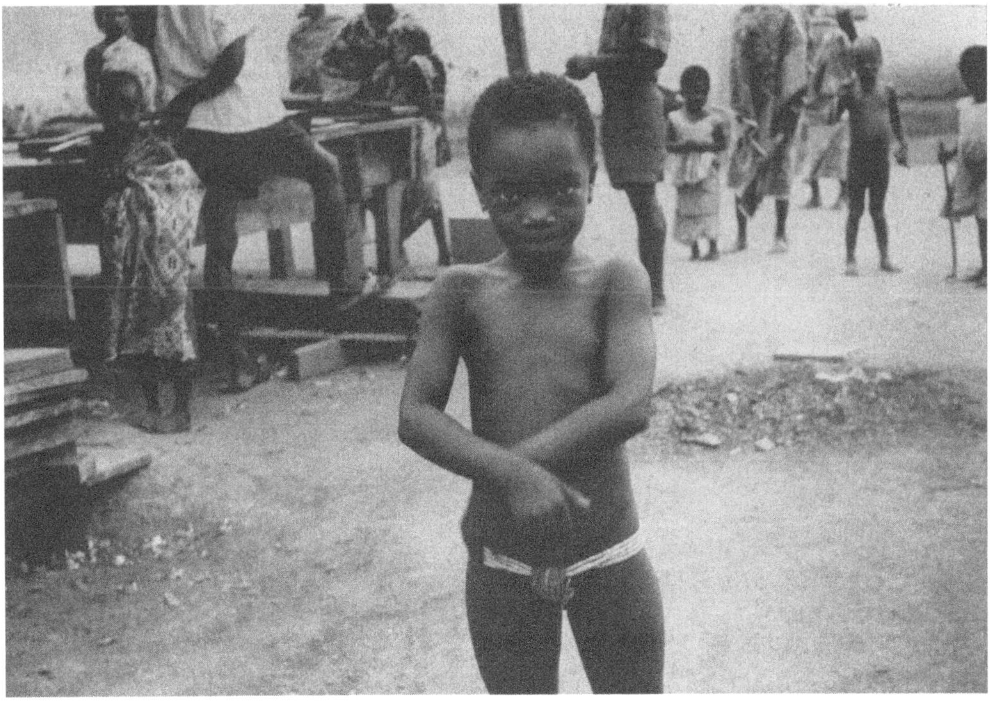

Children's dress. 47. A group of boys in Berekum, wearing their cloths round their shoulders to counteract the early morning chill.

48. When asked why he wore his cloth in this fashion, this boy replied that he was keeping his ears warm. Also taken in Berekum, in the early morning.

embrace, tickle and rock a young child. They are not kissed, however, as saliva is believed to carry evil influences. In JAISI (Asante) all through babyhood, children are continually petted, kissed and tickled by all; a common method of fondling an infant is to tickle its buttocks and penis. After they can walk, however, children are rarely embraced, except by their mothers on a return from a journey. In SUPOWMU DUNKWA (Fante) cuddling, kissing, stroking and fondling of babies 'continues until the mother has a new baby'. In TEMA (Ga) the young infant is kissed and fondled by everyone, 'especially touching the sex organs and sensitive zones of the skin, which are good enough stimuli that will produce a smile'. In OTROWE (Adangme) the child is fondled by its parents, relatives and friends; 'people who are suspected of witchcraft are not allowed to carry the child, touch it or have any of these physical contacts with the child'. In APIREDE (Cherepon) the baby is kissed and fondled by everyone; 'after the third year he is seldom kissed, if at all'. Among the ISALAS 'kissing is unknown. Parents show affection towards their children by stroking, embracing and placing them on their laps. The father and the mother are not the only people who show their affection in this manner, but also the grandmother and the father's other wives.'

The giving of special attention to children's genitals during bathing is an almost universal practice in Ghana. Warm water, and sometimes ground ginger, are used to clean them; this is thought to prevent disease, and is regarded as particularly important in the case of girls. In DWINYAMA (Asante) special attention during bathing is given to the genitals, especially those of girls. The vagina and penis are cleaned out with hot water to avoid sores. In JAKOBO (Asante) girls' vaginas are carefully washed, and ground ginger is pushed into them from time to time in order to cure any diseases. In GBLEDE (Ewe) the washing of children's genitals, especially those of girls, is regarded as very important. In CENTRAL ACCRA (Ga) parents give special attention to the genitals when bathing their children. Warm water is dribbled into the opened vulva; the end of penis and foreskin are cleaned with warm water. In TESHIE (Ga) during the child's bath, hot water is dribbled into its genitals and rectum, to heal any sores. Herbs and roots are ground and pushed into the vagina and rectum to heal sores, and to give girls strong firm hips. Among the ISALAS 'in bathing the child, special attention in the case of girls is given to the genitals, which are bathed with warm water.'

In some areas children use special words when referring to their genitals, in others they use the same words as do adults. In ABURI (Akwapim) genitals are referred to by children in an indirect way; 'any child who will mention the genital organs by name is hushed to stop, warned strictly not to say that again'. He is beaten if he continues to do so. In JAISI (Asante) there are no special children's words, and children must learn accepted circumlocutions; e.g. 'a crab', 'a man', 'that which is not mentioned', 'a treasure', 'a great god'. In KOFORIDUA (Asante) 'the adults are not embarrassed when, for instance, the young ones use everyday terms relating to sexual subjects or organs. "Your mother's vagina" is the commonest oath heard from most lips.' In GOVIEFE (Ewe) special children's words for genitals are used. In APIREDE (Cherepon) there are no special children's words, though young children may invent their own. In WINNEBA (Efutu) there are no special words for children to use.

Practices regarding the circumcision of children vary in Ghana.[1] Among the Akans, the circumcision of boys was formerly tabooed. Nowadays a great many boys arrange for their own circumcision, often without their parents' knowledge. It is still tabooed for a member of the ruling clans to be circumcised in most areas, however.[2] Among the Ewe-speaking tribes, the circumcision of boys is customary, and it is usually performed in infancy or young childhood.[3] Among the Ga-Adangme speaking tribes, boys have always been circumcised. Formerly this was done at a public ceremony at, or some time before, puberty. Nowadays, however, boys may be circumcised at any time from soon after birth until they are twelve years old, and there is no public ceremony, though they may be given pennies by their relatives.[4] In the Northern Territories, the circumcision of boys is not widely practised except in one or two

[1] See Plates 12 and 41–42.

[2] Christensen notes that, among the Fantis, boys are not circumcised; (5) 85. Meyerowitz in *The Akan of Ghana* (London, Faber, 1958) says that the Akans abhor circumcision because it involves the shedding of blood; page 31.

[3] Manoukian notes that, among the Ewes, 'circumcision commonly takes place today at about four or five years, although formerly it was done between the ages of six and ten. All suitable boys of one town quarter are circumcised professionally on the same occasion, but apparently without particular ritual. Such boys are to some extent afterwards regarded as a special group'; (26) 42.

[4] Field describes a public ceremony that is held among the Gas when a royal or important male child is circumcised at about a week old. She notes that ordinary

tribes.[1] In ABURI (Akwapim) boys are not circumcised; to be so is tabooed. In BANKO (Asante) in the middle school 'the boys in class six had become interested in sex matters. All of them began to go to the Hausa man at the Zongo to be circumcised. Some did the circumcision privately without their parents' knowledge. If an uncircumcised boy came to their group, they drove him away and shunned him. When they went to the river to swim or wash themselves, they drove all the uncircumcised boys of their age downstream, and they swam upstream. They said those people were too unclean to join them at the same spot. The girls in the class too knew of this, and looked interested. They laughed and jeered at those who feared to go for the circumcision.' In KOFORIDUA (Asante) 'there are no tribal initiations for the boys, but what most of them do is to go to a private place to be circumcised. This is the growing practice. It is afterwards that a parent may get to know that his boy has been circumcised.' In GOVIEFE (Ewe) some boys are circumcised. In TESHIE (Ga) boys are circumcised at any age up to twelve, but usually during infancy. Uncircumcised boys are derided. In former times circumcision used to be done at a public ceremony, but now there is none, though relatives usually give the boy pennies. Circumcision gives the boy the right to enter the yard of the high god of the town. In OTROWE (Adangme) boys are circumcised during early infancy. In APIREDE (Cherepon) circumcision is not customary.

The circumcision of girls, or clitoridectomy, is widely practised among the tribes of the Northern Territories, at ages varying from one week old to six years.[2] This custom

boys are usually circumcised in early infancy, though the operation may be performed at any time up to the age of twelve. 'An uncircumcised lad is an object of derision'; (8) 176. Manoukian notes that, among the Gas, the circumcision of a foreigner implies naturalization; (25) 89. She also notes that Adangme boys are circumcised; (25) 108.

[1] According to Manoukian, the circumcision of boys is practised universally among the Dagombas. Among the Walas, it is the custom of the majority, and done seven days after birth. It is also practised by the Gonjas and the Mamprusis. Among other tribes of the Northern Territories, the circumcision of boys is not widely practised; (27) 73. According to Rattray, members of the Kusasi tribe do not circumcise their boys; (32) 397.

[2] According to Manoukian, '*clitoridectomy* is practised by the majority of tribes in the Northern Territories, and in most cases the operation is performed in infancy or early childhood, at ages varying from a week old to six years. The Gurensi, Kasena, Builsa and Namnam perform the operation at puberty. . . . The Dagomba, Mamprusi, Kusasi, Tallensi, Konkomba and Bedjelib do not practise clitoridectomy'; (27) 73. Rattray includes the Dagabas, the Lobers, the Isalas and the Walas among tribes in which clitoridectomy is practised. Reasons given include

is not practised in other parts of Ghana, except among Muslims.

In most parts of Ghana, though not all, parents strongly disapprove of their children masturbating.[1] Children are scolded and beaten for doing so, and threats of castration are made if the offender is a boy, but the commonest punishment is for ground red pepper or ginger to be smeared on the genitals. In some areas the practice of masturbation is thought to lead to sexual precocity, immorality or even madness. In TUTU (Akwapim) masturbation 'is very common among infants and toddlers, and more among children between the ages of two and six years. Children beyond six years of age and under sixteen do secretly practice masturbation in pairs, usually at night, when two friends of the same sex sleep together; it is practised more often by girls than boys. It is believed that if masturbation is practised in excess the inevitable result is sterility and madness.' Young children who masturbate are scolded or slapped; older children are beaten, or have red pepper smeared on their genitals. In BENIM (Asante) small boys who hold or play with their genitals are often threatened with castration. In BOMPATA (Asante) only a few parents were aware that their children masturbate. Among adolescents 'confessions of homosexual activity among such groups [15-18 years old] are not easy to obtain but it appears masturbation at least is almost generally practised. This is said to relieve the intense sexual excitement which follows undesirable lessons on sex and vivid descriptions of sexual experiences from older members of the groups.' Parents believe that masturbation in children leads to a bad life, and boys are punished by being beaten, girls by having pepper rubbed in their genitals and sometimes in their eyes. In JAKOBO (Asante) masturbation, both by boys and girls, is said to be common. In APAM (Fante) masturbation among children is

'because the thing is not beautiful to see and is visible even through leaves' (Dagabas); because 'if this were not done, there would not be room for a man to have connexion with a woman' (Lobers); '(a) that its non-removal would obstruct the entrance of the penis, (b) that its removal makes delivery more easy, (c) ridicule, if not "cut" ' (Isalas); (32) 409, 439, 498, and 454.

[1] Rattray notes that, among the Ashantis, 'a son is warned by his father against the evils of masturbation'; (30) 13. Christensen says that, among the Fantis, a boy will be censured for masturbation; (5) 99. Rattray quotes a Gurensi informant as saying that, formerly, there was much rivalry between lads who acted as cattle herds, who competed in wrestling and archery, and 'youths who attempted early sexual intercourse or masturbation, lost their prowess and skill, and were derided'; (32) 137. According to Fortes, among the Tallensis, parental indulgence is extended to masturbation, 'which is overt until puberty in boys'; (12) 36.

thought to be very rare, and believed to have no effect. In GOVIEFE (Ewe) 'masturbation in children is recognized as being common. Masturbation will make the child grow into a highly-sexed personality and it will lead to the development of premature, or precocious, sex appetites and, therefore, immorality.' Children who masturbate are scolded and threats of circumcision are made. 'Boys are usually punished with drops of ginger juice into their nostrils, followed by beating. Girls are punished by having red pepper pushed into their vaginas.' In VAKPO (Ewe) it is thought that no children masturbate over the age of three. In TESHIE (Ga) the attitude of parents towards young children who masturbate is one of indifference, though if the child is a boy he may be told that his penis will be cut off if he holds it again. Some parents may scold or slap their children for masturbating. In AGOMANYA (Krobo) it is said of masturbation that 'the freedom enjoyed in the love life of the young makes the practice of it unnecessary'. In APIREDE (Cherepon) it is thought that a child who masturbates will be spoiled, and it is beaten and red pepper is applied to its genitals and anus and sometimes rubbed on its face. In LARTEH KUBEASI (Guang) masturbation is said to be rare among girls. Boys are 'gently rebuked' for handling their penises in public. This rebuke is never addressed directly to the boy but is made to a third person; 'Why does he finger his penis in that way?' Among the ISALAS 'masturbation in children is recognized as exceptional. Parents are of the opinion that their children do not practise it.'

Make-believe games in which children play at 'fathers and mothers' are widely played in Ghana; these are sometimes said to lead to sexual experimentation, or to actual intercourse. In nearly all areas, children who are caught by their parents indulging in sex games are severely punished, by being beaten, or by having red pepper rubbed on their genitals, or by both.[1] In TUTU (Akwapim) make-believe games are approved by parents, but sexual activities are forbidden. In BOSOFO (Asante) children often play such games when they are left alone, involving mutual masturbation and actual sexual intercourse. The investigator cites the case of a girl of seven who had sexual intercourse with a boy of two and a half years of age by directing

[1] Christensen notes that, among the Fantis, boys are warned against sexual play with girls approaching puberty; (5) 99. Among the Tallensis, according to Fortes, parents take it for granted that children will indulge in sexual play; (14) 100.

his actions. In JAISI (Asante) 'sex games are common and frequent among children', involving mutual examination of genitals. In GBLEDE (Ewe) mother-and-father make-believe games are not encouraged but are viewed with suspicion by parents who think that they might lead to sexual play. In CHRISTIANSBORG (Ga) children play sex games which are severely disapproved of by the parents. If they are caught doing so, red pepper is put in their genitals. 'It usually happens that there is always a very old woman in every house whose official duty is to deal with such cases.' In TESHIE (Ga) make-believe games of husband and wife often lead to attempts at sexual intercourse. 'More often than not, parents take a serious view of such actions.' They are punished in many cases with red pepper on the genitals. While such organized games are not common, boys of eight, nine and above sometimes have sexual intercourse with the girls in the room during the night. When children sleep in the same room, boys on one side, girls on the other, 'this usually leads to sexual activities during the night'.

CHAPTER THIRTEEN

SEX DISTINCTIONS

'From about the age of four, boys and girls are supposed to behave differently in many ways.'

THE attitude towards nakedness in children varies considerably in Ghana according to the child's sex and according to the degree of urbanization of the area. In the cities and large towns, children are taught to be modest from an early age.[1] In smaller towns, nakedness is allowed in young children about the house and compounds, but they are expected to cover their loins in public and before strangers; older girls are expected to cover their breasts. In villages and rural areas, parents do not worry about their children's nakedness, and may even encourage them to go out without cloth, partly because it is thought more healthy, partly to preserve the cloth. In some of the tribes of the Northern Territories, very scant clothing is the normal wear of the adults, and children may go completely naked until puberty.[2]

In all areas, the attitude regarding nakedness is severer towards girls than towards boys, and for a girl to appear without a small cloth or 'pad' covering her genitals is almost universally deplored.[3] In most areas, older girls are expected to cover their breasts in public, except during the puberty rites, when the breasts may be ornamented with shea butter and left uncovered. It is, however, not uncommon to see adolescent girls with bare breasts even in the main cities.[4] In ABURI (Akwapim) children are not allowed on the street naked.

[1] See Plates 43-46.

[2] See Plates 67-68.

[3] By 'pad' is meant a small strip of cloth, usually red, which is worn covering the genitals, and tucked into the string of beads worn round the waist. Rattray notes that, among the Ashantis, young children, both male and female, are taught always to wear a loin-cloth under their cloths; (30) 13. See Plates 84, 92, 94.

[4] See Plate 44.

'Parents say it is in the villages that children go about naked but in the towns they should put on dresses to show that they are civilized.' In BOMPATA (Asante) all children of from two to six years of age are naked most of the time, though girls wear pads from infancy, in order to prevent the wind from entering the vagina and causing inflammation. Children are clothed to go to school, but they remain naked in the home until they are about ten. Girls are said to be modest earlier than boys. In JAKOBO (Asante) not long ago children appeared naked in public up to twelve or thirteen years of age, but nowadays they are rarely seen over ten. A girl of eight years old may go naked inside her house, but not in public; a girl of about ten years of age should feel ashamed to appear naked before boys or men. Adolescent girls are upbraided if they expose their breasts. In SUPOWMU DUNKWA (Fante) children are expected to show modesty from about the age of eight, after which lapses are treated by threats to use red pepper or to cut off the genitals. In GOVIEFE (Ewe) modesty is taught from the age of three, especially before members of the opposite sex and before elders. 'It is considered that a girl who continues to appear naked will grow eventually into a bad girl, morally.' In CHRISTIANSBORG (Ga) the attitude towards children's nakedness varies. In illiterate homes, the girls usually wear only a narrow strip of cloth to cover their genitals. Exposure of the body is believed to strengthen a boy's chest, especially among fishermen. There is no definite attempt to teach modesty; one reason is that it is thought that formal training will direct a child's attention to its genitals at an early age, which might not be conducive to its moral upbringing. Girls usually become self-conscious earlier than boys; uncircumcised boys become modest earlier, as they are ridiculed by others. In APIREDE (Cherepon) children between the ages of two and six years may play about in the street naked, except that girls must wear their pads. 'Children are not taught to feel ashamed of nakedness until girls begin to develop breasts and boys pubic hairs.' Girls well over the age of ten are commonly seen naked to the waist. Among the ISALAS 'children are not trained to feel ashamed of appearing naked before anybody. They are allowed to play about naked except on special occasions such as market days and during funeral ceremonies of old men and women.'

Attitudes regarding parents undressing in front of their

Children's dress. 49. A fisherman's son on the beach at Ahenboboi, near Cape Coast.

50. This little girl wears her cloth as a skirt. Notice her elaborate ear-rings. Taken in Tamale.

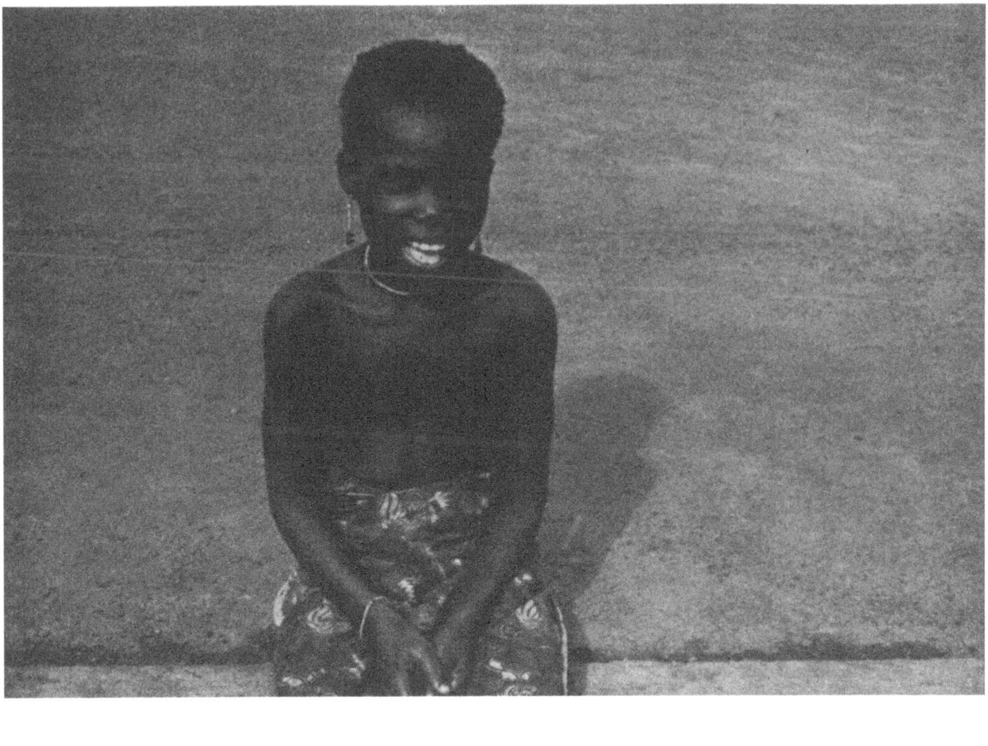

Children's dress. 51. To wear the cloth knotted at the back of the neck is the traditional style for young boys. Taken at Wa.

52. Taken at Keta Krachi

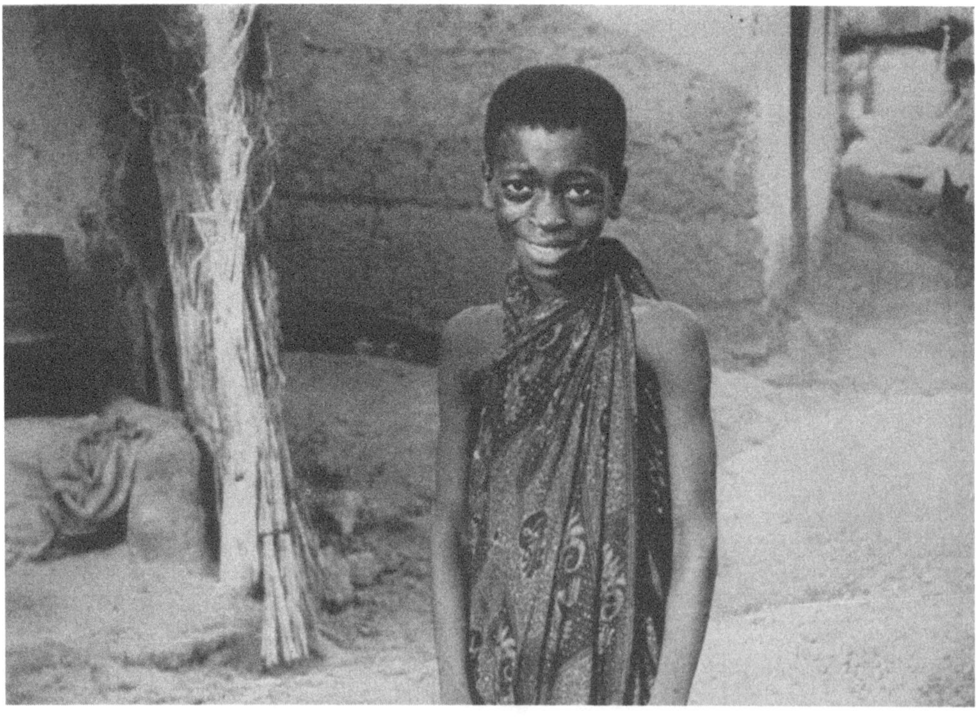

Children's dress. 53. Shoulders are kept warm in the early morning. Taken at Bosofo.

54. This boy has wrapped his cloth round his waist with studied unconcern, in imitation of the elders of the village. Taken in Bosofo.

Children's dress. 55. The carpenter's children, the boy aged four, the girl five, wearing Western style clothes. Taken in Winneba.

56. An eight-year-old schoolboy wearing his school shorts for playing in. Taken in Gblede.

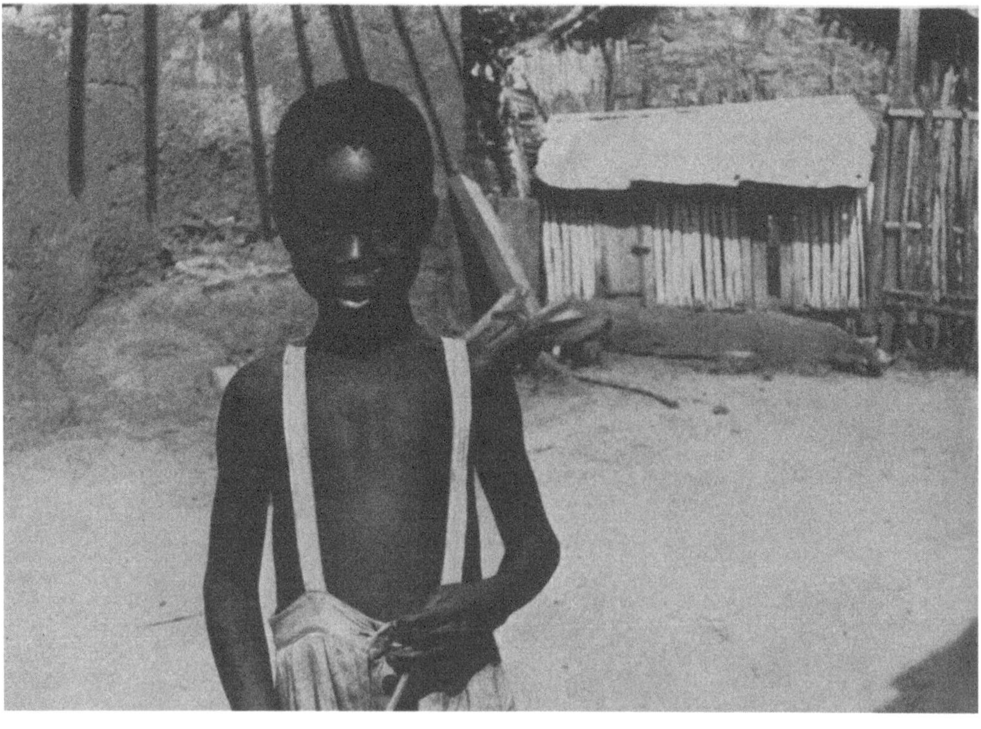

children appear to vary considerably. According to some informants, parents undress and even eliminate in front of their children without hesitation; according to others, it is forbidden for children to see their parents undressing. Nor does there appear to be any correlation between attitudes and the degree of urbanization, though in the Northern Territories, where near-nakedness is the normal rule for adults, there is a general feeling of indifference on the subject. In those areas where parents are said not to allow children to watch them undressing, the reason commonly given is the fear that the children should see their genitals, and talk about them. In TUTU (Akwapim) 'some parents sometimes appear naked before their children under five years of age but parents feel it indecent to appear before their children who have attained the age of six and over'. In BOSOFO (Asante) parents may undress before their children; mothers undress in front of their sons until they reach the age of puberty. In DWINYAMA (Asante) 'parents do not in any circumstances undress before children'. In APAM (Fante) some mothers undress before their children. In GBLEDE (Ewe) parents do not undress before older children for fear of gossip. In TESHIE (Ga) parents undress before their children, though boys of eight and above usually feel shy and leave the room although they are not told to do so. In KODIABE (Shai) women do not usually undress before their children, and men do so very rarely. In APIREDE (Cherepon) the attitude varies very much. 'On the whole, a parent may undress before the children of her own sex, but not normally before the opposite sex.' Among the ISALAS 'the parents are careful not to undress before their children because they feel their children should not see their sexual organs'.

In most parts of Ghana, children are expected to start to behave differently according to their sex from the age of three or four. After about the age of six, children form play and work groups of their own sex, and those who prefer the company of children of the opposite sex are disapproved of.[1] Boys who behave girlishly, and girls who behave boyishly are openly derided and called nicknames. In BENIM (Asante) children are expected to behave according to their sex by the age of seven. Boys are taught to look on girls, even their own mothers, as fools. Girls who play with warlike boys after the age of seven

[1] Fortes says that, among the Tallensis, children of six or seven are laughed at if they play with those of the opposite sex; (12) 42.

are considered disgraceful and a sign of their mothers' neglect in child training. In JAKOBO (Asante) boys are supposed to be brought up by their fathers, girls by their mothers. Boys are discouraged from associating too much with their mothers. If a boy calls for his mother instead of his father in a time of crisis, he will be called by a nickname throughout his life; it will be said that he has been brought up by his mother instead of by his father. If a girl calls for her father, however, she is regarded as brave. In AYANZILI (Nzima) boys and girls who behave in a manner of the opposite sex are laughed at and called by derisive nicknames. In GOVIEFE (Ewe) 'from about the age of four, boys and girls are supposed to behave differently in many ways'. Boys are expected to choose more valiant and energetic games; girls more rhythmic ones. In their make-believe games, boys are expected to choose male roles, girls female ones. They are expected to fight differently (girls with open hands, abuse, biting and running away), and to choose toys appropriate to their sex. Children who behave in a manner more fitting the opposite sex are jeered at and chased out of the company. In DOME (Ga) children are expected to behave according to their sex from the age of four. Those who persist in preferring the company of children of the opposite sex, or who behave in the manner of those of the opposite sex, are scolded, and may have red pepper smeared on their genitals. Such children are called by abusive names. Among the DAGABAS a boy of about twelve years of age 'who behaves like a girl may be rebuked by his father, or taunted by his friends and told to behave like a boy, or scolded as being too fond of women; similarly, a girl with boyish inclinations may be scoffed at by her play-fellows, or told by her parents to behave like a girl'.

While there is little formal separation of young children according to sex, from about the age of six, boys and girls begin to move apart. At this age, or soon after, in many parts of Ghana boys leave their mothers' compounds to go to live with their fathers, and learn their trades. In both formal and informal gatherings, boys are expected to sit with the men, girls with the women. They are expected, and they themselves expect, to undertake different domestic chores according to their sex, and to play different games, and if they do not, their parents may order them to do so. In following the parents of the same sex, they learn the occupations appropriate to that sex, and, as a matter of course, except between siblings and at school, contacts between children of the opposite sex diminish considerably.[1] In TUTU (Akwapim) 'at the age of about ten, boys are separated from girls in many activities in the house. At meals, the girls are given a separate dish and they eat in groups according to sex. The girls always remain with their mothers at the kitchen while the boys play either inside or outside.' Children are rigorously separated except for certain traditional games at puberty. In BOMPATA (Ansante) children are separated for games after the age of four, and 'boys and girls of five and above can hardly be seen playing together'. Children prefer to eat with members of their own sex. In JAKOBO (Asante) boys of twelve and over are discouraged from playing with girls, though there is no rigid segregation. Children themselves exclude those of the opposite sex in most games. In APAM (Fante) after three years of age, 'girls are gradually advised to withdraw from strenuous boys' games such as tennis, football, jumping and wrestling. "Esi, you are a woman, you can't wrestle with men." "Aba, you are a woman, you must not play football with men." "Ekua, you are a woman, you must stop jumping with men." "Araba, you are a woman, you must stop fights with men otherwise you will one day have your jaws bashed in!" ' In GOVIEFE (Ewe) children eat, sleep and bathe separately from the age of five. 'In informal social gatherings, where women traditionally congregate together and the men also form their group, boys are actually expected to join the men, and girls the women.' Among the ISALAS children tend to form into groups of their own sex after about the age of five.

While many parents claim to like their children of either sex equally, there appears to be a general preference for those of the same sex as the parent, particularly as it is from them that the parent gets help in his or her work.[2] In areas in which descent is by matrilineal succession, this fact is adduced as an additional reason for mothers preferring their daughters to their sons. In BOMPATA (Asante) 'all informants said that they had equal love and affection for all their children irrespective of their sex';

[1] Fortes notes that, among the Tallensis, siblings of different sex are often together until the age of nine or ten; thereafter their different occupations separate them, and they tend to become scornful of one another; (14) 248 and (12) 16.

[2] Rattray quotes a Gurensi informant as saying that unless a man has a son, he will feel inferior to other men, no matter how many daughters he has, as it is the sons who will sacrifice to him when he is dead, whereas daughters will go to other houses as the wives of other men; (32) 137-8.

but in fact, it is reported, most parents prefer children of their own sex, fathers for the help they get from their sons, mothers for reasons of the clan lineage. In JAISI (Asante) men prefer sons, women their daughters, because they help them with their chores. In AYIKAI DOBORO (Ga) there is no general rule, and parents have individual preferences. In OTROWE (Adangme) parents prefer their children of their own sex, since they help them in their work. In APIREDE (Cherepon) fathers prefer their sons on account of the patrilineal system of inheritance; mothers prefer their daughters who help them in the house.

CHAPTER FOURTEEN

CHILDREN'S RELATIONS WITH THEIR PARENTS

> 'Like all Akans, parents in Dunkwa feel that they owe it to their children to provide all their needs for them. They feed them, clothe them, send them to school, find jobs for them and even marry for them. In return for all these, the children are expected to show their gratitude by taking care of them financially and in all other respects, when they start earning money.'

THERE are three main factors which affect the nature of the relationship, and the extent of the contact, between a child and its parents in Ghana: these are, the family practice with regard to living compounds; whether or not the family is polygynous; and whether or not the tribe is matrilineal.

In many parts of Ghana, it is the practice for the men to live in one compound, while the women and young children live in another. These two compounds may be next door to one another, or they may be some distance away.[1] With such living arrangements, the usual practice is for young boys, when they reach the age of six or seven or thereabouts, to leave their mothers' compounds and go and live with their fathers, who are then responsible for their upbringing. The males living in the house are usually related to one another; they may be agnatic kin. Each man's wife or wives sends his meals to him by the hand of one of his young children. A wife will come to the man's room to sleep at nights, and bring her infant with her. The man may pay a formal call to his wife's compound, and he may take charge of one of his younger children from time to time. Apart from these, there may be no other contacts between a man and his young children or his older daughters.

[1] 'Traditionally, Ga men live in one building and their wives and children in another. Usually in the past, these two establishments were adjoining'; (1) 47.

A second factor affecting relations between parents and children is whether or not the family is polygynous. Living conditions among polygynous families appear to vary widely. With some, the wives live in separate compounds, or with their mothers or other blood relatives, while the husband lives apart, and sends for his wives when he requires them. With such an arrangement, the children may see little or nothing at all of their fathers. In some families, the husband lives with one wife, and visits others; or he may live with each in turn. In other families, and this is the usual practice in the Northern Territories, a man and his wives all share the same compound, usually with other agnatic relatives, but each woman has her own bedroom, and often her own kitchen; the man may have a room of his own, though it is used more as a guest room than as his bedroom.[1] The extent of contact between children and their parents in polygynous families can be seen to vary according to which of these living arrangements is followed.

The third important factor governing these relations is whether or not the tribe is matrilineal; that is to say, whether descent is reckoned through the female line, or through the male line (patrilineal). In matrilineal tribes, considerably greater importance is paid to the bond between a child and his mother's kin, who form the child's clan. The nearest adult male blood relative, according to this system of descent, is the mother's brother or maternal uncle.[2] While the relationship between the child and its father is recognized as an important one, its importance is held to depend upon totemic and not upon blood kinship. The father is a member of a different clan from his own children, and many of his own relationships with, for example, his sisters' children, are thought to be more important, in certain respects, than those with his own. Virtually all the Akan-speaking people are matrilineal; the Twi name for the clan is *abusua*, and for the totemic group which unites child and father, *ntoro*. In the traditional Akan family, the *ntoro* relationship was

[1] 'The characteristically domestic family of the Tallensi is the agnatic joint family . . . a joint family consists of two or more close agnates . . . together with their wives, children, and other dependants, if any, occupying a single homestead'; (14) 64-5. Among the Konkombas, according to Tait, households are in a constant state of change; joint households split up to form simple family unit households; these become joint households as the sons marry and bring their wives in; they then split up again; (34) 247-8.

[2] The maternal uncle may be an important relative in patrilineal tribes, as well. According to Goody, among the LoWiili a young child sees a great deal of his mother's eldest brother; (19) 58.

thought to be of great spiritual importance, and some writers speak of a double descent system to indicate the two relationships governing the child's life. Today, however, the importance attached to the *ntoro* has considerably diminished, and it is said that there are Akans who do not even know to what *ntoro* group they belong; there can be very few if any Akans who do not know the name of their *abusua*.[1]

In traditional Akan family life, the child's upbringing was the responsibility of its father, who derived his authority from the *ntoro* relationship. At the same time, the maternal uncle showed great interest in the child's development. He was responsible for his debts, and he could remove the child from its father's custody if the latter was too poor to look after him properly. He could also pawn the child against his own debts. The areas of responsibility between child, maternal uncle and father were all clearly defined and universally recognized. Today the traditional culture is in a state of rapid change; the *ntoro* relationship has diminished in importance, and also the overriding importance formerly attached to clan ties is beginning to give way to European influence, which stresses the bond between husband and wife, and their joint responsibility for their children. Some educated married couples are preferring to live by themselves on the European pattern, instead of as a part of an extended family household, and this must have a great effect on the nature of the relations between themselves and their children. As the majority of the investigations in this book were carried out in villages in the rural areas, these changes are not so apparent.[2]

A further factor affecting child-parent relations is the frequency of divorce and the provisions made for the care of the children. It is very difficult to get any reliable figures for the frequency of divorce in Ghana, but it is clearly sufficiently

[1] Fortes says that, among the Ashantis, 'about half of the children under fifteen live with their fathers, a large proportion because their parents are living together, and the other half live in households presided over by their mothers' brothers. . . . It is not uncommon for a man to have both his own children and his sister's children residing with him, but the preference of most men is to have only one class of filial dependants living with him'; (11) 262.

[2] Acquah, in her survey of Accra in 1953, found that, among the Gas, the traditional sex segregation for living purposes was still prevalent and the only inhabitants who lived in small family units were the more educated clerks; (1) 47. Busia, in his survey of the Sekondi-Takoradi area notes that 'the effect of monogamy as enforced by the Ordinance and Christian teaching is to strengthen the bond between husband and wife at the expense of the strong sibling bond in the old matrilineal society'; (4) 44.

frequent for it to be an important consideration when considering the whole question of child-rearing. Marriages contracted under the Marriage Ordinance can be dissolved only by the legal procedure necessary to obtain a divorce. Such marriages, however, represent a very small percentage of the total, and the dissolution of customary marriage is often a very simple procedure.

In most parts of Ghana, the children of a divorced couple remain with the mother if they are young; older children go with their parents of the same sex for their training. In a matrilineal tribe, with the children of divorced parents as with those of any married couple, it is recognized that ultimately the children belong to the mother's clan or *abusua*.[1]

While in all parts of Ghana the universal practice is for the mother to be chiefly responsible for the early care of her children, this responsiblity is felt to extend to other members of her family, particularly in the case of a first-born, when the child's grandmother may take over the major part of looking after it. In any case, the grandmother and other female relatives are always nearby to advise the mother, and to act in her absence.[2] In TUTU (Akwapim) 'when the child is born, there is always a

[1] Manoukian says that, among the Akans, 'a divorced wife leaves her husband but the children remain subject to the custody of their father. Usually the older children live with their father while the younger ones stay with their mother until they are old enough to go to live with the father. A man may remove his children from their mother as soon as they are weaned if he wishes, or he may provide money or meat for the divorced mother to feed the children. He also clothes them and is responsible for curing them when ill and for all other paternal obligations. Some men refuse custody of their children who are then under the care of their mother and her *abusua*. A man who marries a divorced woman may feel it his moral duty to adopt her children. Parents are afraid that separation from the father may have a bad effect on the child's *sunsum* or spirit, which it inherits from its father and which is under the protection of his *sunsum* (modern version of the *ntoro*) when the child is young and weak'; (25) 33-4. She says that, among the Ewes, if the parents get divorced, 'young children remain with their mother, but should go to join their father when they are old enough. Nevertheless, children, especially daughters, may remain with their mother by their own choice, or because their father has repudiated them, or because their mother's next husband feels it his duty to take on the responsibility of bringing them up'; (26) 28. Among the Gas, 'in every case of separation and divorce the husband is the possessor of the children, provided he has paid the full marriage fee to his wife's relatives. If he has not, they can claim the children. It is not clear what happens when the marriage fees have been refunded. The child of an adulterous union may also be claimed by the wronged husband, and it has full rights of inheritance and succession in his lineage'; (25) 80. Fortes speaks of the instability of early marriages among the Tallensis; see (14) 84-5. 'By Tale custom, if a woman leaves a husband by whom she has had a child and is properly married to another man, the child lives with her during its infancy. When it is five or six years old it can be claimed by its natural father. This is called "separating" it from its mother. Tallensi think it immoral to separate a child from its mother before it is well able to fend for itself'; (14) 137.

[2] Christensen says that, among the Fantis, a child is completely under the control of its mother for the first two or three years of its life; (5) 97. Manoukian notes

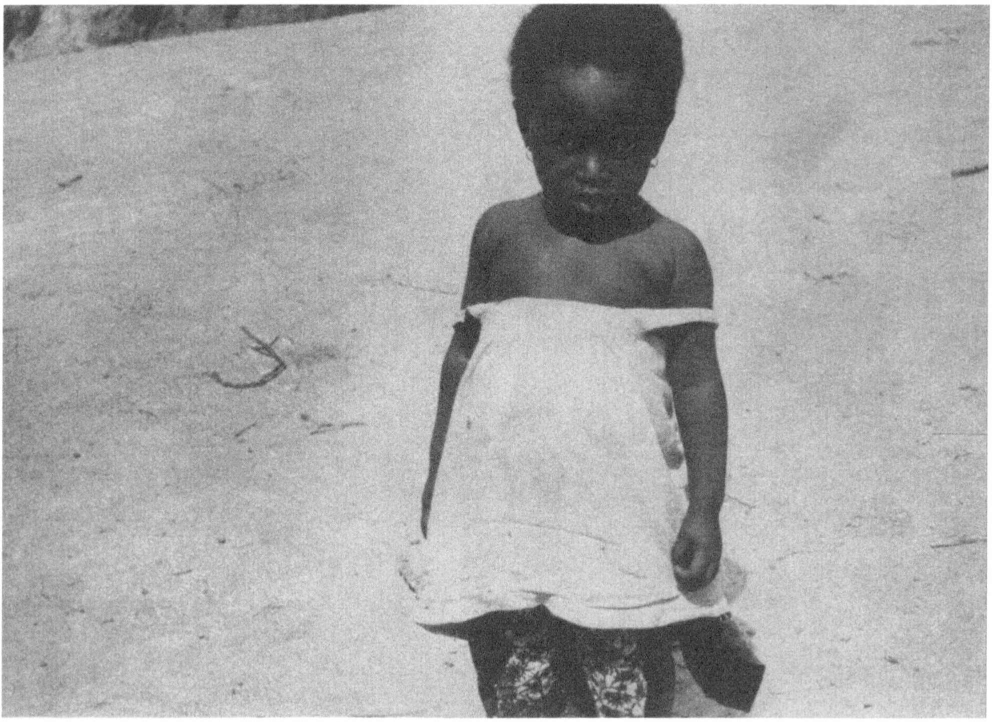

Children's dress. 57. Three-year-old girl in Bosofo.

58. Four-year-old boy in Gblede.

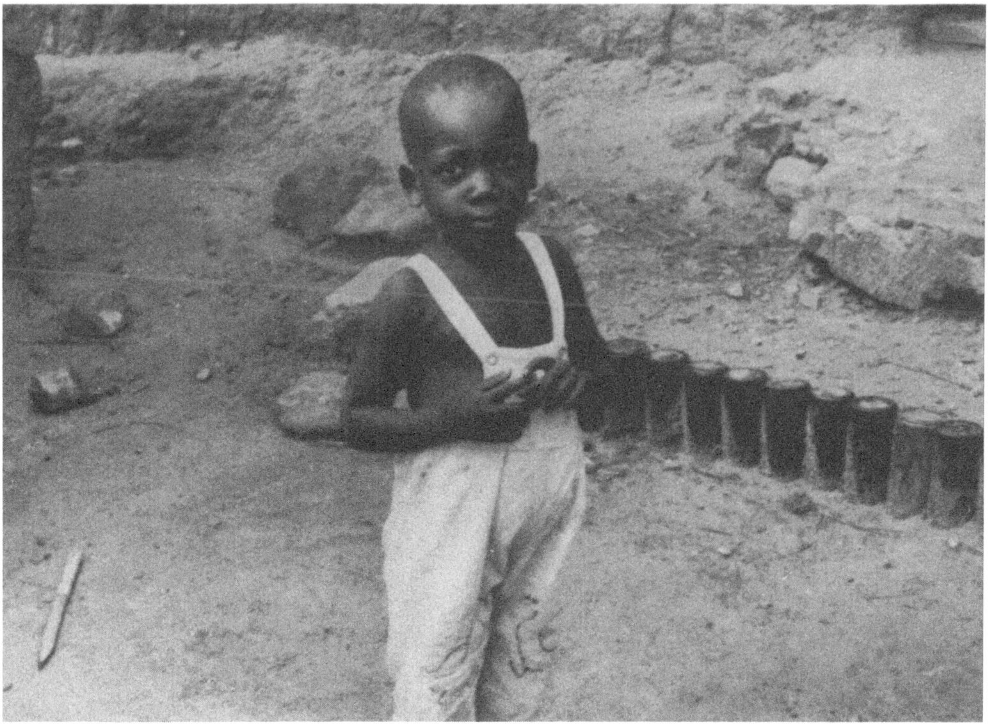

Children's dress. 59. Blouse worn with a skirt of a different cloth in Ahenboboi, near Cape Coast.

60. Blouse worn with a skirt of the same material in Apam.

Children's dress. 61. Boys may wear their cloths in many different ways. Taken in Berekum. Notice chewing-stick.

62. Notice the complicated folds of this boy's draped cloth. Taken at Wa.

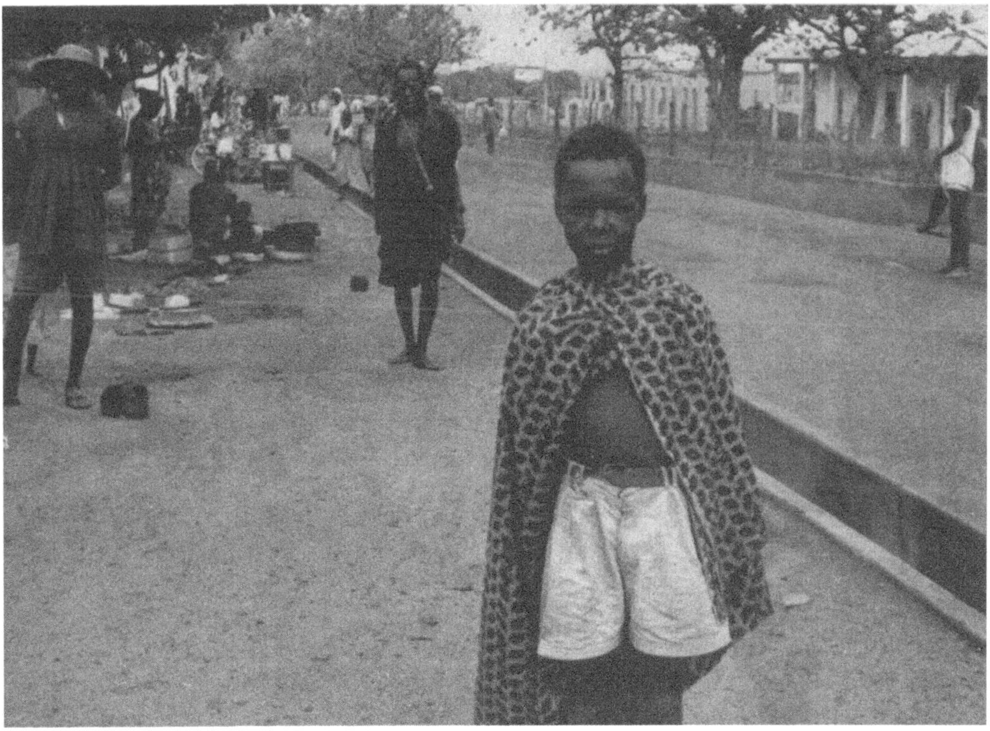

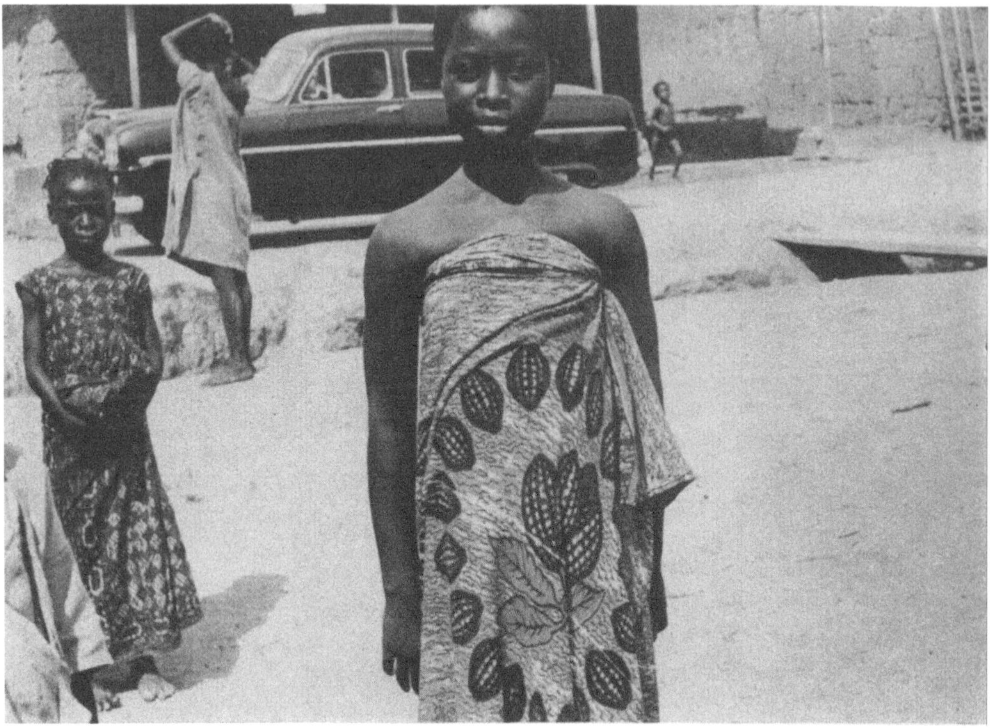

Children's dress. 63. Girls may wear a single cloth in sarong-style. Notice cocoa-pod motif. Taken in Bosofo.

64. The same style, worn with a head-kerchief, in Tamale.

close relative of the mother who assists her in caring for the new baby; usually the grandmother is the first person to shoulder this responsibility. She may continue to render this service till the end of the first month.' In BOSOFO (Asante) during the first three months of infancy, the mother is helped by the grandmother, who often takes chief responsibility for the child's care, leaving the mother only the nursing. The head-shaping is left to the grandmother. When children are about two and a half years old, they are left at home from after breakfast until late afternoon while the parents go to the farm. Some may be left with friends. In JAKOBO (Asante) the responsibility for the early care of the child belongs to the mother and the other clan relatives; this depends to some extent upon the dwelling system. In BEREKUM (Brong) 'a year old child who can eat solid food is sometimes left in the house for the entire day with the three to five year old children. The parents will be away on their farms and the children just roast either cocoyam or plantain and eat it. Sometimes the parents return home late in the evening, and the evening meal will be ready when the child is already asleep.' In GBLEDE (Ewe) the care of the infant is the midwife's responsibility during the first week after birth; thereafter it is the responsibility of the mother and the grandmother. In CENTRAL ACCRA (Ga) the mother is chiefly responsible for the early care of the child, 'but the family structure makes people of close relationship equally responsible'. With a first child, the mother takes care of it under the direct guidance of her own mother or another elderly experienced person; 'many mothers leave the child to the care of the housemaid or grandmother'. In DOME (Ga) the mother is chiefly responsible for the infant's care. As soon as her child can eat solids, she may give it to the other adults, so that she can go out. Among the DAGABAS 'the care of the baby is almost everybody's concern; older siblings, grandparents, co-wives, the father and above all, the mother'.

It follows from the fact that it is mainly the mother who is responsible for the early care of the child, that young children of both sexes have considerably greater contact with their

that, among the Ewes, children belong exclusively to their mothers in the first two or three years of their lives; (26) 42. Fortes says that, among the Tallensis, while 'looking after baby is everybody's job', children are mainly in their mothers' care until they are weaned, at about the end of their third year. At the same time, it is thought important that young infants should remain under their fathers' roofs and hence strong objections are raised if a mother goes to stay with her own parents while her child is still in arms; (14) 187 and 29.

mothers than with their fathers.[1] In those areas or families where the husband lives in a separate compound from his wife, there may be very little contact at all between a young child and its father. In many parts of Ghana, young boys go to live in their fathers' compounds when they reach the age of six or seven, and even where this is not the custom, the contacts between an older child and his parents tend to be increasingly those with the parent of the same sex. In matrilineal areas, the tie between the mother and her children, even when they are older, remains very strong.[2] In BOSOFO (Asante) 'a child's real contacts with his father starts at the time he starts to walk. Earlier than that, the father occasionally takes the child, and the child recognizes him as his father from his interesting him, or from the fact that the mother calls him "your father". The father seldom carries the child because he lives apart from the mother. He carries the child in the evenings when he comes on a visit to the mother or when the mother goes to sleep in his house; but even this does not last long. The child generally sees less of his father. When the child starts to walk the father sometimes takes pleasure in taking his hand and walking with him into the streets or to his own house. If that is done very often, the child becomes so attached to the father that he very often cries to be taken to him. A child's attachment to his father at the age of about two or three can be very strong, as I was informed. A mother told me her daughter does not give her father any rest at all. Any time she is given food, she waits until her father comes and eats with her. She even does not want anybody to take away her stool other than her father. If the father refuses to do it, she cries and refuses to stop until her father tells her to. Any time the father goes on a journey the child is ill and remains so until the father returns. These parents stay together in one house, the only couple staying together in the village.' In JAISI (Asante) young children have more contact with their mothers, and those children whose

[1] See Plates 81 and 82.

[2] Fortes says that 'through the whole gamut of social relations in Ashanti there is no tie so fundamental and so strong as that of mother and child. Though it has the sanction of the whole of customary law, on account of the principle of matrilineal descent, Ashanti think of it as an ultimate and irreducible moral and psychological fact which needs no sanctions. A woman and her children constitute the indissoluble core of Ashanti social organization'; (13) 72. (Here, and elsewhere in his writings, Fortes analyses the psychological and sociological aspects of family relationships with a far greater degree of subtlety than is attempted in the present book, and the reader is referred to the books listed in the bibliography for a profound discussion of these relationships in Ashanti, and among the Tallensis of the Northern Territories.)

fathers live in separate houses may see very little of them until they are older. In DOME (Ga) parents mostly live in separate compounds and up until they are seven years of age, children live with their mothers. When they reach the age of seven, boys go to live in their father's homes. In APIREDE (Cherepon) young children spend their time with their mother; older children have more contact with the parent of their own sex. Among the ISALAS 'as the children grow older they have more contact with the parent of the same sex'.

The amount of contact a very young child has with its father varies from family to family.[1] A polygynous father may see very little of his children; he may feel it sufficient to fulfil his responsibilities towards his infants by 'a brief and rather stiffly formal visit to his wife at sunset'[2] to inquire after them. In some families, the main contacts that a father has with his young children are in relation to discipline. In other familes, however, fathers are to be seen looking after their infants while their wives are away, playing with them and carrying them round in their arms.[3] As their sons grow older, so their contacts with their fathers increase until, at about the age of six or seven, the father assumes complete responsibility for his son's training.[4] Girls remain their mothers' responsibilities until they are married. In ABURI (Akwapim) 'up to the age of four

[1] In Ashanti, according to Fortes, pre-adolescent children live in their fathers' households only when their mothers are also members of those households; in polygynous families where wives live by themselves, their children tend to live with them. At adolescence, a number of children then go to live with their maternal uncles; (13) 82-3. At the same time, according to Danquah, a child belongs to its father until its marriage, and a mother cannot beforehand take a child away from its father against its wishes; (6) 187.

[2] Field (9) 8.

[3] Fortes notes that an Ashanti father has no legal authority over his children; (11) 268. Christensen says that, among the Fantis a father will often care for and fondle an infant during the first two years of its life, and may tend it for long periods while the mother is elsewhere. From the time the child is able to walk, the father may begin a 'constant association' with him, and as soon as practicable, the child goes to live with him and he assumes full responsibility for him; (5) 97. Among the Gas, according to Field, the father's contacts with his infant children are regular though rather formal; (9) 30-1 and 7-8. Fortes says that a Tallensi father, though he sees less of his young children than does the mother, is as loving and indulgent a parent; (14) 189.

[4] Fortes stresses the responsibility of the Ashanti father to bring up his children, especially his sons, for whose training he is wholly responsible, even though they belong to different clans; (11) 268. (But see pages 180-4 below for a discussion of the problems that the cost of formal schooling entails.) Christensen says that a Fanti boy spends virtually all of his time, except when he is playing with other children, with his father at about the age of four; (5) 97. Field notes that, among the Gas, the father is responsible for the training of his sons; (9) 31. (See also Chapter 21 below.)

years, fathers play with their children a lot'. They seldom beat them for wrong-doing, and the mothers are sometimes annoyed when they merely laugh at their children's misbehaviour; it is felt by the mothers that the fathers spoil the children. In APA (Asante) the father rarely sees his children, and may not visit his wife's house for a whole week. In JAISI (Asante) the child's early contacts with its father are irregular, especially in polygynous homes, where 'marriages whether recognized or not are unstable. Many of the women have had several broken marriages.' In VAKPO (Ewe) 'before the child is four years, he has learnt to play with his father, chat with him and laugh with him'. In CENTRAL ACCRA (Ga) some fathers leave home early to go to work and come home late, and therefore have little time to play with their children, 'and in many cases the children do not know their fathers'. Among polygynists, the children live with their mothers, who only take their babies to their husbands' homes when they go to sleep with them. In some families, however, 'a father especially spends his leisure time playing with the infant', since the mother is often busy with housework or with her trading. In APIREDE (Cherepon) the father plays with his young children on his return home from the farm. Among the ISALAS 'the child's early contact with its father is mainly through play. After the day's work on the farm, the father sits in the compound with the child on his lap and plays with it.'

In most parts of Ghana, the mother is regarded as the main authority for the discipline of young children. As they grow older, children come under the rule of their parents of the same sex, who are responsible for punishing them. Mothers may report their sons' misconduct to the fathers, who will then punish them. Some mothers, on the other hand, may conceal their sons' misdemeanours for fear they will receive too severe punishment. In polygynous families, as has been said above, fathers may have very little contact with their young children beyond matters of discipline. Threats of bogy men, circumcisers and monsters, and of beatings, are the chief sanctions used to maintain discipline; beatings and the applications of ground pepper or ginger to the genitals or the eyes are the most common punishments.[1] In some homes, the child is expected to cry

[1] Though, according to another survey, the application of red pepper juice is not so popular a form of punishment as is suggested in the original investigations; see *Child Training in Ghana*, p. 455. Busia notes a case of a housemaid who had red pepper rubbed in her eyes for coming home late from an errand; (4) 36.

and run away when it is being beaten; not to cry and to endure the beating is regarded as disrespectful.[1] In APA (Asante) the mother has chief authority in disciplining the child, as the children usually live in clan houses and do not often see their fathers. 'The fact that the father is responsible for the discipline of his children is only theoretical to most of the fathers.' A red pepper enema is a common form of punishment, especially since excessive beating might harm the child while the enema has also medicinal properties, and the child who is given one 'loses nothing but gains'. Threats of being captured by dwarves, or being taken to an imaginary place of torture are also used. In BANKO (Asante) the mother is the chief authority and main agent of discipline. When children are older, they are disciplined by their parents of the same sex. Sometimes, however, the parent of the same sex allies with the child to conceal an offence from the other parent; 'whenever the boys (of from three to seven years of age) did something wrong and they feared punishment, they ran away to the father's house and sought refuge there'. Beatings and red pepper are common forms of punishment. In BENIM (Asante) the mother is the main agent of discipline for young children; after the age of seven, fathers are responsible for their sons' behaviour. When a son disobeys his father, he is sent away to his maternal uncle. This is considered very serious, and his mother, his maternal uncle and other members of the clan have to go to the father and apologize and pay a compensation, to appease the soul's anger, which can cause the death of the son. 'The child's instructions are in most cases given verbally, directly or indirectly through such expressions

[1] Fortes says that the Ashanti father derives his right to punish his sons from his responsibility for training them. Ashanti fathers, according to Fortes, tend to be over-strict; (11) 268. Christensen says that, among the Fantis, disciplining children is held to be the duty of the father, and this often leads to arguments between parents, as mothers may feel that their husbands are too severe; (5) 48. Fortes says that, among the Tallensis, the father has the right and the duty of disciplining his children. While the mother is entitled to beat her children, it would normally be considered unbecoming and unnatural for her to do so; (14) 138-9. According to Fortes, Tallensi parents are very long-suffering with their children, and allow them much latitude in conforming to the social standards of their society. They are not expected to have 'acquired sense' enough to conform much before eight or nine years of age; before then the punishment of misconduct is due more to anger than to outrage, and is not very common; (14) 191-2. At the same time, no one hesitates to punish when it seems to be merited; (12) 14. Mothers resent very much the punishment of their children by their co-wives; (14) 131. Tait says that, among the Konkombas, children are sometimes beaten by their mothers for misbehaviour inside the compound, but for any misconduct outside the compound, a boy should be taken to his father for punishment; (34) 333.

as "Stop that! Don't say that!" or "If you do that, a ghost will catch you", or "The policeman will arrest you". At times when a child has once been treated by a doctor, and has, for instance, been once given an injection, the mother might make use of that. When she wants to threaten her child because she wants discipline and obedience she will say "If you don't stop, the doctor will come again and give you another injection". Sometimes a member of the household may stand outside the house or room in which the mother and child are and will pretend to be either the ghost, the policeman, the doctor or whatever person or thing the mother has used for threatening the child. This person changes his or her voice and says, "Who is that child crying or misbehaving? I shall come there just now, if he does not stop!" Then you will see the child full of fear cling to his mother for safety. At once peace will be maintained. The mother will then comfort the child by saying, "Stop, so that this bad policeman or doctor will not come and catch you." ' There are three main forms of punishment: scolding, slapping the buttocks and putting pepper or ginger into the rectum or genitals. Fathers beat their sons over the age of seven with the stick. Mothers may threaten their daughters that they will have their first menstruation during the day-time, which is considered to be very unlucky. Good behaviour is rewarded with praise, a penny or fruit. In DWINYAMA (Asante) the mother has the chief authority in disciplining the child in the early stages, but later the father is recognized as the final authority. The mother may sometimes decide that the child is to be punished, while the father carries out the punishment, especially with older children. Parents usually inform one another of cases of misconduct; the mother may not bother to inform her husband of small offences, but she would not conceal a major offence, which might involve parental pardons to avoid civil actions. She may also quarrel with him, for taking the child's side, if he uses excessive severity in punishing his children. While appeals to the child's self-esteem, and encouragement and flattery are sometimes used, the most common sanctions are those of force and fear. Beatings are often given in order to get the children to submit to parental authority. If this is found to be ineffectual, parents may appeal to school-teachers. Other forms of punishment in common use are threats of ghosts, bogy men and the use of ridicule. In JAKOBO (Asante) while both parents have authority in disciplining their children, severe punishments are left to the father. It is not usual for the mother to conceal her children's offences from the father, though some sympathetic mothers may do so. To squeeze ground pepper and ginger into the rectum is a common form of punishment, widely approved of because of its medical effects. In SUPOWMU DUNKWA (Fante) 'although the father has the final say in the disciplining of the child, the mother is the main agent of discipline. It is she who teaches the child from its early age what it should do and what it should not do. When it is naughty, she scolds and beats it, and sometimes threatens to report it to the father. In monogamous homes, most of them Christian, the parents regularly discuss the child's behaviour and decide together what should be done, but in polygamous homes, the mothers often conceal their children's bad behaviour from the fathers, so that the father may not be prejudiced against their children. In some monogamous homes too, when the mother is weak in her control, and thinks the father is too severe in discipline, she often conceals her children's misdemeanours from the father. And often the mother will say to the child, "If you fetch me a kerosene-tin full of water, I will not tell your father about what you did this morning when he was away", and the child will run to perform the task at once.' When a child is being punished, he 'is considered stubborn and rude if he does not cry or run away when being beaten by an elder'. Among the KWAHUS both mother and father discipline the children, but the father is recognized as the final authority. In KPANDU (Ewe) while both parents are responsible for their children's discipline, the father is recognized as the final authority. The mother may sometimes conceal cases of misconduct for fear of over-severe punishment. In CENTRAL ACCRA (Ga) the mother is the main authority for disciplining the young child. Some mothers are very strict and 'go to the extent of beating them, stripping them naked and putting pepper into their eyes, anus and penis or vagina'. Stories of ghosts, white men, circumcisers, and masked men are used to maintain discipline; 'children obey as soon as the mother says "I shall call the man to circumcise you if you do not stop crying" '. Serious cases may be reported to the father for punishment. As the child grows older, its discipline becomes the responsibility of the parent of the same sex. In some cases, with the last-born, for instance, the mother may conceal a child's offence from its father.

In TESHIE (Ga) the mother has chief authority in disciplining the child; her relatives have the right of punishing the child during her absence, though some mothers disapprove of their sisters administering punishment to their children, especially if the sister happens to be barren. Sometimes the mother decides that the child should be punished, and the father carries out the punishment, while at other times the mother conceals the offence from the father for fear of his brutal treatment. 'A very common mode of punishment is the rubbing of pepper into the eyes or lips and then exposing the child to the ridicule of other companions.' In APIREDE (Cherepon) 'it is believed in this village that the mother's duty is to bring up the girl, and the father's to bring up the boy'. In cases of elder children the mother may report them to the father who punishes them. She does not conceal any cases from him. Younger children are slapped, older children are beaten with a cane. In WINNEBA (Efutu) the mother is the main agent of discipline, but the father is recognized as the final authority. Mothers report serious cases to their husbands, though they may conceal them sometimes for fear of too-severe punishment. Among the ISALAS 'the father is the chief authority as regards the disciplining of the child. The mother informs the father of any misbehaviour of the child and the father decides what punishment is to be given to the child and carries it out himself.'

In many parts of Ghana, parents quarrel openly in front of their children, sometimes resorting to blows. Such quarrels are frequently over questions of disciplining the children, but quarrels over other matters, such as the mother's domestic incompetence or the father's adulteries, are not concealed from them. Nor, according to the answers received during the check-list survey is this necessarily regarded as a bad practice.[1] In BANKO (Asante) 'parents do not mind quarrelling in front of their children. Sometimes the mother puts the child down from her back and fights with the father.' In BOSOFO (Asante) quarrels about discipline are frequent; 'most fathers reported that mothers are generally too harsh and punish them for every mistake', referring to the children. Family squabbles are common, and are held in front of children. 'When such quarrels or

[1] See *Child Training in Ghana*, p. 458. Field notes that, among the Gas, married couples very rarely show open affection towards each other in public, and she argues that this is not merely a question of etiquette but a reflection of the genuine lack of warmth between them; (9) 8.

Children's dress. 65. A boy in Tamale market.

66. A boy in Tumu, Northern Territories.

Children's dress. 67. One pair of shorts between four boys in Kani, Northern Territories.

68. A boy from a Northern Territories tribe in traditional dress, with bow and arrow Taken outside Navrongo.

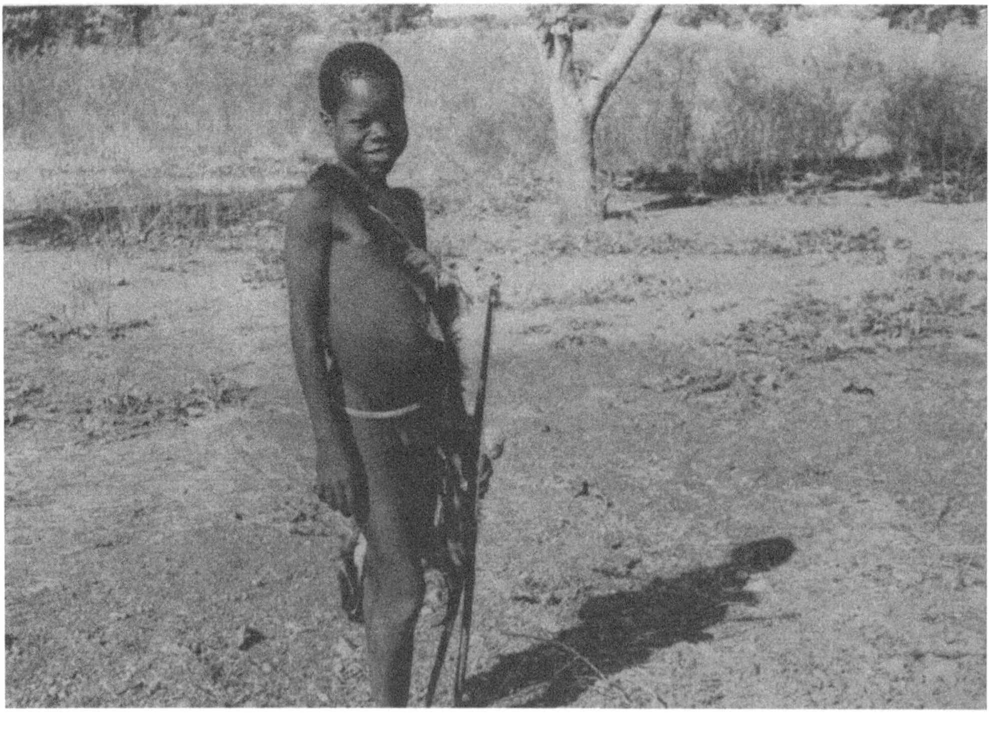

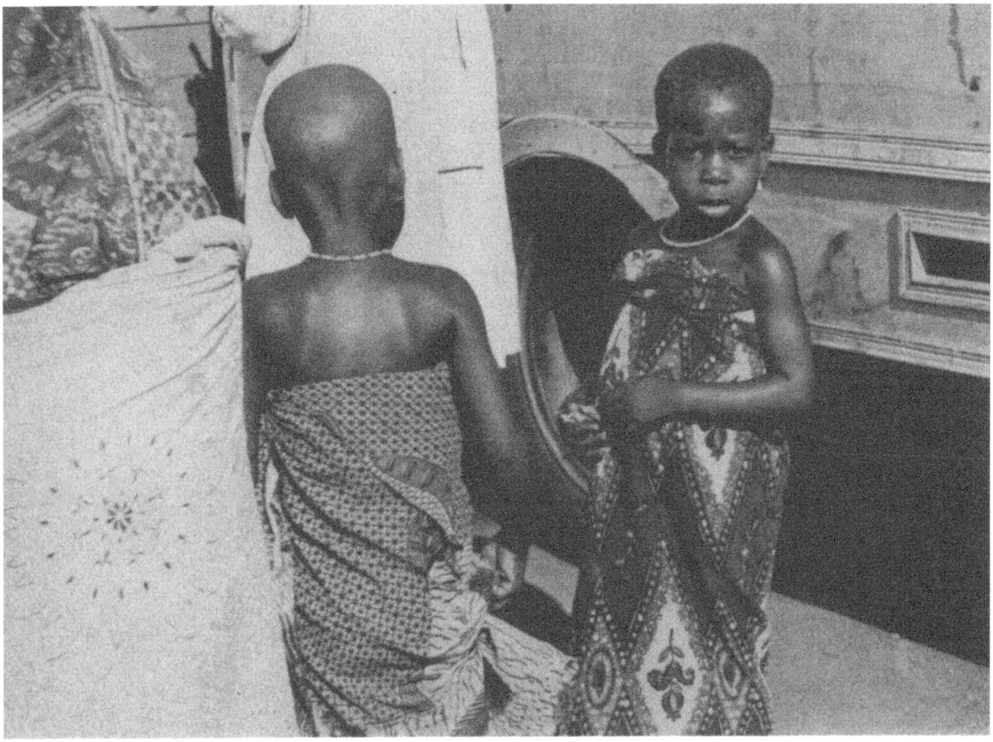

Children's dress. 69 Young children in their best clothes in Bawku market.

70. Two toddlers in Goviefe, one in her best cloth, and one in her beads.

Children's dress. 71. Schoolgirl in Bawku market.

72. Two friends in Wa.

fights occur, the young children are usually very much troubled and cry. I was told that sometimes they throw stones at their fathers when they beat their mothers.' In JAISI (Asante) parents quarrel at times in front of the children, including shouting at one another and quarrelling over the mother's domestic incompetence or the father's adulteries. In APAM (Fante) 'while there may be occasional disagreement, or even open quarrels and fights over matters of discipline, especially where mother's favourite is concerned, parents generally live peacefully, giving due respect to each other in the presence of their children'. In SUPOWMU DUNKWA (Fante) 'the parents do not bother to put on their best behaviour when the children are about. It is common to see a fight between a man and his wife, and the children either weeping or trying to separate them.' In AYIKAI DOBORO (Ga) parents may openly quarrel in front of their children, especially in polygynous households. In TESHIE (Ga) a father may beat his wife in front of the children. Obscene language is freely used in front of them. In OTROWE (Adangme) 'quarrels between husband and wife over the treatment of children and over other things are very common. Such quarrels may result in fights between husbands and wives; when this happens children are often sympathetic towards their mothers. They cry, weep and call other adults to come and defend or save their mothers. They may shout too. It is a common practice for parents to disagree before their children.'

Quarrels between children and their fathers are rare in Ghana.[1] Between children and their mothers, quarrels are more frequent, particularly with adolescent girls, who resent the lack of freedom they may be allowed. In a survey carried out in Apam by one of the investigators, the majority of children appeared to have no complaint over their parents' treatment of them. In BOSOFO (Asante) quarrels between parents and children are not usual, at least until the age of adolescence. In BEREKUM (Brong) in literate homes 'it is not uncommon to find a young educated girl showering abuses on her mother who tells her that she should not go out very often in the night'. Formerly, and still today in illiterate homes, children dare not say that their fathers have wronged them, and there is no open argument or disagreement. In APAM (Fante) quarrels between

[1] Fortes says that, among the Ashantis, 'to insult, abuse or assault one's father is an irreparable wrong, one which is bound to bring ill luck'; (11) 268.

mothers and daughters are common; between fathers and sons, very rare. In TESHIE (Ga) quarrels between a mother and her daughters are frequent, particularly over the girl's keeping late hours, or using the mother's cloth, or because the mother disapproves of her daughter's boy friends. Quarrels between a father and his children are few, as the father's word is law in the family. In APIREDE (Cherepon) 'children scarcely quarrel with their parents until they reach the age of adolescence'. Such quarrels as then arise are mainly concerned with parental restraints on their outside activities. In WINNEBA (Efutu) quarrels are largely between mothers and their daughters, especially where the mothers and their husbands also quarrel. 'Whatever the circumstance, there is always a reserved store of respect for one's parents whom it is more or less a curse for one to vilify.'

When quarrels between parents and children do occur, however, the matter may become serious, particularly if the child has been formally cursed by the parent. In such cases, a go-between, usually a relative, is asked by the child to intercede on his behalf. Gifts of rum or schnapps are needed, and the repentent child may have to appear before a court of elders, and provide a sacrificial sheep before the curse is withdrawn. On such occasions, and also with less important quarrels, it is usually held by both parent and other elders that the fault rests with the child. It is very rare, though not unknown, for a parent to admit that he or she was wrong.[1] In TUTU (Akwapim) 'it is the accepted opinion that in the matter of disputes between the parents and their children, the parents are never at fault and it is the children who are always found guilty'. In DWINYAMA (Asante) quarrels are settled by consulting the clan elder or head, and by the propitiation of the offended parent if necessary. Parents may admit to children they are wrong and ask forgiveness, either directly or through an elder. In JAISI (Asante) older children who have offended their parents must apologize through a go-between, especially if the father is offended, when a pacification including a sacrifice may be

[1] Fortes quotes an instance of a Tallensi father admitting to his eleven year old son that he had been wrong; (12) 32. But he goes on to say that 'if anyone who has reached years of discretion behaves in such a way as to incur the resentment and hostility of a parent, some calamity will certainly befall him or her unless he comes formally to beg forgiveness and the injured parent ritually abjures his or her anger'; (12) 34.

necessary for fear that otherwise the father's totem will bring disaster on the family. In such cases of ritual pacification, it is always assumed that the child is wrong, and he asks for forgiveness. But in the case of minor disputes, 'among the Jaisi community parents often admit their wrong before their children'. If the parent's action has cast a slur on the daughter's character, or embarrassed her before her husband, it may be necessary for the parent to make a public propitiation. In APAM (Fante) 'quarrels between fathers and sons are extremely rare; while occasionally there may be quarrels between sons and mothers. Common cases of quarrels are between mothers and daughters, and are usually precipitated by scamped work through laziness such as late rising, neglected work through disobedience, or misuse of things in the house such as pomade powder, coal or firewood, matches or kerosene. Improper dress such as uncovering the breasts in public may also precipitate quarrels. The father generally settles household quarrels between sons, daughters and mothers by pointing out, and reprimanding, the wrong-doer. Where children feel they have not been fairly treated, they may refer the matter to an uncle, aunt or grandmother. As a rule the matter generally ends there. Where children feel they are wrong, and want the parent's forgiveness, an aunt or grandmother is approached for the intercession. Where parents also realize that they have wronged their children, a friend of the family who is on very good terms with the children, an aunt or grandmother is usually asked to appease the children. Children who are wronged and feel that parents owe them an apology may leave the house, and go to live with the relative such as an aunt or uncle or grandmother. The relative who takes in the children for a few days is the one who usually settles the quarrels, and returns the children to their parents.' In SUPOWMU DUNKWA (Fante) 'when a child is very rude and insulting to the father, the father may disown him. The father cuts a broom into two to signify his separation from the child from that moment, and pours libation, swearing that he will never again call him son. The child is then turned out of the house to fend for himself. If ever reconciliation is sought, the child finds two or more elderly people, who go and implore the father's forgiveness. If the father is willing to forgive, the young man is asked to slaughter a sheep. He and the elders go to the father's house, where he prostrates before his father and begs his forgiveness. The sheep he provides is then slaughtered over the broom, and libation is poured cancelling the oath of separation and disownment. Then the father receives his child back, either by shaking hands with him or by embracing him. In the case of a mother disowning her child, at reconciliation the mother puts her breast in the child's mouth to signify that he is once more her child.' In AYIKAI DOBORO (Ga) when a serious quarrel has taken place, the child asks a relative to act as a go-between. In some cases, three or four elders may be assembled to try the case. The child, however, is always adjudged wrong by both relatives and other adults. When a reconciliation has been made, a libation is poured and the offended parent and the child drink from the same cup. In TESHIE (Ga) quarrels between a mother and her daughter are usually resolved by the husband, though sometimes the grandmother or an elderly person in the neighbourhood may intervene. The offending child must always ask forgiveness, even if the mother was right, as the arbitrator insists that the daughter has no right to retaliate. In APIREDE (Cherepon) serious quarrels between parents and children are settled through the intervention of a go-between, usually an elderly relative. 'There is a general tendency however to put the blame on the child, especially when quarrel is between son and his father; for they say that it is not good that a boy be begged for forgiveness by his father.' In LARTEH KUBEASI (Guang) quarrels between parents and children are settled, in the case of serious disputes, by go-betweens from among the elderly members of the family. It is not always assumed that the child is wrong, and the elders may point out the mistake to an offending parent. Among the ISALAS quarrels between parents and children are expected to end with the child's asking for forgiveness. 'It is traditionally held that one's parents are always right and in all quarrels with parents, the child has to ask for forgivenness; parents never admit they are wrong in dealings with their children.'

The almost-universally held view in Ghana towards parental responsibility and filial gratitude is that, in return for bringing up their children, parents have the right to expect support from them in old age and the provision of a fitting burial. The having of children is therefore widely regarded as a form of insurance against old age and obsequial neglect.[1] In addition to

[1] Fortes notes that, among the Ashantis, there is no legal obligation on a son or daughter to support a father in old age, though it would be regarded as 'an

financial support, children are expected to demonstrate their gratitude towards their parents by filial obedience.[1] In TUTU (Akwapim) 'almost all the parents whose opinions on the subject was obtained expressed the view that the care of children, from babyhood to adolescence, entails a great deal of strenuous effort and constant vigilance, and in return for all the hardships undergone by the parents towards the welfare of their children they expect their children to be grateful; this gratitude should be shown by obedience.' In GBLEDE (Ewe) it is the parents' duty to support their children, and it is the children's duty to support their parents in old age. In GOVIEFE (Ewe) a similar view is held. 'Once a schoolboy, for instance, has completed his Middle School course and will not pursue further learning, the parents expect him to get into a job and so they stop giving him any financial support. They expect that as soon as he gets settled he should begin "to extend his arms to them" and help in looking after his younger siblings at school.' In CHRISTIANSBORG (Ga) filial gratitude is expected. Parents provide for their children only on the underlying understanding that they will in turn provide for the parents in old age. In LARTEH KUBEASI (Guang) 'a great deal of the parents are quite aware of their responsibilities towards their children. Many of them strain every nerve and deny themselves of their comfort in order to provide for the needs of their children or to educate them. If some children seem to be neglected, the situation usually arises out of inability rather than from unwillingness on the part of their parents. Later, when the children grow up, they are expected to be grateful not necessarily directly to their parents, but to the whole family in one way or the other. There are many children who depend upon their brothers and sisters for their education.'

The children's financial responsibilities towards their parents are only part of the widespread net of clan responsibility, and children on whose education money has been spent are expected

evil act' if he or she did not do so; (11) 268. According to Fortes, the ancestor cult practised by the Tallensis gives a man 'a moral compulsion' to pass on his private property and the knowledge of his craft to his sons, and a woman has the same feeling with regard to her daughters; (12) 12.

[1] In matrilineal societies, the loyalty and respect owed towards their mother by her children is augmented by the ties of the clan. Fortes says that the Ashantis look upon the bond between mother and child as an absolutely binding moral relationship. 'To show disrespect towards one's mother is tantamount to sacrilege'; (11) 263.

to repay the debt by contributing in turn towards the education of their younger siblings, nephews and other relatives. Among the Akans, this clan responsibility theoretically does not extend to the father-son relationship, since, by virtue of matrilineal descent, a man's children belong to a different clan from his own. He may therefore find that his own clan responsibilities towards his sister's children are regarded as of greater importance than those towards his own. In Akan customary law, a father is responsible only for those of his son's debts arising from sexual misconduct; all other debts are the responsibility of his wife's family, who are the child's clan elders. At the same time, the father is traditionally responsible for the upbringing of his sons, for their training in a craft, and for the provision of the means for their livelihood. Since the coming of formal schooling, the question of who should pay the school fees has given rise to a great deal of controversy, and there is no universal agreement on where the responsibility lies.[1] Moreover, despite the provisions of customs regarding the paramount importance of clan ties, many Akan fathers wish to provide for their sons beyond the minimum allowed for by tradition; to do so brings them into conflict with their own clans, who feel that any gifts of property a man may make to his sons are in fact alienations of clan wealth. A man may now give away up to half his wealth to his children in the presence of accredited witnesses, whether or not he has the consent of his clan.[2]

The traditional responsibility of an Akan father towards his children ended, with his sons, when he had provided for their livelihood and found them wives, and with his daughters, when they were married. While they were under his charge, he had the right of punishing them; he also had the right to any profits from their work, though he was expected to put by some of these to provide against marriage expenses. He had a right to expect support from them in his old age, though this right was not based on legal obligation, and would appear to be more or less proportionate to the trouble and money he spent on their

[1] See below, pages 180-4, for a further discussion of this point. According to Fortes, among the Ashantis it is strongly felt that the responsibility is the father's. In an investigation of nearly seven hundred children he found that half the children attending school were supported by their fathers; 25% by their maternal uncles; 10-15% by their mothers. He goes on to say that an uncle, mother or other relative will take on this responsibility only if the father fails to do so; (11) 268.

[2] The Ashanti Confederacy Council ruled in 1942 that the approval of the man's relatives was not necessary.

upbringing.[1] Traditionally, if a man was deprived of the service of any one of his children (to take up service with a fetish priest, for example), he was entitled to a monetary compensation from the child's clan.[2]

This division of responsibility for a child's upbringing does not, of course, extend to those tribes in which succession is by patrilineal descent, where the responsibility rests squarely with the father, who has the concomitant right to the service of, and the support in old age by, his children.[3]

Parental ambitions for children in Ghana largely centre round the securing of a good job, so that the child will be able to contribute towards the support of the parents in old age. The importance of becoming a respected member of the community and a credit thereby to the family, is also stressed. In ABURI (Akwapim) 'all the parents are anxious for their children to grow up to become good men and women doing honourable jobs. So the children who do not go to school are made to learn a trade; carpentry, blacksmith or gold or silversmith in the case of boys, and sewing for the girls. The mothers are more anxious for the well-being of their children than are the fathers. The fathers just do not care.' In BOMPATA (Asante) parental ambitions for children are that they shall become cultured persons, hard-working and good neighbours. 'All parents agree that an industrious child is a source of pride and an asset to the family.' In AYANZILI (Nzima) the main ambitions that parents have for their children is that they shall make money and have children of their own. In AYIKAI DOBORO (Ga) parents have high hopes of good jobs for their children, preferably in government service. They also look forward to their children's providing for them in old age. In TEMA (Ga) the main parental ambitions for children are that they shall have secure livelihoods and be able to support their parents in old age.

In most parts of Ghana, parental authority lasts until the child is married, and in some matters persists until the parent's

[1] Danquah says that, among the Akims, 'the duty of a child towards a father would seem to wane in proportion to the diminution of the parent support'; and that such support that a father receives from his children is an act of filial affection rather than legal obligation. The only absolute duty is the provision of a coffin on his death; (6) 187. This is confirmed by Fortes; (11) 268.

[2] This compensation was called *Tamboba* among the Akims, according to Danquah; (6) 188-92.

[3] The bond between a Tallensi parent and child, according to Fortes, can be neither obliterated nor repudiated; (14) 169.

death.[1] Parents may interfere with the affairs of their married children in such matters as impending divorce, barrenness, misconduct and disrespect towards elders. In ABURI (Akwapim) 'parental authority lasts, in theory, as long as the parents are alive'; but nowadays there is little of such authority left. 'The following are the matters in which the parents may interfere: decision of the choice of a husband or wife, deciding to take a career, showing disrespect to elders, laziness.' In BOSOFO (Asante) parental authority lasts in most matters until marriage. Parents, and especially the maternal uncle, have authority over the marriage, adultery, divorce and other rites of their children until their death. In BEREKUM (Brong) 'parental authority is a life-time affair'. Fathers may call on their sons' assistance at any time they need them, and the father is the first person to be informed of any trouble which has arisen. In DOME (Ga) parental authority lasts until adulthood, and after in lesser degree. Parents can interfere with marriages if their offspring are being maltreated, and 'they can break marriage by such interference'. Parents may encourage their sons to choose another wife if the first one is sterile, and mothers may even beat their married daughters. In AGOMANYA (Krobo) parental authority is lifelong, though it is diminished after marriage. In APIREDE (Cherepon) 'in the village, the child is under full parental control until his marriage. Even then, matters dealing with divorce, adultery, new marriages and other customary rites are referred to the parents or to an elder relative; and it is expected their opinion and advice should be respected.' Among the ISALAS 'the parents' authority lasts until the boy or girl is married. Even after marriage the son is still under the authority of the father, for the father bears all financial responsibility for the marriage and the maintenance of the son and his wife.'

[1] Fortes says that, among the Tallensis, a woman's parents continue to have a good deal of influence over her for some years after her marriage, and that is why her husband must not offend his parents-in-law; (14) 78.

Children's dress. 73. A Lobi girl with mother in Bole. The girl is wearing the traditional tribal 'horsetail', while the mother has adopted the cloth, though she wears it so as to show off the radial scarification on her belly. Both mother and daughter have pierced lip ornaments.

74. A variety of clothes worn by boys in Bawku market.

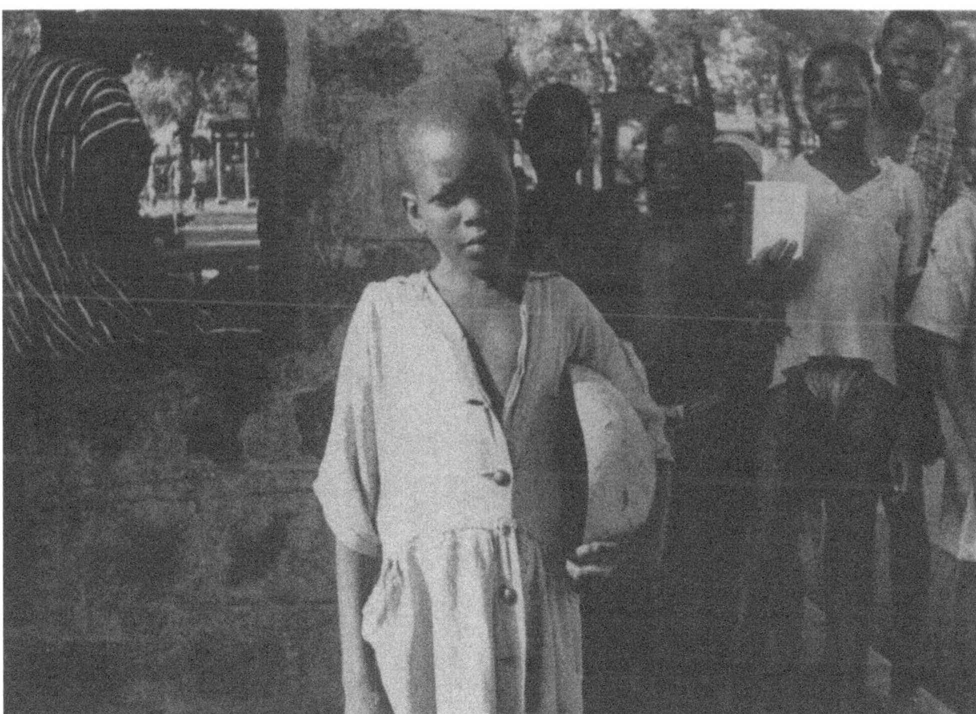

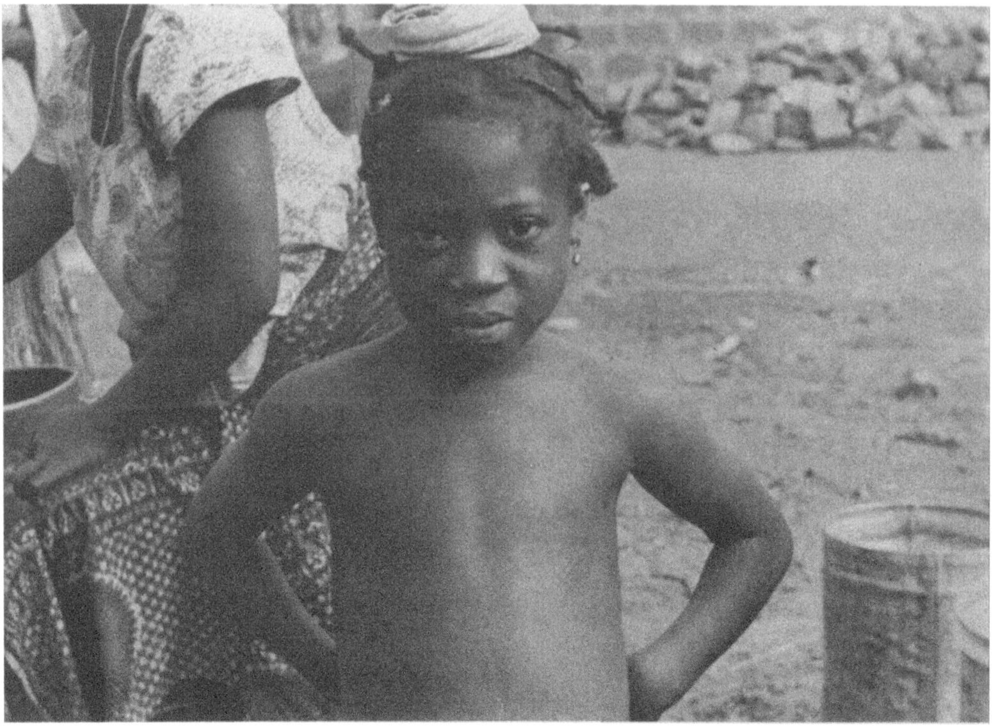

Children's hair styles. 75. Grown-up hair style on a six-year-old girl in Tamale.

76. Taken in an Ashanti village

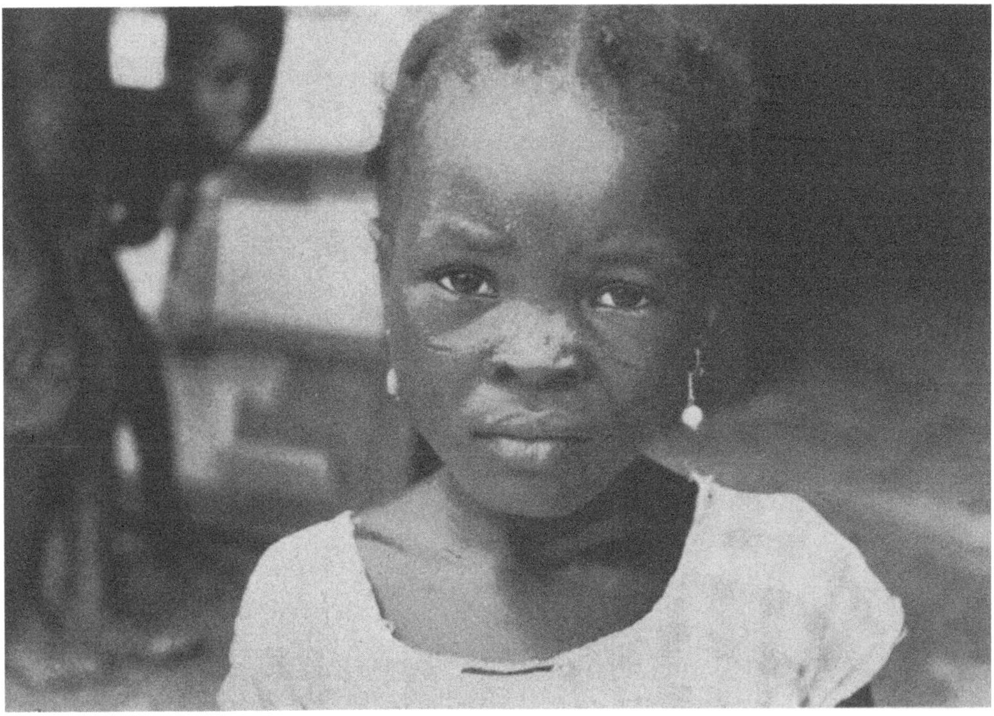

Children's hair styles. 77. Taken in Kpandu.

78. This little girl, of about seven years of age, was having her hair plaited in a grown-up style, in order to try to get her to behave better. Taken in Teshie.

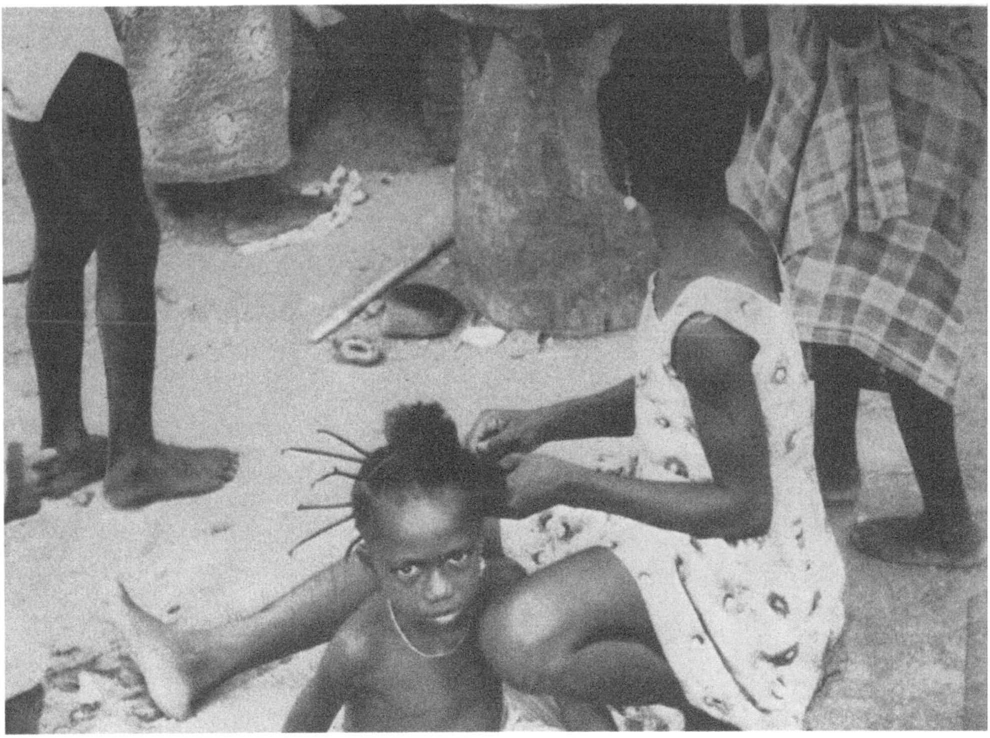

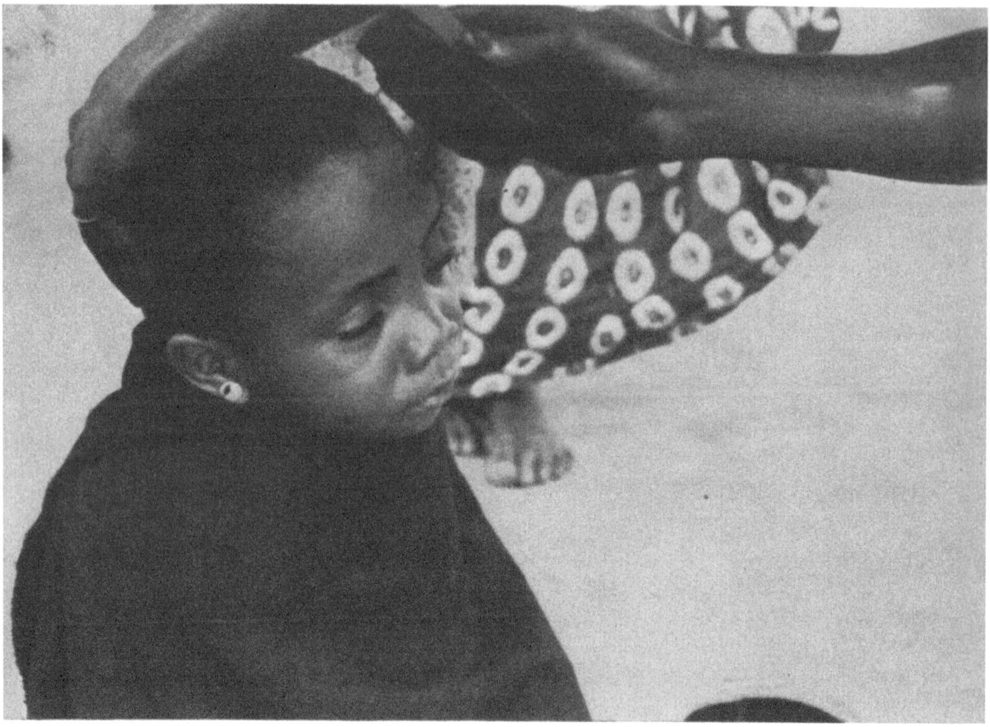

Children's hair styles. 79. Child having her hair blackened in Vakpo market. She is wearing a piece of cloth to prevent the blacking from spoiling her dress.

80. She looks up for her parents to admire the result.

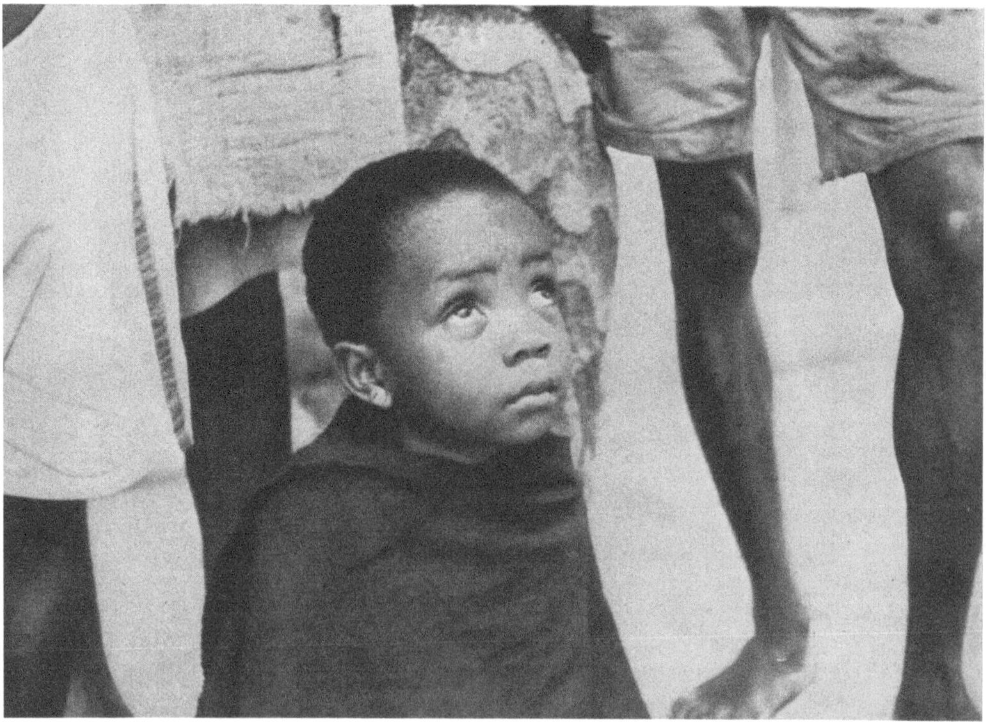

CHAPTER FIFTEEN

CHILDREN'S RELATIONS WITH ADULTS OTHER THAN THEIR PARENTS

> 'The child's life is practically woven into that of the mother's family and all along he is expected to recognize his relationship with and dependence upon them.'

THE Ghanaian child grows up under the direct surveillance, not only of his parents, but also of his other relatives, both those living in the same compound and those living nearby. Grandparents, uncles, aunts, other relatives and even friends of the parents, all feel some degree of responsibility, more or less according to their relationship with the parents, towards the upbringing of the child, and all participate, more or less, in the process. During the early months of life, particularly in the case of a first-born, the child's grandmother may virtually take over the care of the child, leaving only the nursing to the mother. As it grows older, its relatives take part in rearing it, not only directly, by command and restraint, but also indirectly, by giving authoritative advice to the parents.[1]

In matrilineal tribes, the rules of succession give a place of special importance to the child's maternal uncle, who is the nearest adult male blood relative. While the father is recognized to have the responsibility of bringing up and training the child, yet the maternal uncle has the right to remove it if the father is too poor to discharge this responsibility satisfactorily.[2] More-

[1] Fortes notes that, among the Ashantis, grandmothers play a great part in child-rearing, and can be very dictatorial in this respect, arguing that the child belongs more to the clan than to the parents; (11) 263. Field mentions the influence of the grandmothers in the upbringing of the Ga child; 'two groups of old women stand between the child and its parents'; (9) 28. See Plates 89-90.

[2] Rattray says the Ashanti maternal uncle has the right to remove the child from its father's care if the latter is too poor to bring it up properly; (30) 10.

over, the maternal uncle had the right, formerly, to 'pawn' his nephew or niece as a pledge for the discharge of his debts. In such cases, the child was removed from the custody of its father, and sent to the maternal uncle's creditor until such times as the debt was redeemed, which might on occasion prove to be for the duration of the entire childhood.[1] While this practice is now illegal, it would not appear to have died out altogether, and it may be that the widespread custom of sending a young child to live with a guardian during its middle school years is, in a few cases, a form of concealed pawning; the reason usually given, however, is the advantage the child gains from contact with a literate household. Girls may be sent to other households as servants in order to learn to work industriously, thus fitting them to be good wives.[2]

In matrilineal tribes, the child's clan relatives are of special importance, and it has little to do with any of the members of its father's clan, apart from the father himself.[3] In patrilineal tribes, however, the child has two extended families, that of his mother and that of his father, both of whom are concerned with his upbringing.

Contact with all these relatives is daily in the case of those who live in the compound and nearby. With close relatives who live some way off, many parents take care that frequent visits

Christensen notes that the bond between a child and his mother's brother rarely if ever approaches the father-child relationship in intimacy. The reason given is that a maternal uncle may feel that his nephew wishes him a short life, so that he can succeed him, while a father need never fear this; (5) 50-1.

[1] Manoukian notes that, among the Akans, if the maternal uncle intended to pawn his nephew or niece, the father expected to be given 'first refusal' in the case, though he had no right to object; (25) 27. Fortes says that, among the Ashantis a maternal uncle cannot discipline his sister's child unless he is asked to to do so, though he had the right to pawn it; (11) 270. Christensen mentions the custom of pawning children among the Fantis. The services of the child are considered as equivalent to interest. Should a female pawn become pregnant, the debt is cancelled. He says that, although illegal, pawning still occurs; (5) 40-1. Pawning is not confined to matrilineal tribes; Field mentions it as practised by the Gas, who may pawn their children. The work done is taken as interest. Girls sent as pawns will probably be seduced by their masters; (9) 57-8. See p. 19 above.

[2] Busia, in his survey of Sekondi-Takoradi, says that to send one's daughter away to live with neighbours or relatives was a recognized form of training for marriage in the past. He notes that public admissions were made that pawning is still practised and that some housemaids are obtained from this source. Busia goes on to give case histories of severely ill-treated housemaids; (4) 34-7. Rattray notes that especially naughty or unruly children might be handed over to the custody of someone known to be good at disciplining young children; (30) 13.

[3] Fortes says that, among the Ashantis, there may be an affectionate relationship between a child and its paternal aunt, but there are no binding obligations on either side; (11) 277.

are paid, so that the bond between them and the child shall be recognized.[1]

With polygynous families in which two or more wives live in the same compound, the upbringing of the children may be to some extent shared; in some households, however, mothers may resent their co-wives' interference with their children.[2]

Another member of the household with whom the child may come into contact a good deal is the housemaid, who may herself be a 'pawn', held by the head of the household against some debt.[3]

In many families, where the parents spend most of the day away on their farms, the younger children, excluding the baby, may spend the greater part of the day in the charge of the grandmother,[4] or the housemaid, or simply an older sibling. Cases are also reported of young children being left by themselves in their compounds, with a few cold roasted plantains for nourishment, from the early morning when the parents set off for the farm until late in the afternoon, when they return. In BENIM (Asante) as soon as the child can walk, it is left with older siblings while the mother goes to farm. Children of two to four years of age are left in the charge of an older sister. 'The mothers usually carry their younger babies on their backs to the farms with the older children walking in front of them. The little boys and girls of two to four years are left behind with an elder sister or grandmother and sometimes unattended. In some cases where the farm is not very far away, the babies are left very often in the care of the older children or sometimes in the care of the old women in the family, in which case the mother comes home as early as possible. Very often the child cries for some time while the mother is away.' The mother plays with her baby when she returns. 'She sits down when she has reached home, puts her child on her lap and plays with the child

[1] Manoukian notes the frequency of visits, of both short and long periods, made by Ewe children to their mothers' relatives; (26) 42. Beckett says that, in Akokoaso village in Akim, out of 507 children, 421 were living with their parents, 38 were with other relatives and 48 were temporarily away from the village; (3) 6.

[2] Fortes notes that, among the Tallensis, the responsibility for looking after infants may be shared by co-wives; (14) 187. He also says, however, that there are some women who very much resent the disciplining of their children by a co-wife, and in any case, 'a woman cannot have the same feelings towards her co-wife's child as towards her own child'; (14) 130.

[3] See footnote 1 on page 154 above.

[4] See Plates 89 and 90.

after it has been fed. Mothers enjoy this play with their babies so much that at times they forget that they have got to cook something for their husbands.' In BOMPATA (Asante) the child's maternal grandmother is usually the best-known relative, though other relatives, especially those of the parent in whose compound the child lives, are also very important. 'The time when the maternal uncle was more important to a child than the father is past and in spite of the fact that the child is expected to be polite and courteous to maternal relatives, the father has the first claim on his services and obedience.' In KOMENDA (Fante) 'it is a general notion that children who stay with people other than their own parents are comparatively better in their manners, behaviour, conduct and discipline than children who stay with their parents. For this reason some parents have sent their children to stay with people like teachers, clerks and other women of the family who are staying outside the family house with their literate husbands.' In KPANDU (Ewe) 'the grandfathers and grandmothers, the aunt, the clan native doctor, the uncles and other relatives; these are free to have a say in the child's training and can direct him, abuse or flog him when they find him misbehaving, and can also send him on errands'. In CHRISTIANSBORG (Ga) the father's elder brothers are accorded equal or greater respect by a child than his father, since they may become his guardians; similarly, a child's mother's sisters are accorded equal status with her. In the young child's household, it is the old women who discipline the children. In LARTEH KUBEASI (Guang) 'many of the parents at Larteh live for a greater part of the year in the villages where they farm. There are therefore many schoolchildren who stay in the town with their aunts, grandmothers, teachers and other relatives and friends who occasionally receive substantial help from the parents of the children.' Among the ISALAS 'the grandparents, father's other wives, aunts, brothers and their wives all live in the same compound and play prominent roles in the early life of the child. All the adults maintain friendly relationships with the children of their blood relations living in the compound and are kind to the children.'

In all parts of Ghana it is said that grandparents are more indulgent towards children than are the parents; in many parts, a 'joking relationship' is allowed between old people and their grandchildren. To a somewhat lesser degree, this indulgence is characteristic also of the other relatives who take part in a child's upbringing.[1] Of these guardians who look after pawns and other children committed to their care, while some are said to be considerate, others ill-treat and abuse their charges, and the seduction of girls by their guardians, or their guardians' husbands, appears to be no uncommon thing.[2] In MAMPONG (Akwapim) 'the essential feature of the relationship between a grandchild and grandparent is that they can tease and joke with each other. Between the parent and the child this would be almost equal to sacrilege.' In GOVIEFE (Ewe) and KPANDU (Ewe) grandparents and other relatives are generally said to be more indulgent towards children than are the parents. In TESHIE (Ga) the grandmother is usually over-indulgent and she 'is in every child's life, the best friend'.

Children are universally required to respect no less than their parents all the relatives with whom they come into contact.[3] Children are not usually excluded from the room when the parents are being visited, but they are expected to sit still and be quiet. If the conversation is about family matters or some private affair, they are sent out. They may accompany their parents on visits, when they are expected to behave politely.[4] In BOMPATA (Asante) children may either leave the room when their parents are being visited or, if they remain, they must give up their seats and be quiet. If they are spoken to, they must use the polite forms of address. In BEREKUM (Brong) children are not excluded from visits, and a point is made of taking a child round to visit all his relatives so that he knows them; he is expected to visit his grandmother at least twice a week. He must behave with politeness on the occasion of such visits; any offences by him need the parents' apology and possibly a paci-

[1] Fortes says that Ashanti grandmothers 'lavish affection on their grandchildren, who are their greatest pride'; (11) 276. Fortes describes in detail the joking relationship between a Tallensi grandchild and grandparent in (14) 236-8. 'There is . . . a kind of freedom and equality between grandparents and grandchildren which could not exist between parents and children'; *idem*.

[2] See Busia (4) 34-7 for case-histories. Christensen notes the provisions for a pawn's pregnancy among the Fantis; (5) 40-1. Field says that, among the Gas, while a great affection may grow up between a pawn and his master, it is exceedingly common, and almost to be expected, that a girl in these circumstances will be seduced; (9) 57-8.

[3] This attitude is, of course, implicit in the use of a classificatory kinship terminology.

[4] Manoukian notes that Ewe children are taught at an early age how to behave in front of elders; (26) 42. Christensen stresses the importance of this training among the Fantis; (5) 98-9.

fication fee. In TESHIE (Ga) visiting is unusual with the children, and if there is some serious talking to be done, children will probably be excluded. On formal visits, however, the eldest child is expected to pass round the drinks and to act as his father's linguist. In APIREDE (Cherepon) children are not excluded from visits, but they are required to sit quiet. Among the ISALAS 'if the child is taken to visit relations or friends, he is expected to behave himself well and not to disgrace the family. He is warned against bad behaviour because parents are blamed when their children behave badly on such occasions.'

CHAPTER SIXTEEN

RELATIONS WITH SIBLINGS

> 'The first-born is regarded as the head of other children in the house; he has the right to punish or reprimand a younger brother or sister.'

In most parts of Ghana, children are not told when their mothers are expecting another child, and their questions about the increased size of their mothers' bellies are hushed, or else such answers are given as that they have over-eaten, or have pillows inside their clothes. In a very few cases, the child may be given the correct answer. Similarly, children's questions about where babies come from receive evasive answers. They are told that God sends them, or that they come from the farm, the store, or from abroad. Some parents believe that children who persist in asking such questions may grow up into perverted adults. However, some parents give their children the correct information. In TUTU (Akwapim) children are not told when a new baby is expected in the family. Children's curiosity about the size of pregnant mothers is not satisfied, and they are sometimes made to feel that it is rude to ask such questions, because 'if children are told facts about birth they will grow to become morally perverted adults'. Hence the parents agree with any unlikely suggestion from the child as to where babies come from. In BANKO (Asante) some parents tell their children when a new baby is expected and some do not. In DWINYAMA (Asante) children are on no account told when a new baby is expected. A child who asks questions about the size of its mother's belly is silenced and sent away, or may even be smacked. Children are never told where babies come from. In JAKOBO (Asante) children are generally not told when a new baby is expected. Children are told that their mothers' bellies are large from over-eating or they may be told not to be inquisitive. Children who ask questions about where babies come from are silenced; it is said that they want to know what only adults should know. Once a new baby has been born, however, its sibling may be told that it has come out of the mother's stomach, though it will be said that God put it there. In SUPOWMU DUNKWA (Fante) 'both men and women told me that the children never show any curiosity when they see the mother's abdomen unusually enlarged, and they do not ask the cause. It would be considered very improper if a child was so curious as to ask why the mother's abdomen was so enlarged or where the new-born baby came from. But from my observation, children hear adults talk about pregnancy and marital relationship when they are quite young, and, therefore, do not bother to ask questions about that. When they see a woman with an enlarged abdomen, they know that she is expecting a baby. I asked a child of four why a woman who was passing by had such a big stomach, and he answered promptly, "She is pregnant". When I asked him how she became pregnant, he replied, "My father built her stomach". I asked him how, and he said, "He slept with her" meaning that he had sexual intercourse with her. So, though parents prefer to believe that their children do not take any notice of pregnancy, I think that the children do notice it, and get to know somehow. Since the parents often sleep in the same bedroom with the children, it is possible that the performance of marital intercourse is seen by them.' In VAKPO (Ewe) the child is not told when a new baby is expected; curiosity about the size of the mother's belly is treated by saying that she has eaten too much. Sometimes, however, he is told that there is a baby in it. In CHRISTIANSBORG (Ga) children are not generally told when a new baby is expected. Children's curiosity about the size of their mothers during pregnancy is answered by telling them that the mothers have over-eaten or drunk too much. When a child asks where a new baby has come from, he is told that somebody brought it as a gift during the night. In OTROWE (Adangme) children are not told when a new baby is expected. The child's questions about the size of his pregnant mother's belly are answered by telling him that he will know when he is older. Children who ask where babies come from, however, are told that they come from their mothers' bellies. In WINNEBA (Efutu) children are not told when a new baby is expected; some people

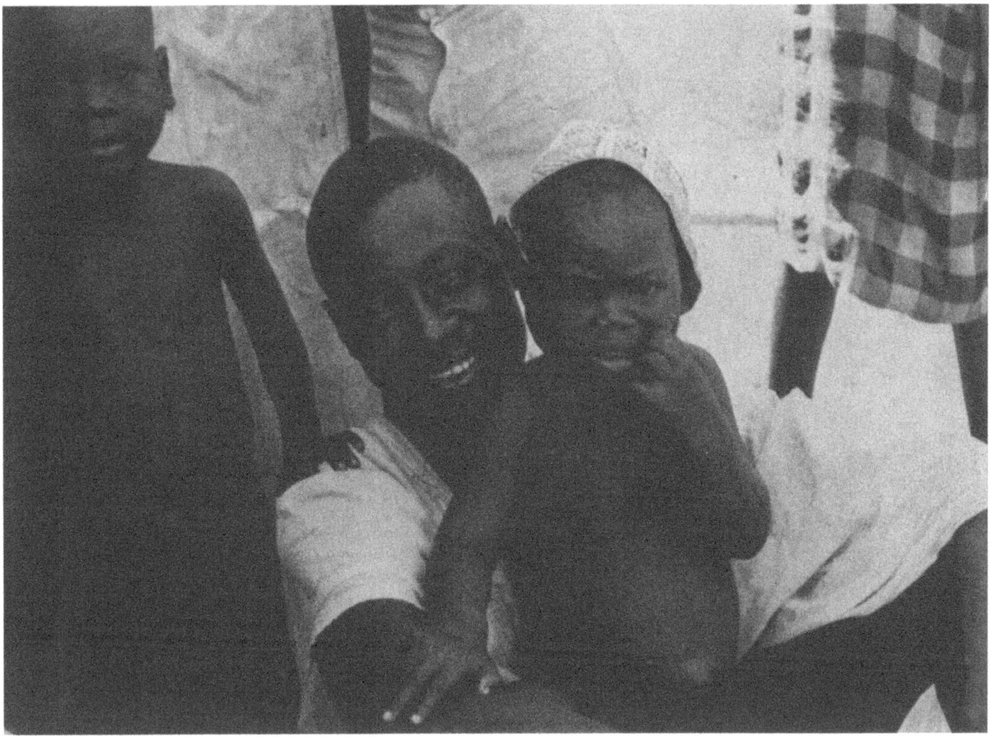

Care of the children by fathers. 81. A tailor with his son in Tamale. Notice belly keloids of child standing.

82. A carpenter and his fourteen-month-old daughter in Vakpo.

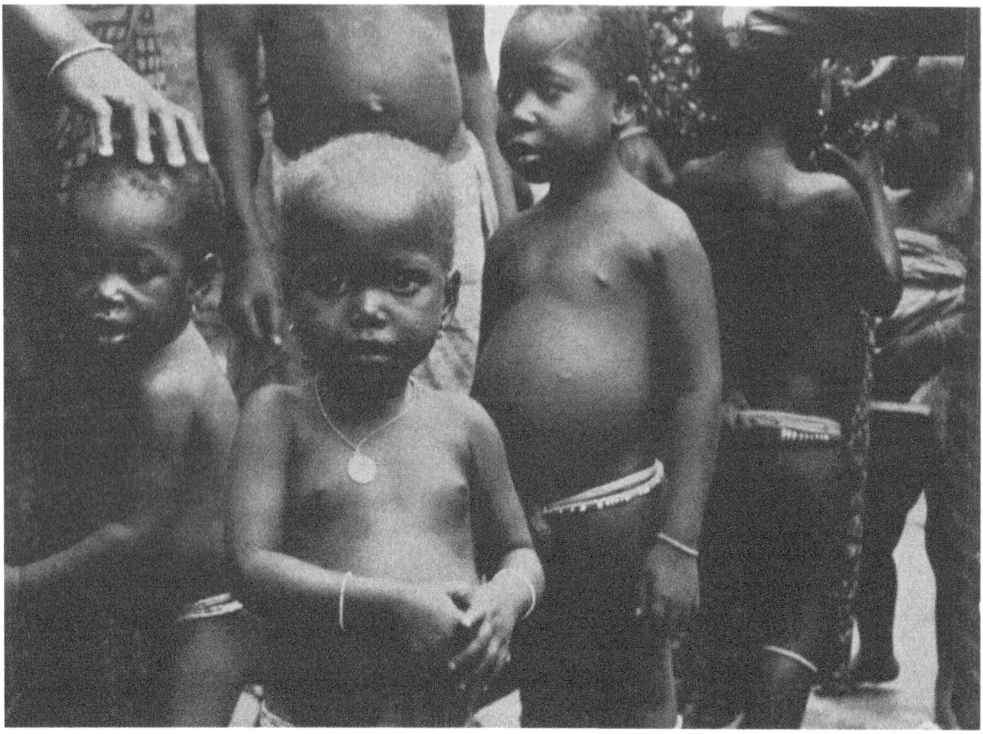

Children's contacts with adults. 83. Adults are nearly always about. Here a young child stares fearlessly at the camera; adults are just behind. Taken in Komenda.

84. An adult is near to run to if the child is anxious. Taken in Goviefe.

Children's contacts with adults. 85. Children are taken by their mothers to their place of work. Here a toddler hangs on to its mother's cloth in Salaga market, Accra.

86. A little girl with her mother, a kola-nut trader, in Lawra market.

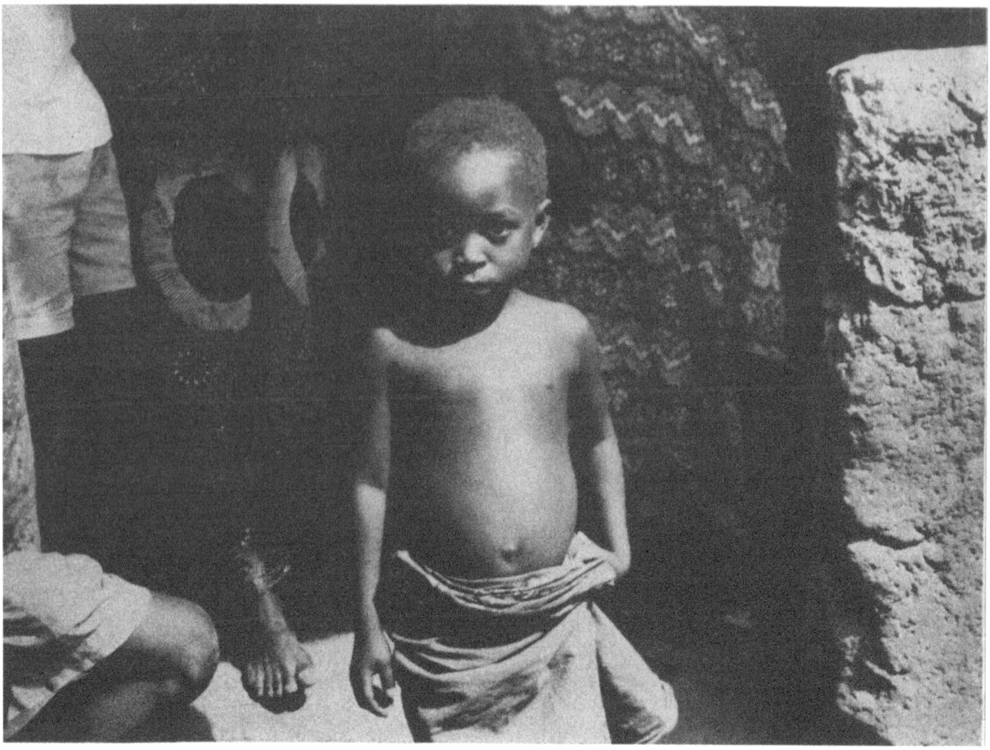

Children's contacts with adults. 87. Child among adults in Gblede.

88. Child among adults in Bosofo.

say 'that when they are told, their spirits within them which would not like to be supplanted in the affections of their parents may sorrow and die'. Questions about where babies come from are usually ignored and the condition of pregnant mothers is explained by saying that they have eaten too much. Among the DAGABAS 'a child is not told when a new baby is expected neither is he informed where babies come from'.

Children are universally excluded from the scene of child-birth. They are usually looked after by an aunt or grandmother, to whose house, if she does not live with the parents, they may be sent to stay. One reason for this prohibition is that it is believed that young children can talk with unborn babies; if they were to describe the troubles of the world, the babies would refuse to be born, resulting in a difficult delivery or even the mother's death. In JAISI (Asante) children are not present at child-birth. Most frequently they are sent away from the house. It is believed that young children who have not had any teeth are able to talk to the unborn baby, and it is feared that such children might delay birth and cause a difficult delivery by telling the unborn child of the troubles of this world. Older children may become afraid of child-birth, or describe the mother's labour in public. Consequently, children are usually sent to stay with relatives, where they may be left to the care of their children who, resenting the extra treatment given to the visitors, may torment them. In APAM (Fante) children are not allowed to be present during child-birth; they are looked after by their grandmother or maternal aunts. In GOVIEFE (Ewe) 'the boy is sent away for it is feared that the sight of his mother's birth-canal would bring ill-luck, even death to him, apart from its being improper for him to see it'. He is sent to stay with his maternal grandmother. In TEMA (Ga) children are looked after by other adults in the home during the time of their mothers' confinements, or they are sent to relatives in a different house. In LARTEH KUBEASI (Guang) children are not present during child-birth. 'A few parents allow the older child to be taken away by his grandmother at the birth of the new baby, because some children are said to be so jealous of the new arrival that they tend to cry too much and pine away with grief.' Among the DAGABAS a child 'is never present at the birth of a younger one; he is usually sent away to remain with a grandmother'.

Among the Gas, jealousy towards a new-born baby on the

part of its displaced sibling is expected. The jealousy is called *kwashiorkor*,[1] and it is associated with various symptoms, including irritability, refusal to eat, loss of bladder and bowel control and loss of weight. Such cases are treated with great care; the child is made a great fuss of by its parents and grandparents, and compared favourably with the new-born baby, which is said to be ugly and worthless. In other parts of Ghana, jealousy may be permitted and the child made a fuss of, or it may be discouraged or even punished. In BOMPATA (Asante) it is recognized that many children show hostility to their newly-born siblings. Children cry a lot at this time, and cases of attempts to kill the new baby are reported. When the weaned child is comparatively young, it may be pacified, but older children not. In DWINYAMA (Asante) 'no expressions of jealousy are permitted; they meet with flogging or smacking'. In GOVIEFE (Ewe) children are expected to show tenderness towards new-born babies; however, expressions of jealousy are permitted, since it is believed that if the jealous child is scolded, punished and especially beaten for any expression of jealousy, he may die. In VAKPO (Ewe) jealousy towards new-born siblings is said to be common. When it occurs the child is spoilt by its grandmother and parents in an attempt to win over its love. In CHRISTIANSBORG (Ga) despite the fact that children are not told when a new baby is expected, it is sometimes claimed that a child can sense that it is going to be dispossessed as early as the second month of pregnancy, and that it then becomes very jealous. Several cases have been cited where a child's jealousy has been the first indication of conception. This jealous state is called *kwashiorkor*, and it is assumed that all children pass through it, though it is more marked in some. After the baby is born, children suffering from *kwashiorkor* refuse to eat; they get thinner, wet and soil the bed, forget words and may harm the baby. Bad cases are treated by the herbalist who bathes the child with herbal water, and recites various chants. The child gets better, though he may steal the meat from the stew and commit other similar acts. A child suffering from *kwashiorkor* gets more attention and is told: 'You are more beautiful than this ugly thing, you are born by your mother, he is only stolen, you have many things while he has nothing, he is a fool and that is why he wets and soils his bed

[1] See also page 74 above.

without warning'. This treatment is usually successful. In KORDIABE (Shai) an attitude of affection towards the new-born baby by its older sibling is encouraged; 'often the child is easily persuaded and he becomes so fond of the new baby that he would not even allow other inmates of the house to touch the baby'. Children who show jealousy are discouraged and teased. If this is unsuccessful, they are treated harshly. Among the ISALAS 'the child is expected to show a kind attitude towards the new baby. Expressions of jealousy are not permitted nor provoked.' Parents stress the good fortune of their children in having a new baby sibling.

Ghanaian parents tend to favour the baby of the family, who is usually made a great fuss of.[1] Other children who may be favoured by their parents are the first-born and the last-born, the third and tenth children, those who are named after well-loved relatives, those whose delivery was attended with excessive pains and, conversely, those whose delivery was unusually easy, and helpful and courteous children.[2] In TUTU (Akwapim) 'more often than not, greater attention is diverted on to the youngest child, especially if he is the last-born. If the mother is giving them food, the youngest child is always given the largest share, and he is always given the best of everything.' In BOSOFO (Asante) the baby is the favourite. Children with whom the mother had an easy delivery are sometimes favourites, or if the father gave her many presents at the time of child-birth. Tenth children and those named after loved relatives may also become favourites. In GOVIEFE (Ewe) 'the baby itself is the darling of the family; it can do no wrong and is adored and favoured'. Other children who may become favourites are the last-born, a child who has survived a serious illness, and the most respectful and the hard-working child. In AGOMANYA (Krobo) 'the married couple with many children have great affection for the youngest. The mother shows the greater concern for her "knee child", and the father to his first son, whom he instructs in the household

[1] Field says that, among the Gas, 'the mother usually seems to be interested in a child only while it remains the youngest'; (9) 31.

[2] Fortes says that, among Tallensi parents, 'youngest children are the favourites, upon whom they lavish all their tenderness when they have long ceased to make a show of affection for the older children'; (14) 231. He goes on to say that, when it is a question of rights, Tallensis say that it is sinful to discriminate, but in practice one cannot help preferring an industrious or obedient child to a lazy or disobedient one; (14) 270. He notes that a latent antagonism is recognized to exist between a father and his eldest son; (14) 226-30.

responsibilities and other economic activities. They, however, love all of them because they supply the labour on the farm and also raise their social status in the neighbourhood.'

The advantages of older children are that they are entitled to the respect and obedience of their juniors,[1] and have the right to the first helping of meat or fish which, since they themselves share the food, is always the largest. At the same time, they have more domestic chores than the younger children, and are expected by the parents to give in to the younger ones in quarrels. The youngest child in the family is always the favourite of everybody.[2] In APA (Asante) 'the smaller children are always favourites of the family', and are favoured at quarrels by the mother. But older children have privileges, and younger ones must clear away after meals, sweep the yard and empty the chamber pots. In BOMPATA (Asante) young children are taught to respect their older siblings. In CENTRAL ACCRA (Ga) younger brothers help their older brothers by sweeping their rooms, carrying water for them, helping them to carry their fishing gear, etc. In return for these services, they expect the elder brothers to give them food, buy clothing for them and pay their school fees. In OTROWE (Adangme) 'the first-born is regarded as the head of other children in the house. He has the right to punish or reprimand a younger brother or sister.' In APIREDE (Cherepon) the oldest child gets the most meat. Younger children must show respect towards their elder siblings.

Relations between siblings of the same sex are generally said to be better than between those of the opposite sex. At the same time, in several areas it is said that quarrels are more frequent between siblings of the same sex, largely on account of greater frequency of contact and division of domestic chores. Another reason given is that boys who attacked girls would be mocked. The division of food, property and favouritism by parents are said to be the most common causes of quarrels between siblings.[3] In BOMPATA (Asante) as children grow older,

[1] Fortes says that, among the Ashantis, 'an older sibling is entitled to punish and reprimand a younger brother or sister and must be treated with deference. He is, conversely, obliged to help his juniors in trouble'; (11) 273. Fortes also notes that, among the Tallensis, 'from the authority of parent over child is derived that of elder sibling over younger. It is equally absolute'; (12) 35.

[2] Fortes says that a Tallensi baby 'can not do wrong; for, as Tallensi say, "it has no sense"'; (14) 189.

[3] According to Fortes, in Ashanti, 'brothers and sisters may joke with each other, tease each other, and even quarrel, as they are prone to do in childhood,

they come to prefer the company of their siblings of the same sex. There is a belief that children of the same father, though of different mothers, who hardly ever meet during infancy, come to be fonder of one another as adults than children of the same mother. In APAM (Fante) it is usually though not invariably the case that siblings of the same sex are closer to one another. In GOVIEFE (Ewe) children of the same sex are said to be closer to one another; twins, however, are closest of all, regardless of sex. In DOME (Ga) children of the opposite sex are supposed to be closer to one another, since those of the same sex quarrel. However, often children of the opposite sex but of the same age may quarrel over things, and it is said that the relationship between an older boy and his younger sister is always satisfactory. In DWINYAMA (Asante) siblings often quarrel and fight, though no serious harm is done. Quarrels are usually between siblings of the same sex, rarely between those of the opposite sex. In BEREKUM (Brong) quarrels between the children of different co-wives are common, and 'children of the same mother help to beat the child of a different mother if he unfortunately happens to be there alone'. Quarrels between siblings of the opposite sex are said to be more frequent, though parents usually support their daughters in such quarrels. In SUPOWMU DUNKWA (Fante) quarrels are more frequent between siblings of the same sex; 'occasionally, there may be a fight between a boy and a girl, but when this happens, the boy is mocked, ridiculed, and told even by his own friends, that only cowardly boys fight with girls'. In GBLEDE (Ewe) quarrels are more frequent between siblings of the same sex; 'this, to some extent, is due to the fact that everybody accepts the inferior position that women are made to assume as a natural state of affairs. Therefore when women are being cheated they hardly complain. They consider it their lot.' In TESHIE (Ga) quarrels between siblings occur over toys, or because younger ones neglect their chores and the older siblings are asked to do them. Quarrels are more frequent between children of the same sex than between those of the opposite sex; boys are not allowed to fight girls,

without causing offence. This accent on equality is not found in any other kinship relationship'; (11) 274. He also notices that 'men and women are usually very fond of their half-siblings by the same father; but there is no sense of inescapable obligation about this, as there is about all social ties through one's mother'; (11) 270. Among the Tallensis, according to Fortes, it is expected that children, irrespective of sex, will quarrel with their successive siblings: that is with their siblings born immediately after and before them; (14) 253.

and if they did so everyone would side with the girl and would call the offending boy a sissy.

In most families, parents interfere with quarrels between siblings, and they usually take the part of the younger. Children may be scolded or even beaten for quarrelling.[1] In ABURI (Akwapim) children who are stopped from quarrelling by their parents may be invited to state their case; this is one of the times when to talk to adults is not regarded as a sign of disrespect. In TUTU (Akwapim) 'in the home when two siblings quarrel or argue the parents always intervene. If the two siblings go to the extent of fighting each other the parents, especially the mothers, always defend the younger sibling. If in the course of the fight the younger sibling is beaten by the older sibling the parent will, without enquiring into the cause of the fight, get hold of the older sibling and beat him too, either with the hand or with a stick.' In JAISI (Asante) the younger children are protected by the parents. The quarrels of children often lead to quarrels between parents. In BEREKUM (Brong) in the case of children's quarrels, the guilty party may have to pacify the other, for example by giving up his share of meat. In AYANZILI (Nzima) if siblings quarrel over the food, the mother redistributes it. In DOME (Ga) when a quarrel occurs between siblings, it is settled in favour of the older child by their mother in order to console it, because it is thought that if it is ill-treated it may die. Quarrels are only dealt with fairly when the siblings are old enough to understand one another. In AGOMANYA (Krobo) with regard to siblings' quarrels, 'the moment there is the slightest dispute, an adult sets in'. In LARTEH KUBEASI (Guang) 'some parents, in order to please the crying baby, pretend to beat the older children'. There is a tendency for parents to get involved in quarrels with other adults on account of disputes between their respective children.

In estimating the significance of the data set out in this chapter, the responsibility which, in many cases, older children are obliged to have for their younger siblings must not be forgotten. Looking after his or her younger siblings is one of the commonest duties given to a young Ghanaian child, and from a very young age he or she is held responsible for their welfare.[2]

[1] Among the Tallensis, however, according to Fortes, 'squabbles between children, whether they are successive siblings or not, are laughed away'; (14) 255.
[2] See Plates 91-96.

CHAPTER SEVENTEEN

CHILDREN'S SPEECH

'A good child is the one who does not say anything until he is told to do so.'

MOST mothers in Ghana interpret their infants' cries and distinguish between various kinds of cry, such as those of hunger, rage, fear or physical discomfort. The almost universal reaction of a mother to a crying baby, whatever her interpretation, however, is to suckle it. A mother who allows her baby to cry for a long period without attempting to comfort it may earn social disapproval. It is thought that too much crying in young infants makes them sickly. Crying at night is particularly to be avoided, for fear it should attract the attention of evil spirits. Persistent crying is generally attributed to a stomach-ache, the usual remedy for which is an enema, normally of ground ginger or pepper juice. If the crying still persists, a herbalist or fetish priest may be consulted.[1] In ABURI (Akwapim) all infants' cries are interpreted as those of hunger. If a child still cries after being fed, illness is suspected. In DWINYAMA (Asante) crying in the early weeks is taken to be a sign of hunger and 'the least whimper brings the mother to the baby'. By three months or so, different cries will be interpreted and reacted to; for example, sharp shrill cries of pain, irritable cries after meals attributed to stomach-ache, and other cries to hunger or anger. All cries are immediately responded to and 'a mother who is indifferent to the child's cries is severely criticized and scolded by relatives and neighbours'. In KOFORIDUA (Asante) babies are not allowed to cry for long 'because much crying makes the child sick and the voice broken. Therefore to place a child on the ground and leave it to cry for long is considered gross neglect. The only means of pacifying a child is to breast-feed it.' In SUPOWMU DUNKWA

[1] Rattray notes this latter practice among the Dagabas; (32) 419.

(Fante) a child is suckled as soon as it cries. Among the KWAHUS, 'an infant is almost always treated with constant indulgence, it is never left to cry'. In GOVIEFE (Ewe) 'adults seem to suppose that infants should not be allowed to cry at all and that their cry is to be avoided at any course'. In AYIKAI DOBORO (Ga) the first cry that an infant makes is interpreted as one of disgust and regret at coming into a world of hardship and sorrow. Cries of hunger, pain, and anger are differentiated, but all are cured with the breast. In KORDIABE (Shai) the reaction of mothers to their children's crying is to breast-feed them. Children are not allowed to cry at night in particular, for fear of witches. In LARTEH KUBEASI (Guang) 'any woman who allows her child to cry without paying attention to him is regarded as a bad mother'.

As children, and boys in particular, grow older, they are discouraged from crying by threats of bogy men, wild animals and the repetition of unpleasant experiences, such as vaccination. Older children who do not stop crying when told to do so, may be thrashed or given rectal suppositories of red pepper as a punishment. On the other hand, not to cry when being beaten may be taken as a sign of disrespect, and children, and girls in particular, are expected to cry at the funerals of relatives. Little attention is paid to children's crying while they are being bathed. In TUTU (Akwapim) children are taught not to cry at night; 'when a child between the ages of two and five years cries at night he is frightened with bogies and told that there are some animals going about the town at night that eat children who cry'. In APA (Asante) 'very often, the mothers take no notice of their children's cries'; at other times they are soothed with promises, or threatened with bogy men or wild animals. 'The child cries when he is hungry, when he is whipped, when he is being scolded and teased, when he is sick, when he is sleepy but there is no light in the room, or when the mother has not made the mat ready, when he cannot find his property, when he knocks his foot against a stone, when he is being bullied by a stronger child and when the mother or an elder sister he loves is cunningly leaving him behind to go somewhere.' In BANKO (Asante) 'it is considered good preparation for a woman's life to be able to cry and weep at funerals, so if a little girl cries, the mother does not heed her, provided that the little girl is not ill or hungry'. Boys are taught not to cry by being told that men

Care of infants by grandmothers. 89. A woman oiling her six-month-old granddaughter. Taken in Winneba.

90. A woman looking after her grandchild in Apam.

Looking after siblings. 91. Here a young girl, about eight years old, wraps a carrying-cloth round her to secure her infant sister. The baby wears a bought dress; she herself is wearing only her waist beads and pad. Taken in Winneba.

92. Although this little girl is only just two years old, she has been given charge of her baby sister of eleven months. (Ages given by an older sibling, who was chopping firewood some hundred yards away.) Taken in Teshie.

Looking after siblings. 93. A young girl taking her infant sibling to market to buy food. As it is a very young baby, the carrying-cloth covers its arms and shoulders, to give support to the neck. Taken in Bawku, Northern Territories.

94. A young girl, about six years old, looking after her baby brother. Taken at Teshie.

Looking after siblings. 95. A young girl looking after her infant sibling at home. Taken at Winneba.

96. A girl carrying her infant sibling on her back on her way to visit a relative. Taken at Kpandu.

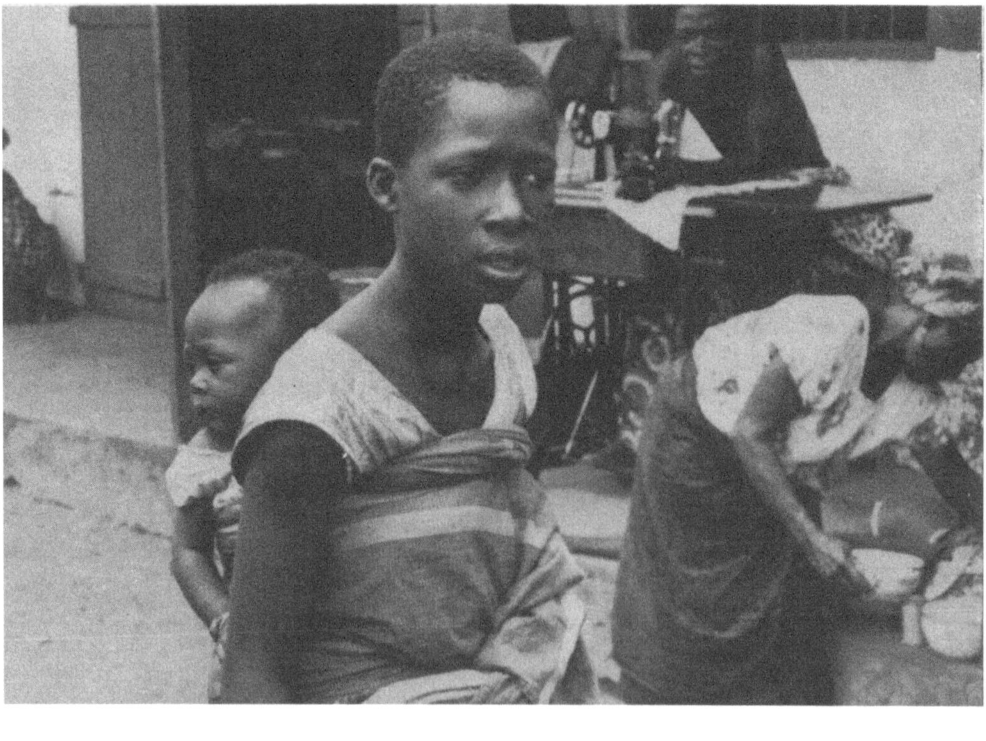

should not give way to tears. In SUPOWMU DUNKWA (Fante) 'when a child falls down, the ground becomes the offender, and the mother asks him to spit into her hand so that she may hit the ground with it. As the child grows older, he is not expected to cry so often and when he continues crying for a long time, the mother loses her temper and either frightens him with stories about bogies or beasts, or spanks him. A child is considered stubborn and rude if he does not cry or run away when being beaten by an elder.' Crying in young children is often stopped by 'punishing' the ground or any other inanimate object with which the child has harmed itself. No attention is given to crying during bathing. In GOVIEFE (Ewe) children are not allowed to cry for long lest they become ill, and their souls leave them. They are threatened with bogy men if they do not stop crying. Children are expected to cry, however, on the death of a relative, though 'it is supposed that a boy should be able to control his passions much more than a girl' on such occasions. In KPANDU (Ewe) 'male children of about four years old are told that men do not cry, and they stop. If a child however means to cry, and to make a noise in order to have his way, he is beaten severely. If this yields to more weeping and crying, ground ginger is put into his nostrils as a punishment'. Girls are expected and allowed to cry, however. In AGOMANYA (Krobo) children are dissuaded from crying by bogy stories and beatings. To prevent them from crying if they fall down their mothers 'punish' the ground by hitting it after the child has spat into her hand. Boys particularly are expected not to cry and told to be men. In APIREDE (Cherepon) older children are expected not to cry, but weeping is legitimate for girls as women are expected to have causes for sorrow, and they are also required to weep at the funeral of a close relative.

Infants' early vocalisations and attempts at speech are generally encouraged in Ghana, and mothers and the other adults in the compound often talk to the baby of the house and repeat its babblings. In MAMPONG (Akwapim) everyone talks to the baby, especially its elder siblings; 'generally the older sister or brother is the principal teacher of the child'. In DWINYAMA (Asante) infants' attempts at speech are encouraged; parents try to get their infants to repeat words. Baby-talk is enjoyed by all and any adult who is near will talk to the baby. Among the DENKYERAS the baby's early attempts at speech are highly encouraged and everyone in the home, especially the mother, talks to the baby. In VAKPO (Ewe) 'the parents and other children in the house are all interested in the child's attempt to speak and so they speak to him a lot'. In DOME (Ga) the baby's own sounds are encouraged and applauded, and everyone in the house talks to the baby while playing with it. In TESHIE (Ga) adults are very interested in the baby's efforts at learning to talk, and they compare them and discuss them. Baby-talk is regarded as amusing and the mother usually replies in kind. In LARTEH KUBEASI (Guang) 'visitors as well as members of the family, especially the child's mother, delight in talking to the young child'.

It is generally considered a sign of disrespect for a child to address an adult, except in reply to a question. Children are expected to lower their voices politely when replying to adults' questions. In the presence of visitors, children are required to sit quietly without saying anything, or to leave the room.[1] On the other hand, parents and grandparents enjoy conversing with their offspring if they are not busy, and on evenings when Ananse and other stories are being told, children are expected to contribute.[2] In ABURI (Akwapim) children are allowed to talk to adults when, after quarrelling, they state their case; when they are delivering a message; and when they are invited to tell a story. At other times to talk to adults is a sign of disrespect. A child who reminds an adult he has forgotten something is scolded. It is thought he will grow up a gossip; 'a good child is the one who does not say anything until he is told to do so'. In BENIM (Asante) children are taught not to talk about everything they see; 'if you always talk about what you see a chicken will be hung on your lips'. They are also taught to be silent in the presence of adults. In DWINYAMA (Asante) adults may listen to what children have to say from time to time, but if a serious conversation is going on, children must be quiet and they are taught to remain silent before elders. In the olden days 'precocious and inquisitive older children had either their lips, ears or nose removed to show others to be wary of their words and actions'.[3] But 'soft speakers are considered feminine'. In KOFORIDUA (Asante) children are taught never to interrupt when

[1] This is confirmed by Rattray (30) 13. See also pages 157-8.
[2] Fortes notes that Tallensi children have considerable freedom of address towards their classificatory fathers; (14) 196-7.
[3] Cp. (30) 13.

adults are speaking, and they are smacked on the mouth for doing so. In SUPOWMU DUNKWA (Fante) 'people often talk to the child and listen in return to him talking, but no child is expected to join the conversation of his elders, especially when there are visitors. At such times he is expected to sit still and speak audibly and politely when spoken to, or leave the room.' In GBLEDE (Ewe) children are taught to lower their voices when talking to adults. In CHRISTIANSBORG (Ga) children are taught to speak quietly before elders, as to speak loudly is regarded as a sign of low breeding. They may be listened to by parents and encouraged to talk, but they are not encouraged to ask too many questions, except when riddles are being asked when 'both adults and children forget themselves'. In AGOMANYA (Krobo) children are expected to lower their voices when speaking to relatives and elders. In APIREDE (Cherepon) 'adults like to speak and listen to children because they find it entertaining'; they are taught, however, not to interrupt adults.

Grammatical correctness in their children's speech is not generally held by Ghanaian parents to be of great importance, though the investigators in Accra reported that parents there tended to correct their children's mistakes. In ABURI (Akwapim) children are not expected to speak correctly under the age of five. 'When a child is saying something incorrectly and another child says the correct thing for him the latter is considered a prospective liar.' In DWINYAMA (Asante) no importance is attached to grammatical correctness on the part of children. In KOMENDA (Fante) there are 'children with some speech defects, especially stuttering, and these get severe treatment in terms of scolding and punishment'. In GOVIEFE (Ewe) children are not held to high standards of grammatical correctness, but mistakes are corrected casually. In CENTRAL ACCRA (Ga) mistakes in speech of children are corrected by their parents. In CHRISTIANSBORG (Ga) children are expected to pronounce their speech correctly from an early age, and correctness of expression is held to be more important than content. In TEMA (Ga) children are not held to high standards of grammatical correctness, since it is thought that to do so would confuse them. In WINNEBA (Efutu) no importance is attached to grammatical correctness on the part of children among the fisherfolk.

Truthfulness is not generally expected from very young children in Ghana. In most areas there is a generally recognized critical age, after which lying is punished, often with severe beatings or the application of red pepper; this critical age varies from four to eight. While high standards of truthfulness are expected thereafter, the parents themselves may tell their children to deceive the tax collector as to their whereabouts.[1] In TUTU (Akwapim) a child at the age of four 'knows when he is telling the truth and when he is telling a lie. Factual precision in a child's speech is not given any prominence by adults, for all that is demanded is the expression of a general idea of facts. Some trivial lies are ignored by parents. On the other hand, there are certain lies which are not ignored by parents. For example, if a child steals food or some money, and on being questioned he tells a lie, the mother considers this a serious offence; she badgers the child into telling the truth, and punishes him severely.' In BANKO (Asante) parents expect their children to tell the truth, and sometimes beat them if they discover that they have been deceived. But sometimes the parents tell lies to the children. If a creditor comes to demand some money from the mother, she tells the children to inform the creditor that she is not in the house, in order to evade him. In BOSOFO (Asante) children are regarded as liars, and are not expected to tell the truth under the age of ten. Parents 'believe that their children have visions and what they sometimes tell them is correct. A woman told me how she is afraid of her child Yaw, who has been speaking about fire-burning, and houses falling in and such things. She believes the child is foretelling events that are to happen, therefore believes everything he says. I was told by an old woman, that when you suspect a child has done something wrong, he would never tell you the truth when you ask, as children are known for their lies, so you just beat him and tell him not to do that again. But when you do not know the particular child, you punish all the children in the house, and one of them who knows the wrongdoer would point him out.' In JAISI (Asante) children are not expected to be factually precise in what they say under the age of six; from seven onwards, however, 'the emphasis put on truthfulness is very great indeed', and a lying child is punished by flogging, red pepper and other punishments. In SUPOWMU DUNKWA (Fante) 'a child suspected of lying is severely scolded or beaten'; however, 'sometimes too,

[1] According to Fortes, among the Tallensis lying 'is considered merely foolish and contemptible'; (12) 38.

unscrupulous parents request their children to tell the lies for their own benefit'. In GBLEDE (Ewe) a distinction is made by parents between fantasies and lies; lying proper is regarded as a serious matter. In GOVIEFE (Ewe) children are expected to distinguish between fact and fantasy after the age of five or six and considerable importance is attached to truthfulness. 'Though parents expect their children to be truthful at all times and under all circumstances, they themselves do not always bother to tell the truth to their children.' In VAKPO (Ewe) children are expected to distinguish between fact and fantasy at the age of five, and they are always checked for lying. Ananse and other stories are told to them to teach them not to lie. In DOME (Ga) children are not expected to be factually precise in what they say under the age of four; after five, however, a great deal of emphasis is placed on truthfulness, and the child is threatened and beaten if it persists in lying. In APIREDE (Cherepon) 'when a mischief such as breaking of a plate has been caused, adults generally assume that the child responsible will never tell the truth'. In LARTEH KUBEASI (Guang) children are expected to tell the truth from the age of five or six, but many parents themselves deceive their children.

CHAPTER EIGHTEEN

CHILDREN AND PROPERTY

> 'Young children have no right to choose any dress that they want to put on. The mothers decide for them for fear they will grow to be vain.'

NOT many children in the areas investigated were bought toys by their parents, and of the few that were, most were likely to have them taken away again as a form of punishment, or if they maltreated them. The majority of children in Ghana have to make do with such toys as they can make themselves out of the collections of miscellaneous waste materials which they all amass. Most children are allowed complete freedom over these collections. They include old tins, bottles, lids and stoppers, paper, wire, broken pots, sticks, boxes and other debris.[1] Such other possessions that Ghanaian children have are few. Very young children may have toilet articles reserved for their exclusive use; as they grow older, they will probably have to share them. Towels, combs, brushes and sleeping mats are all shared by children once they have passed infancy. Most parents feel it their responsibility to provide clothing for their children; when they are older, this may become part of the reward for helping their parents with trading, farming or fishing.[2] Ghanaian children are regarded as owning their clothes; in poor families these may consist simply of two changes, one of which is reserved for best use, and kept in the mother's box. The attitude towards the choice of clothing seems to vary from one family to another. Some parents allow their children to please themselves as to which clothes they wear; others keep a strict control over their children's dresses. In ABURI (Akwapim)

[1] See Plates 97-104.

[2] Fortes notes that a Tallensi father is not obliged to provide his children with clothes, though a 'good' father will probably do so; (14) 138.

'the young children have no right to choose any dress that they want to put on. The mothers decide for them for fear they will grow to be vain.' From the age of eight, children may be allowed to choose their own clothes, though if they change them too often, then this right may be taken away again. Toys may be taken away and a child scolded or beaten if he damages them. In BANKO (Asante) 'between two to three years, children have very few possessions. The chief possessions are their clothes.' Some children have simple toys, but these may be taken away as a punishment, or used as bribes. In BOSOFO (Asante) a child may own its cloth, a toy cooking pot and possibly an eating bowl. A locally-made doll may be given when the child is able to walk. All children have their own collections of bottles, tins, etc. The baskets or boxes of adolescent children are searched when they are away, and explanations are demanded on account of anything thought to be stolen. In JAISI (Asante) babies have special toilet articles reserved for their use. From two to six years of age children may possess a few toys, such as imported or locally-made dolls, rattles, drums, toy hoes and cutlasses. They often make 'lorries'[1] from cigarette tin lids and sticks. In KOMENDA (Fante) children have their own collections of odds and ends; 'some of these possessions are paper, match-box, nails, cigarette tins, sardine tins, sticks, rope, toys, wheels, guns, boxes, packing cases, pipe, pieces of cloth, hammer, buttons, walking stick, canoe toys, paddles, stones, sand, broken plates, cat, dog, pictures, newspaper, wires, books, whistles, mouth-organ'. In VAKPO (Ewe) the child must consult its mother before using a special cloth. In CENTRAL ACCRA (Ga) children collect plates, stones, pots, pieces of cloth, and pieces of stick. Apart from these and from his clothes the child has no possessions. At about the age of four or five, the young boy owns a pair of pants, a piece of cloth, and one or two Sunday dresses if his parents are Christians. At ten a child shares a bathing sponge, comb, brush, towels and sometimes clothing with its siblings. They have a common sleeping mat. Some parents buy toys for children when they are very young. 'Children go to the public dustbins and take home things that have been thrown away. They bring home broken bottles, bottle-stoppers, biscuit tins,

[1] 'Lorries' are made by nailing a round tin lid to the end of a stick. The stick is then pushed along using the lid as a wheel. Articles to be carried may be hung from a nail higher up the stick. See Plates 105-106.

papers and anything at all in the dustbin that may attract their attention at the moment. These things are brought home and are kept secretly at a corner in the house. Parents collect these things and send them back to the dustbin. Children go back and collect them again. When parents get fed up with their children they either beat them or leave them to themselves.' The child has no freedom with his best clothes, which are kept in the mother's room. In OTROWE (Adangme) 'children have very few possessions'. Toilet articles may be reserved for the sole use of a very young infant, but 'at the age of seven, he shares bathing sponge, towels, soap, comb, brush and sometimes clothing with brothers or sisters'. 'The mother keeps the belongings of the child which she considers valuable. His extra clothes and cloths are kept by the mother and he is allowed to use them only when the parents see the need for it.' In WINNEBA (Efutu) 'a child's possessions in literate and semi-literate homes usually consist of clothes, toys, shoes and hats and some necklaces, ear-rings and beads in the case of girls. These are kept either in the mother's box to be brought out when needed or in small boxes and baskets belonging to the children themselves. Among the fisherfolk, most children have rarely any possessions besides clothes, dolls, ear-rings and beads, and these are kept in the mother's box till needed.'

Thieving by children is severely punished in Ghana. Common punishments are beating, tying the hands together, making cuts in the finger tips and rubbing ground pepper in, or putting red pepper into the child's rectum.[1] Children who pick up things they find lying about are told to return them to their owners; one of the more important reasons for insisting on this is the fear of any curse which might have been placed by a lost article's rightful owner on anyone who keeps it. In ABURI (Akwapim) 'if at the age of ten the child still takes things that are not his, he is considered a thief and he is punished severely. If beating fails to make him stop the following punishments are inflicted: small cuts are made on the tips of the finger nails and red pepper is rubbed in.' In BOMPATA (Asante) stealing is considered a very shameful habit, but there is a general laxity about articles that are found, and people are expected to compen-

[1] Rattray notes this last form of punishment among the Ashantis for children who pilfer within the family circle; see (30) 12. Fortes says that, among the Tallensis, a thief incurs disgrace and universal opprobrium; (12) 38.

Children's playthings. 97. Young children play with such waste material as they find lying about. A fourteen-month-old child with a stick. Taken in Vakpo.

98. An infant playing with a used tin.

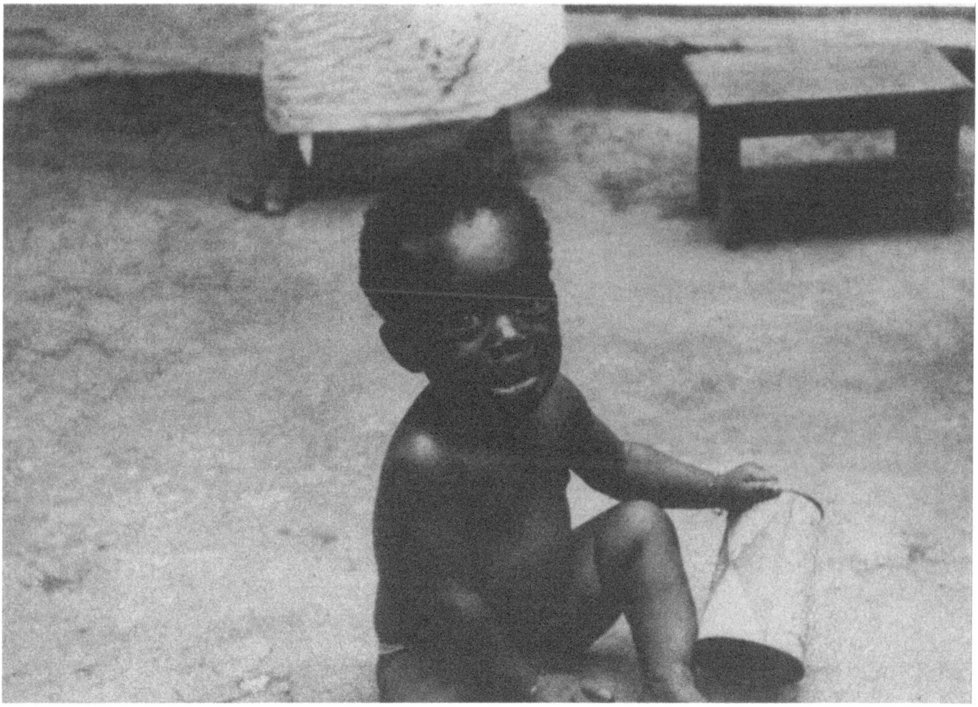

Children's playthings. 99. A one-year-old playing in the gutter with a bit of stick. Taken in Gblede.

100. A child surrounded by the world he lives in; old tins, stones, pieces of scrap iron, rubble. Taken in a lane between houses in Christiansborg.

Children's playthings. 101. A boy with a hoop made from a bicycle inner tube. Taken in Berekum.

102. Children with hoops made from bicycle tyres. One is using the inside of a pump as a driving stick. Also taken in Berekum.

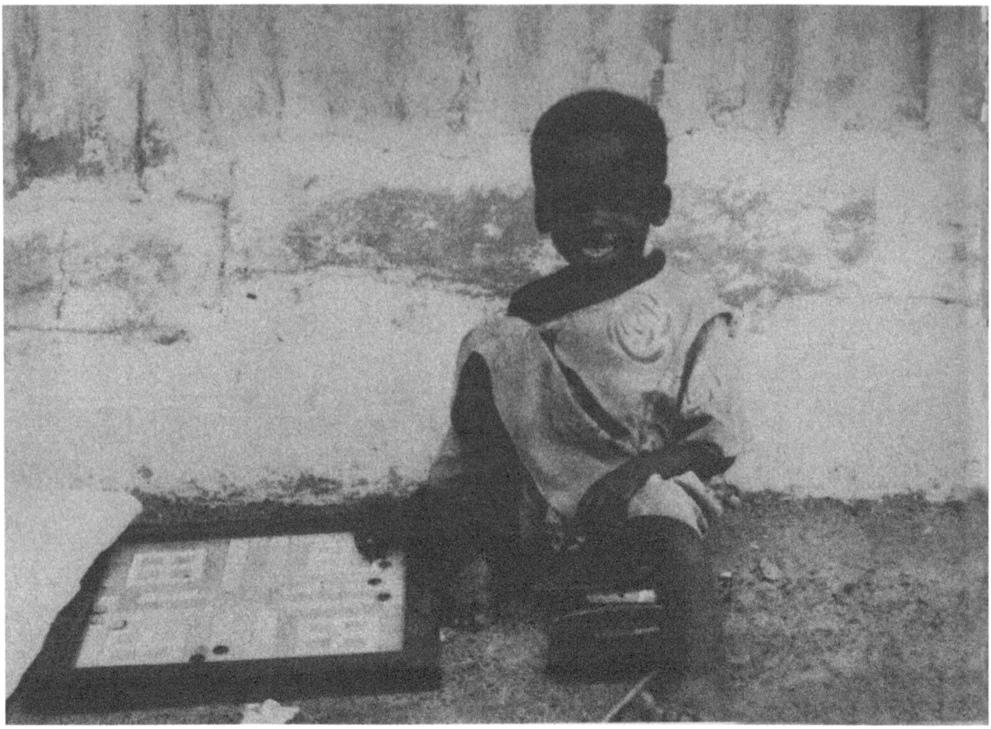

Children's playthings. 103. A boy playing ludo by himself, on a manufactured board. Taken in Christiansborg.

104. A little girl with her manufactured doll. Notice the western dress of both children. Also taken in Christiansborg.

sate finders of their property. In DWINYAMA (Asante) children are warned not to steal and if they do so are beaten. If they continue to steal, they are severely flogged and red pepper is pushed up the rectum. The habit of cutting their finger tips is now dying out. Stolen objects are returned by parents who apologize for their children; however, valuable objects that are found are regarded as a gift from 'Mother Earth' if the owner is not known, and in any case a reward for their return is expected. In SUPOWMU DUNKWA (Fante) if a child 'persists in taking other people's things, he may be beaten or starved or, as a last resort, his fingers are incised by the mother and smeared with pepper to warn him against stealing'. In VAKPO (Ewe) children are questioned about things they have picked up and made to return them for fear of death which may operate through a curse placed on the lost object by its owner. In AYIKAI DOBORO (Ga) children are taught from infancy not to steal. They are scolded or beaten for doing so and made to give the things back. A few cases occur, however, in which mothers may connive at their children's pilfering by not asking any questions. In AGOMANYA (Krobo) 'a child who is found to have stolen a penny receives a severe beating'. In WINNEBA (Efutu) younger children are scolded, shouted at and threatened with policemen for stealing; children of four and over are beaten, their hands are tied together or they are denied food, for doing so.

Toddlers are prevented from touching dangerous things by being shouted at, or the objects are placed out of reach. Sometimes they are made to feel the heat of a fire by being held close to it, or their fingers may be pricked with a sharp knife. Ghanaian children have little opportunity for manipulating objects apart from the household utensils they use in the course of doing their domestic chores, the tools they handle while helping their parents on the farm or at work, and their own collections of home-made toys and waste materials. Some older children manipulate natural materials in the construction of catapults and various kinds of traps. A few instances were reported from the investigated areas of children taking manufactured articles to pieces to see what was inside. Children in Ghana are generally regarded by adults as destructive; they are scolded or slapped for playing with valuable objects. In ABURI (Akwapim) children are generally regarded as destructive; younger children have valuable objects taken away from them, older ones are scolded and punished for taking them. They manipulate various household objects in the course of doing their chores. 'Through curiosity boys cut their sisters' dolls into two and when they are asked why they do so they say they want to see what is inside them.' In BOSOFO (Asante) dangerous objects are snatched away from children and they are given something else. Children are regarded as generally destructive, especially after they are able to walk, and they are taught not to destroy things by being beaten. Children of five or six years of age make 'lorries' and other toys and play with bricks, tin boxes, etc. In BEREKUM (Brong) children are warned away from dangerous objects. The mother of a child is responsible to its father for its welfare, and 'I was informed that a woman was one day severely beaten and divorced because she allowed her infant child to crawl to a pot of hot soup. The child was almost burnt to death.' Children are generally regarded as destructive and for this reason parents do not buy them toys. In APAM (Fante) children are scolded and shouted at if they get near to dangerous objects, or they may be given a short experience of their power, by being pricked with a knife or by being held near the fire. They are regarded as generally destructive and are taught not to destroy things by being scolded or beaten. 'At various ages the child is encouraged to manipulate his own possessions, such as toys, and household objects such as stools which may be used as lorries. Very often children use their own small chairs and stools as lorries, and when broken they try to mend them. When unsuccessful they ask adults to help them. Children also enjoy adding to their possessions on their own by collecting pieces of cloth, coloured paper, cardboard boxes, cigarette tins, biscuit tins, powder tins and small bottles. Between four and six years children here are fond of making vehicular toys. Family groups or small groups of three to six may make cars and lorries from biscuit tins with cotton reel wheels or from soft wood. These are either drawn along with strings, or pushed along with long sticks. The girls make large wooden dolls which they bathe, dress, converse with, scold, beat for their refusals to go on imaginative errands. Sometimes these dolls are elaborately beaded at the legs, waist and neck. When children of both sexes are busily engaged with their toys it is difficult for parents to get them to do something else. These home-made toys are some of the most valuable possessions, and most parents are careful not to destroy them. Owing to the abundance of crabs in the area, children learn to make and use crab-traps from four years onwards. Since the crabs caught are sold, crab-traps are very important items in the children's possessions. These traps are sometimes made and manipulated by small groups of children of ages varying from four to fifteen years. These groups are joined on Saturdays by school-going relatives and friends.' In GOVIEFE (Ewe) children are shouted at to keep them from dangerous objects. If a child cuts its finger with a knife, the mother pretends to beat the knife after the child has spat in her hand. Children are generally regarded as destructive. They manipulate household articles while they are doing their chores, and may construct 'lorries' and other toys. In AYIKAI DOBORO (Ga) children are told not to play with dangerous things and they are generally regarded as destructive. They are taught not to destroy things by being beaten. Girls play with their mothers' clothes and cosmetics; boys with 'lorries' and tins. A case was reported of a boy taking an electric torch to pieces. In TESHIE (Ga) everyone in the compound watches out for young children and shouts if they come near anything sharp or hot. Threats are made of calling in the policeman or the sanitary inspector; 'If you touch that knife again, I will call the sanitary inspector in to take you away'. Children, especially older ones, are generally regarded as destructive, and they are usually beaten for breaking things, even if it was not their fault. 'The children spend most of their time in the air and sun, chasing lizards and birds with stones and sticks. They also use more often, earth, sand and pebbles. They have very little contact, in fact I had no examples, of things to be taken apart and put together.' In APIREDE (Cherepon) children are regarded as generally destructive and are punished for destroying things. They manipulate household objects, dolls, 'lorries', catapults, etc. Dolls are often destroyed by girls in order to see what is inside them.

CHAPTER NINETEEN

SCHOOLING

> 'The main reason why children are educated is to get them good jobs so that they can support their parents and the younger brothers and sisters later.'

THE attitude of parents in Ghana towards formal schooling has undergone a considerable change since it was first introduced, when it was regarded with such suspicion that in some cases slaves were the first school-attenders. Schooling is now highly regarded, and parents are anxious to send at least their sons to benefit from a formal education. In some areas even the traditional belief that it is a waste of time to educate girls has given way to a desire on the part of parents to prepare their daughters for good jobs, or to become the wives of educated men. However, it is still widely argued that schooling spoils girls, who are said to become lazy, extravagant, selfish and sexually lax. Some illiterate mothers tend to treat their school-going daughters with special indulgence, exempting them from household duties and even appointing illiterate sisters as their maidservants. On the other hand, in some homes, school-children have to face a heavy load of domestic chores on top of their day's school-work. In his survey of the municipality of Sekondi-Takoradi, Busia found that 'many of the schoolboys and girls on arriving home from school plunge straight into a round of domestic duties; fetching water, cooking, washing, cleaning, or doing errands. Many of them are sent out into the streets to sell things.'[1]

In matrilineal areas, the introduction of schooling has complicated the relationship between the family of a child's father and that of his mother, or the matriclan. Traditionally, the maternal

[1] (4) 51.

uncle is responsible for the child's debts, except those arising from sexual misconduct. On the other hand, the father is traditionally responsible for the vocational training of his sons. This has led to widespread controversy over who should pay the child's school fees. There is no general agreement; in some families the father pays, in others the maternal uncle pays, and in still others each bears a part of the total cost.

While the general attitude among Ghanaian parents towards formal education is positive, it would seem that it derives largely from materialistic considerations. The money expended upon schooling is regarded as a form of investment, which is expected to pay dividends when the child is in a salaried job. Funeral expenses, traditionally the most important responsibility of a Ghanaian child towards his or her parents, are expected to be large when the parent has paid for his sons' or daughters' schooling. Other motives for sending a child to school are (i) the increase in social status which attends having educated offspring, (ii) the direct value of such children (in keeping accounts, etc.) to illiterate parents, (iii) the supervision in school of troublesome children.[1] In some areas, notably the Akwapim Ridge, there is also a tradition of education. In ABURI (Akwapim) 'many parents are very eager to send their children to school. Parents are anxious to get their children out of the house because they are troublesome at home at that stage; fighting, shouting, destroying things and eating too much are common. The main reason why children are educated is to get them good jobs so that they can support their parents and the younger brothers and sisters later. In fact some of these parents send their children to school just because they see their neighbours doing so. They have no aim for the children and no hope of helping them to finish. These form the majority of the parents.' Parents tend to prefer to send their sons to school to sending their daughters, since boys are thought to be more clever than girls. But some parents can now see in other families daughters supporting their parents and they are beginning to change their minds. In JAISI (Asante) some children are sent to school in order to avoid occupying a useful farm labourer, that is, an elder sibling, in looking after them; others, because they are too difficult to manage at home. The teacher's cane is a

[1] Rattray notes the Ashanti custom of handing over unruly offspring to the care of someone well known at managing troublesome children; (30) 13.

common threat. Parental expectations of high social prestige and a good job for their children are other motives. Some parents may send their daughters to school in order to prepare them for marriage with men of high social standing. Schooling is generally regarded as an investment; 'the purpose of education, therefore, looked at from the point of view of many of the village parents, is frankly materialistic'. In BEREKUM (Brong) the general belief about the aim of schooling or educating a child is that it is to get money. Parents feel that girls' education is a sheer waste of time and money. Schooling makes the girls lazy. Formerly it was believed that schooling was a means 'whereby people were trained to be liars and not fit to live in community'; hence slaves were the first to go to school. Some illiterate parents still think that education is a waste of time, and all parents agree that the education of girls leads to pregnancy, laziness, fancifulness and to their not knowing how to cook. In SUPOWMU DUNKWA (Fante) parents are very keen on education. 'More boys are sent to school than girls because of the idea prevalent in most villages that it is useless educating girls, as they always end up in the kitchen.' Among the KWAHUS the responsibility for the education of children rests sometimes with the child's father, sometimes with his maternal uncle and sometimes with both. In GOVIEFE (Ewe) parents attach importance to education because it is fashionable, because it brings them social prestige, because their children can look after the accounts, and because they hope that their children will get good jobs. Parents feel there is more point in educating their sons than their daughters, as the latter become spoiled. In CENTRAL ACCRA (Ga) 'parents take delight in seeing their sons and daughters reading letters, understanding them and translating them into the local language. It is a common sight to see schoolchildren during thanksgiving or customary ceremonies writing down donations and keeping accounts up to date. An educated child is an asset to an illiterate mother who trades in European goods.' Nowadays 'fishermen choose to send their children to school instead of allowing them to learn fishing, which is not paying these days'. Some fathers, however, do not like to send their children to school because of the cost of uniform and books, and because unstable marriages and frequent divorces often mean that mothers derive more benefit from their children's education than do fathers. If parents cannot afford to send their children to school, though a mother may sell her valuables in order to pay the fees, they may send them to a relative, or to anyone who will send them to school in return for heavy domestic duties. Usually one of a family of children is kept at home to do the domestic chores, and he or she may resent it afterwards. In KORDIABE (Shai) little importance is attached by parents to schooling. 'According to the headmaster, some parents after they have got their children enrolled care very little as to whether the children attend school or not.' In OTROWE (Adangme) children are expected in adult life to repay the expenditure that has been made upon them for their schooling. In LARTEH KUBEASI (Guang) parents 'attach great importance to learning chiefly because the child will, through it in future, be qualified to hold a lucrative job. It enhances his social dignity, if a parent educated his children.' Parents show keen interest in the out-of-door activities of schoolchildren. Generally boys are given a higher education than are girls. Though 'many more girls are given chances today than they had some years ago'.

In nearly all the investigated areas, children who attended primary schools were able to do so in their own villages. In the *Accra Survey*, eighty-four per cent of the children attending Primary schools had to travel less than one mile to reach them.[1] Those who went on to middle schools, however, tended to have to travel some distance, or, alternatively, to have to live away from their homes. This tendency is enhanced by the tradition in Ghana[2] that middle schoolchildren should be sent to live in a literate household while they are at school. In some cases the foster-parents are relatives, in others not. In the latter case, and often in the former, the child's services in the foster-parent's house are recognized as the payment for board and lodging, and for the educational value of living in a literate home. In a survey of over two thousand schoolchildren in Sekondi-Takoradi, Busia found that seventy-two per cent lived with one or both parents; less than five per cent lived with guardians to whom they were not related.[3] 'Nearly all the pupils in the Infant and Junior Schools lived with one or both parents, and it was among the older pupils in the Senior Schools that those living with

[1] Percentage calculated from Table 73, (1) 112.
[2] Which may possibly derive from the custom of 'pawning'; see page 154 above.
[3] (4) 48.

other relations, or with guardians who were no relations of theirs were found.'[1] Some of these foster-children are very badly treated, and several of the cases of juvenile delinquency reported by Busia started off in such foster-homes.[2] In TUTU (Akwapim) 'the parents may sometimes have a friend who takes great interest in their child. Some of the parents who travel to far distant places on business often arrange for their child who may be attending school to live with such a friend of the family. The child may continue to live with the parent's friend during the whole of their absence until the end of this primary school education. There are other instances in which the child is sent away from Tutu to live with a friend of the family who may be living at a far distant place, for example, Accra and Koforidua. Such a child who is sent away from his parents to live with other people usually is between the ages of seven and twelve years. Most of these guardians are very kind and just in their dealings with the children left in their charge. Although the children's own parents provide all their needs yet their guardians will shoulder willingly all incidental expenses without demanding anything in return from the parents. They see to it that the children are well fed, and they do all they can towards their welfare. However, there are other guardians who treat such children miserably. They are very hard on them and ask them to do the most unpleasant work in the house; they will overtask them with domestic duties which may sometimes keep them busy far into the night, thus giving them insufficient sleep at night, and they will mercilessly punish them for the least offence committed.' In GOVIEFE (Ewe) primary school-children live at home, though some may have to walk five miles to school every day. In LARTEH KUBEASI (Guang) 'many of the parents at Larteh live for a greater part of the year in villages where they farm. There are therefore many school-children who stay in the town with their aunts, grandmothers, teachers and other relatives and friends who occasionally receive substantial help from the parents of the children.'

Teachers in Ghana are a highly respected section of the community, particularly in the rural areas, where the village teacher is often the only literate member of the community, to whom the villagers frequently come for advice. Formerly, the relations between a teacher and his pupils were dominated by fear on the

[1] *Idem.* [2] *Ibid.*, 91 ff.

part of the latter; nowadays the prevailing attitude has changed to one of respect. Instances are still reported, however, of children refusing to attend school for fear of an over-severe teacher; such teachers are sometimes transferred. Evidence of friendly and co-operative relations between teachers and pupils were reported from several of the investigated areas. In some schools in the larger towns, the pupils are not above playing pranks on their teachers. In ABURI (Akwapim) 'many children like their teachers a great deal. They have more respect for their opinions than for those of their parents. They say that whatever the teachers say or do is the best.' In BANKO (Asante) the local primary school headteacher had elephantiasis, and was on that account feared. The relations between the schoolchildren and the other teachers were cordial, however, and 'every afternoon every child made it a point to bring some oranges or some bananas as presents to the teachers'. 'At the Middle Schools most of the boys and girls spoke lovingly of all their teachers, particularly the headteacher. Children felt very proud of their teachers and admired them.' In GOVIEFE (Ewe) 'in the community a teacher, provided he behaves himself, commands the respect of both parents and their children and adults generally. Even the local chief and his elders look up to him for advice, however young he may be.' The attitude of the children towards their teacher is primarily one of respect and the fear which was a characteristic of old-time teaching is now dying out. In CENTRAL ACCRA (Ga) the attitude towards the teacher that prevails on the part of schoolchildren is one of fear. Women teachers may be the sexual rivals of schoolgirls, and intimacies between male teachers and schoolgirls may lead to pregnancies. 'There is more fear and respect on the part of the child for the teacher than for the parent. It is therefore common for parents to send their children to school to be punished by the teacher or to use the teacher's name as a threat to stop the child from misbehaving. Young children in the primary school do not often play tricks on teachers but pupils of the middle school do. Usually these tricks are played on teachers who have no sympathy with the pupils. During religious instruction a teacher condemned African supersition and belief in magic as well as charms. A week later, the teacher came to the school and found black powder, a snake's head and some shells spread on his table. He could not go near the table. The children teased him by reminding him of the religious instruction lessons they had had, but still the teacher could not go near. The headmaster was called in. He ordered the prefect to clean the table. A teacher in charge of Middle Form II in one of the schools could not control the class. He was sent to another class and a new teacher was brought from Cape Coast. This teacher did not understand the Ga language. He asked the children to teach him and they taught him wrong words most of which were profane. Whenever he spoke to people outside he was laughed at and the real meaning explained to him. There are many tricks played by pupils at school and in many cases children who play these tricks are punished when they are caught. It is not usual for boys in a class to expose their friends when a teacher is looking for one who has created laughter somewhere.' In TESHIE (Ga) the prevailing attitude among children towards their teacher is one of fear; mothers use the teacher's name as a threat to control their children. In APIREDE (Cherepon) 'the teacher is regarded as an intellectual giant whose great authority should be respected'.

School discipline in Ghana is traditionally more severe than home discipline, and while the custom appears to be on the decline, it is still fairly common for parents to take their children to school to be punished for misdemeanours committed at home.[1] At the same time, teachers are sometimes condemned as too severe, even by parents. In most areas investigated, however, the teachers were respected by the parents, unless they involve the payment of extra charge of contributions. In one or two towns, however, and in Aburi in particular,[2] the relationship between teachers and parents appears to be considerably strained by the unco-operativeness and even outright hostility on the part of some parents. Busia, in his survey of Sekondi-Takoradi, mentions a number of criticisms of the standard of education in primary schools, made at 'meetings with teachers, parents and old pupils';[3] according to the investigators, such criticisms would be beyond most of the parents in the investigated areas. In BANKO (Asante) Christian parents have cordial relationships with teachers and often visit school to discuss

[1] This may not be a result only of the stricter discipline at school. Some illiterate parents feel that once their children start attending school, they no longer have any responsibility towards them; such parents sometimes describe their children as 'Government property'.

[2] It is interesting to note in this respect, that Aburi has a long tradition of formal education and is today the site of several large educational institutions.

[3] (4) 59.

work and behaviour. They report their children to the teachers for having misbehaved at home and similarly teachers report them to the parents for misbehaviour in school. But 'with the pagan or Muslim parents, the situation is quite different. These parents think that school discipline is too severe for their children.' In BEREKUM (Brong) some parents take their children to the teacher to be beaten. On the other hand, 'some of the parents become infuriated when their children are overpunished in school. Sometimes these parents lose their temper, go to the school and start insulting the teachers for the ill-treatment that they give to the pupils. A headteacher who does not exercise patience finds himself exchanging blows with the parent. Mr X who was once the headmaster of one of the middle schools was held in the night by some pupils and beaten mercilessly. There was another instance when a teacher was taken to court for inflicting wounds on the legs of a pupil by the use of the cane.' Children are punished at home for poor performance in school since no one wants to spend money on a child who shows little progress at school. Parents may dispute school decisions if they involve the children being kept at school after school hours. In GOVIEFE (Ewe) the relationship between parents and teachers varies. School discipline is generally regarded as more severe than home discipline, and parents sometimes send their children to the school teacher to be punished. Parents sometimes dispute school decisions, when they involve the children taking part in chores. In VAKPO (Ewe) 'parents admire dutiful and conforming behaviour in school and generally do not dispute school decisions. Many parents show keen interest in their children's performance at school. At the end of the term, they are anxious to see the children's report sheets. The illiterates often take these report sheets to other people to read to them and will not permit their children to read and explain them. When parents realize that the child's performance at school is good, they praise him, and when it is poor, they tease him by saying he is eating too much. Some parents even ask the big children, whose performance at school is poor, to stop schooling and help on the farms.' In AYIKAI DOBORO (Ga) there is a close relationship between teachers and parents and some teachers go round after school hours to see if the children are behaving themselves. Parents sometimes ask teachers to punish their children for misbehaviour at home and children may be punished at home for poor performance at school. Parents do not dispute school decisions as they do not understand the matters involved. In KORDIABE (Shai) parents and other adults report naughty children to their teachers for punishment. School discipline is more severe than at home, particularly since many children stay with indulgent grandparents. Children may be threatened with removal from school if their performance is poor. Parents do not dispute school decisions though occasionally if a child is very severely beaten his parents may remove him.

Relations between schoolmates are generally friendly, though in some cases school inter-section competitions, and particularly those in which the losers are given extra school duties, lead to hostility. Older boys form themselves into gangs for the purpose of fighting rival gangs, pilfering fruit and visiting lovers. Busia notes the many complaints about the behaviour of schoolchildren in Sekondi-Takoradi.[1] In BOMPATA (Asante) relations between schoolchildren are friendly and fights are rare. Older children form gangs, especially for such purposes as the hiring of their labour to cocoa farmers during school holidays. In JAISI (Asante) relations among schoolmates are generally friendly though there is a tendency for hostility to exist between the winners and losers of competitions and gangs are often formed to persecute clever children. In KPANDU (Ewe) children of fifteen to eighteen years old form gangs; 'they attack their opponents, throw stones at teachers in the night, go about plucking fruits and destroying garden crops'. In DOME (Ga) 'a majority of the children are related to each other so that the relationship between them is very friendly'. Competitors sometimes tend to be hostile as a result of jealousy, though there is general admiration of the winner. In WINNEBA (Efutu) relations among schoolmates are cordial and competitions are held in a friendly atmosphere, though competitions in class between sections may lead to quarrels. Boys of from ten to fifteen years of age form gangs for games and activities.

Friendships made in middle schools tend to persist, sometimes even into adult life. Schoolchildren begin to form boy-girl relationships at about the age of fourteen; before puberty, such intense friendships as are formed, are between members of the same sex. Sexual intercourse between middle schoolchildren appears to be fairly common. Busia reports in his survey of

[1] (4) 60.

Sekondi-Takoradi that 'there were instances of pre-marital sexual relations between schoolgirls and working men, as well as between schoolgirls and schoolboys. Authentic cases of conceptions and even abortions were reported. Though pre-marital sexual relations prevail, its extent appears to be much exaggerated by popular report; nevertheless, chiefs, and schoolmasters and mistresses frankly admitted its prevalence, and expressed great concern about it.'[1] In BANKO (Asante) older children develop intense friendship, often in pairs. Boy-girl relations begin after the age of fifteen; before this age they are too shy to make friends with the opposite sex. In JAISI (Asante) early friendships in school are unstable, but in the middle school years more stable relationships, often group friendships, are formed. In later years strong relationships, often revolving around confidence about love affairs, are a feature of school life. Boy-girl relationships flourish after the age of fifteen. In CENTRAL ACCRA (Ga) at the age of thirteen, boys develop intense friendships 'and each one cannot go out without the other one'. Sometimes they become blood-brothers. 'Between girls friendship does not last for a long time because of gossiping, which generally ends in a fight in which sometimes the parents participate.' School friendships between boys often persist after school and sometimes throughout life if they live in the same compound, though the sons of rich men do not become friends with poor men's sons. In KORDIABE (Shai) intense friendships are to be found at about the age of twelve. By the age of fourteen, boy-girl relationships have begun. Some school friendships last after school is finished.

[1] (4) 60.

CHAPTER TWENTY

CHILDREN'S GAMES AND STORIES

> 'Story-telling is generally done in the evenings as it is believed that, if children tell such stories in the daytime, they will grow tails.'

MAKE-BELIEVE games, in which the activities of the adults around them are imitated, are widely played by young children in Ghana, and many parents encourage them, saying that they teach children how to fulfil their roles when they grow up.[1] As children grow older, the emphasis tends to be on team games, most of which are traditional and played only by the members of one sex. For adolescents, however, there are traditional games played on moonlit evenings in which both sexes participate. School games and athletics are played by many children out of school, and in some places these are said to be driving out the traditional games.[2] In TUTU (Akwapim) games played are *amuntumamuntum* or hide and seek; *odo* in which boys form into two teams, and throw and catch a bundle of palm leaves; *ntew*, or marbles played with seeds; and *ampe* and *aso* played by the girls. In *ampe* two or more girls form into two teams. They clap their hands and jump rhythmically landing with either foot forward. One side wins when the same feet of each team are forward, the other when alternate feet are forward. The number of turns is predetermined and the winning team is that which has the most marks. In *aso* a group of girls form into a horseshoe or circle, with one in the middle. They clap and sing, while the middle girl falls back and is caught by the nearest

[1] The attitude towards make-believe games is not always favourable; see pages 125-6 above.

[2] Danquah describes a wrestling game played by the Akims, called *avensin* or *aguma*, but this was, at the time he wrote (1928), being given up for school games; (6) 229. Fortes has drawn up an elaborate chart of play development at different ages among Tallensi boys and girls; see (12) 62-4.

members of the circle who swing her over to the other side and she is pushed from side to side in time with the song. The centre girl is changed as the song is changed. Both these games, *ampe* and *aso*, are played only by girls. Football is also popular and so is bicycle-riding. Among the schoolchildren, athletics are practised during the holidays. In APA (Asante) young children play make-believe games, especially girls, who delight in imitating their mothers. Boys wrestle, run, kick things about, climb and make 'lorries'. Group hide and seek is played, and older girls also play *aso* and *ampe*. A game played by adolescents is *odo benkiti*, in which the children form into two groups, the boys in one and the girls in another. A girl will select a boy and give him her handkerchief, singing the first verse of a lover's song and the whole group will then sing the chorus. In JAKOBO (Asante) the traditional games are gradually dying out in favour of European games introduced at school. Girls of eight years old and over play *ampe*, *aso* and *dwonkor*, a game in which the girls form a circle, clap their hands and take it in turns to sing, while the rest join the chorus. The girls usually sing about their lovers. *Asaadua* is a group singsong held on moonlit nights in which children and adults all join. Boys hunt, fight, play at hide and seek and marbles. Among the KWAHUS the boys play hide and seek and football, and the girls *ampe* and *aso*. In VAKPO (Ewe) hide and seek, marbles, games at which older children sing and choose sweethearts, *ampe* and *oware* are played. *Oware* is played with marbles or beads in a wooden board.[1] It was originally associated with funerals and is therefore not encouraged. The game of football 'has completely eclipsed and replaced many of the boys' games which were played on festivals and national celebrations in the past'. In CENTRAL ACCRA (Ga) young children play games at imitating their mothers' and fathers' activities, such as cooking, fishing and so forth. Boys of about six make 'lorries' out of sticks and cigarette tin lids.[2] Carts are made out of small tables. Hoops are made out of barrels, old bicycle wheels, etc. The emphasis with older children is on team games. Boys of ten or eleven steal pennies from their parents to hire bicycles to learn to ride them. In APIREDE (Cherepon) 'children's games are mainly informal

[1] A description of the game, giving the rules and some elementary strategy, is given in (31) Chapter 32. A board may be seen in the background of Plate 10.

[2] See Plates 105-106.

activities undertaken by groups. Usually the oldest of them takes it upon himself to instruct the younger ones in the rules of the game.' Boys play at football and *ntosa* which is a knee-slapping version of *ampe*. Girls play *aso* and *peewa*, a clapping and singing game. Boys and girls together play 'hunt the ferret'.

The evening is the time for telling stories, and adults and children gather round the fire to listen to traditional folk tales, particularly those about Ananse, the wise spider. Story-telling is a time when the rules of etiquette concerning children's behaviour before adults is relaxed, and children are encouraged to tell stories, and are listened to by all. Ananse stories and other folk tales are highly regarded by many Ghanaian parents, who argue that they are a form of moral training.[1] In some areas children are told that stories should not be told during the day, or the teller may grow a long tail. There are various special children's songs, most of which are sung during the playing of team games.[2] Children take part in traditional drumming and dancing, though there are certain dances in which they are forbidden to participate. There is very little reading for pleasure outside school, and as most parents are illiterate, they neither read to their children, nor concern themselves with what they read. In some areas, however, children are said to read books on sexual matters secretly. In MAMPONG (Akwapim) 'children delight greatly in songs and stories. While at home the mothers and the grandmothers often tell them many interesting Ananse stories. The stories are generally narrated in the evening near the fire. It is a saying that stories should not be told in the afternoon or in the daytime. He who does so grows a long and unwanted beard. The parents say this to the children to frighten them not to spend the day frivolously. Some of the stories are so fascinating that the children laugh until tears begin to run down the cheeks. They dance and play and ask each other riddles. Many of the stories break off into songs, one of the characters

[1] Rattray says that 'a large part of a child's training is derived from listening to the *Anansesem* (Spider Stories) and later reciting them'; (30) 13. Collections of English translations of Ananse stories are to be found in Barker, W. H. and Sinclair, C.: *West African Folk-Tales*, London, Harrap, 1917; and Itayemi, P. and Gurrey, P. *ed.*: *Folk Tales and Fables*, London, Penguin Books, 1953. To European readers, the moral instructive value of many of the exploits of Ananse is somewhat dubious.

[2] According to Danquah, in Akim adolescent children gather in the streets during festivals and social occasions, and sing satirical songs against each other; (6) 228-9.

Children's playthings. 105. A child with his elder brother's 'lorry', made from a piece of bamboo and two shaped cork wheels. Taken in Vakpo.

106. A boy with his 'lorry'. The wheels are made of shaped pieces of wood. Taken in Apam.

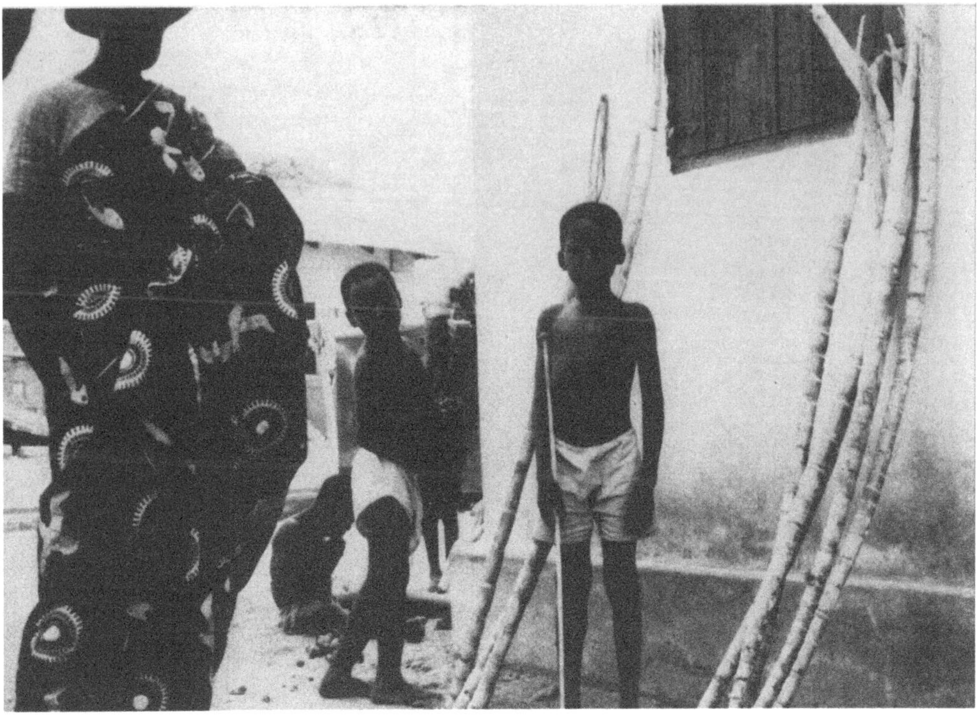

Children's contacts with other children. 107. A group of children on the beach at Teshie.

108. Other children are always about. A group of children in Goviefe.

Children's games. 109. Girls playing *ampe* in Wa.

110. Boys wrestling in Kpandu.

Children's games. 111. Making a high-jump stand in Winneba.

112. Making a high-jump stand in Christiansborg.

singing a line or two and there is a chorus. The narrative proceeds and again the solo and chorus are repeated.' In BANKO (Asante) young children are told Ananse stories and 'children make Ananse their hero'. But later on, in Middle School, Ananse stories are regarded as childish and children prefer stories about explorers. In JAISI (Asante) some children at school are punished for reading books on sex and mysticism. On one occasion, the headmaster of the Middle School told the assembled children not to read books on sex, magic and mysticism, which aroused the children's curiosity and they went to the book shop, got the books and circulated them. Adults when asked to recall their favourite childhood books mentioned *Pilgrim's Progress*, *Gulliver's Travels*, *Treasure Island* and many teachers mentioned *Oliver Twist*, which they read several times in order to give themselves solace for their own difficulties at home. In BEREKUM (Brong) children sing songs to accompany their games. There are special mourning and historical songs which are only taught to those who have reached puberty. At story-telling time mothers and children take it in turn to tell stories, but fathers think it is beneath their dignity; 'to find a father telling stories to his children is very rare'. In CENTRAL ACCRA (Ga) the traditional songs and stories are disappearing. Sometimes adults tell stories to the children. Some time ago, parents used to read and interpret Bible passages, but this is rarely done nowadays. No books are forbidden among children but pictures of 'white ladies standing bare' introduced by Europeans, are forbidden by the parents, who burn them. In CHRISTIANSBORG (Ga) folk stories, riddles, proverbs and other tales are told by both children and adults, and discussed afterwards and these are regarded by parents as an important source of social training and instruction in correct expression and style. In this respect an illiterate child has a considerable advantage over a literate child who has little opportunity to hear these stories. In TESHIE (Ga) the moral value of folk tales is emphasized by parents. Special children's songs are sung to accompany the traditional part of folk tales told by the children. 'Children in the Middle School are fond of reading books on sex.'

CHAPTER TWENTY-ONE

CHILDREN'S WORK

> 'By the end of her eleventh year, every girl at Banko has mastered all the details of housekeeping, cooking, sweeping and carrying water. Whenever the mother menstruates, it is the little girl who cooks for the father or the uncles.'

IN most Ghanaian homes, children are expected to take part in the work of the house from a very early age, and they may have simple household duties allotted to them from the age of three, or even two. At this age they may follow their mothers, and help to bring in firewood. By the time they are five or six, most children have a programme of chores for which they are responsible. In some families, by this age the boy has left his mother's compound to go and live with his father, and he spends most of the day helping him at his work.[1] The amount of work children do increases as they grow older, and by the time they reach puberty, girls who do not go to school are employed full-time in their domestic duties, while schoolgirls may have to get up early to do their chores before going to school, and are required to do more when they return home again.[2] In some illiterate homes, however, children who go to school are exempted from some or all domestic duties, and may even be given the services of a non-school-going sibling, as a maid-servant. In APA (Asante) 'from the age of four, a boy

[1] Christensen says that when a Fanti boy is large enough to handle a cutlass (or matchet), he learns to farm; a fisherman's son of six or seven will be given an oar and goes to sea with his father; (5) 97.

[2] Field says that, among Ga fishermen, sons may begin to help their fathers to carry their fishing tackle as soon as they can walk; by the time they are ten they have a number of duties such as spreading and drying the sails and lines, and repairing the nets; (9) 31. Manoukian notes that, among the Ewes, while girls have to help their mothers from an early age, boys are free longer; (26) 43. According to Tait, Konkomba girls work with their mothers from about the age of eight, and at the same age, or a little later, boys begin to learn farm work; (34) 334.

accompanies his father to the bush'. He is carried when tired. He is taught by his father how to sharpen his cutlass, how to till the land, and etc. Until about the age of seven, he sits tending the fire and watching his father work. After this age he helps with weeding and other tasks. In the home, girls of six or seven are taught to pound fufu. In BOSOFO (Asante) children are sent on errands about the house from the age of two and are sent to other houses at three to four years of age. At the age of five or six the children go with their parents to the farm. In APAM (Fante) girls are allotted household tasks from four years of age; boys from six. In AYIKAI DOBORO (Ga) children help in the home from an early age; at the age of two or over they sweep the floors. Children of six are to be seen carrying their baby siblings. Carrying firewood, water and other chores may be undertaken from the age of three onwards. Boys of eight years or over help their fathers, while girls may cook and bathe the children from the age of twelve. In APIREDE (Cherepon) 'parents regard children as extra hands to make housework or farm-work easier'; children help their parents fetch and carry from the age of two; from three to five years old they are sent on errands and from the age of six or seven they have regular duties.

In all parts of Ghana, children help their parents at those tasks which they will themselves undertake as adults. Thus, boys assist their fathers with the fishing tackle if they are fishermen, or on the farm if they are farmers; girls help their mothers with the work of the house. In this way, they are learning at the same time as they are working, and the usefulness of this aspect of their assistance is regarded as equally important, if not more so, than the direct value to the parents of their help. They start in a small way, by carrying the father's tools, by spreading out nets to dry, by carrying water and firewood, by looking after younger siblings and helping in the preparation of food. By the time they reach adolescence, Ghanaian children are expected to be able to undertake most of the tasks required of the adult; girls to look after the household, prepare and cook the food and mind the young children, boys to cultivate their own farms. For an adolescent not to know these things is regarded as a grave reflection on his or her parents, who have demonstrably failed in their duty.[1] In TUTU

[1] Christensen says that it is the obligation of a Fanti mother to train her daughter as a mother and housewife, and to give her a rudimentary knowledge of trading;

(Akwapim) 'there are many mothers at Tutu who begin to train their children to do some small pieces of work in the home when they are about six years of age. They sweep some portions of the house, for example the bathroom. The boys between six and eight years of age run errands in the house and feed the domestic animals in the house, by giving maize to the fowls and cutting up the peel of plantain into small pieces for the goats and sheep to eat. The girls of about nine years of age sweep larger portions of the house, for example the yard and the kitchen. They fetch water from the water-hole for drinking and other household purposes. They also run errands in the house and are often sent to the market to buy food. If the mother is a trader, her daughter at this age will carry some of her goods to the market, and at other times assist the mother in going about the street and advertising the goods, especially printed cotton cloth, by carrying them on her head. At the kitchen, she learns cooking by assisting her mother in preparing the meals of the household each day; she also pounds fufu. When the children are between eight and twelve years of age, both boys and girls assist their parents in farm work during the planting season. They plant crops, such as maize, rice, cocoyam, plantain, and they also help a great deal in planting cocoa seedlings when a new cocoa farm is being made; they learn how to make mounds for planting yams, and also raised beds for groundnuts. They are provided with cutlasses and this enables them to take part in weeding the undergrowth as crops begin to grow. Boys beyond twelve years of age do hard work on their fathers' farms. In making a new farm, they help in cutting down the

(5) 48-9. Field notes that, among the Gas, 'an unmarried boy has no property of his own. All his earnings belong to his father, and his father provides for all his needs. The boy goes every day to work on his father's farm or with his father's canoe or nets. When he reaches the age of about fifteen his father gives him one day a week on which to "make a farm" of his own. At harvest time he "shows his profits" to his father, his father "takes a little for tobacco" and gives the boy the rest'; (9) 54. Rattray notes that, among the Gurensis, boys are given small plots of land to tend; (32) 137. Fortes says that, among the Tallensis, children are never urged to work beyond their capacities, and may be restrained from over-exertion; (12) 13. Fortes gives a chart, showing the nature of work performed by Tallensi children of different ages and of either sex. They do little beyond scaring birds until they are six; from six to nine they help in sowing and harvesting; from nine to twelve they are responsible for cattle-herding, the care of poultry, and they farm their own plots; from twelve to fifteen they lead the herdboys and begin real farming. Girls from three to six look after infants, help in sweeping and water-carrying; from six to nine have some responsibility for fetching water and help in the preparation of food; by the time they are twelve, 'all domestic duties can be entrusted to them'; (12) 62-4.

virgin forest or the bush, and they take part in the preliminary work to be done on the farm before planting actually starts. During adolescence, some boys become capable of working on their own and so they make their own farms in which they cultivate all different kinds of crops. By means of this, some children are able to build up a reasonable capital of their own before getting married. Sometimes a boy between ten and sixteen years of age is given some domestic animals to rear, such as fowls, sheep and goats. Girls between ten and eighteen years of age are encouraged to trade on a very small scale. On Mondays and Thursdays they walk to Dodowah which is about seven miles from Tutu; on the way they go down a very steep rocky hill. On these days, being market days at Dodowah, they buy many foodstuffs, such as fish, meat, and vegetables, and on their return home sell them at a profit. Other girls travel to Adawso and Asesewa, about fifteen and fifty miles respectively away from Tutu to buy foodstuffs, such as yams, plantain and cocoyam; these also are similarly sold at a profit.' In BANKO (Asante) chores become sex-differentiated as children grow older and by the age of seven, children will refuse to do the work inappropriate to their sex; 'if a mother tells a boy to sweep the house he will refuse to do so saying, "No, I shall not sweep, because I am a man" '. In GOVIEFE (Ewe) 'children begin to work in the real sense of the word about the age of six. They do jobs common to both boys and girls, such as sweeping the parents' room, the house, the kitchen, the compound; fetching water from the water-hole or spring, going on errands, gathering bits of firewood, bringing back from the farm logs for the fire, food in small baskets or pans, and so on. Another very common task of both boys and girls is acting as nurse-maid to a baby. By the age of seven or eight, children are introduced to sexual division of labour customary among the people. The boys begin to do work supposed to be appropriate to men, and girls that which is appropriate to women. Mothers begin to train their daughters to watch and care for the younger children, washing their clothing and swaddling clothes, carrying them and playing with them. They have to fetch water for the household, sweep the house and rooms, take off the ash from the native hearth and smear it with earth and water in the traditional way, set the fire and put bath-water on the fire. They help their mothers in preparing the baby's food as well as food for the whole household. They wash the cooking utensils after the meal. They reduce expenses by the household duties they perform and add to the cash income of the household by selling things, such as farm produce, cooked food, sweets and petty articles in the markets, streets and shops and from house to house or in the neighbouring villages. They also help on the farm, pulling up the weed or weeding with small hoes made for them. They help during the harvest of cocoa, yam, rice, cotton, groundnuts and other products. They are trained to carry heavy loads on the head. From the age of about nine or ten, a girl may begin to do most of the cooking unaided and begins to acquire some skill and competence in other specialized domestic routine of a housewife. By the age of twelve, the average girl begins to feel herself to belong to the women. Similarly, boys are introduced to work appropriate to their sex. A boy begins to follow his elder brother or father to the farm, carrying a gourd of water and his own small cutlass and, often, his catapult. On reaching the farm, when his father is busy working, the boy sets the fire and roasts some cocoyam or yam for their use. He then wanders along the outskirts of the farm, setting traps, hunting birds, squirrels, mice or lizards. When they are a little older, boys are allowed to make small farms of their own and at other times asked to help in pulling up the weed or brush in the farm with their cutlasses. In the house, boys tether the domestic animals and bring the fowls to their coops in the evening. In the morning they let out the animals and fowls. They set and clear their fathers' tables, give them water for their baths. They are allowed to do a little craft work in their spare times. By the age of thirteen, boys also begin to feel to belong to the men.' In DOME (Ga) at the age of seven or so, boys accompany their fathers to work on the farms. By the time she has reached the age of nine, a girl is expected to know all the domestic duties except cooking and by the time she is fourteen she is expected to be able to run the house by herself.

Children are punished for laziness or for refusing to work by being deprived of luxuries and delicacies, by being abused, and by being beaten. Hard-working children are rewarded with praise, delicacies and gifts; they earn their parents' affection and respect.[1] In ABURI (Akwapim) 'a child may receive a special

[1] Among the Ewes, according to Manoukian, with regard to work 'there is little punishment; laziness and lack of knowledge are simply laughed at by the others, boys and girls alike'; (26) 43.

gift for working well and the same child will be punished severely if he fails to do the right thing the next day. But all the parents agree that they punish their children more than they praise them because they believe that if a child is praised often he becomes self-conceited and a bad child.' In APA (Asante) when a child is sent on an errand 'the mother drops a speck of spittle on the ground and tells the child that if this spittle dries before he arrives his navel will rot and he will die consequently'. Children are sometimes rewarded for doing household chores with meat and fish at meals. Children who refuse to obey are beaten or denied their share of appetising foods, such as sugar-cane, coconuts or groundnuts. In DWINYAMA (Asante) 'refusal to work may result in corporal punishment; but children who do additional work may be rewarded or praised'. In APAM (Fante) children who work hard may be rewarded with new clothes after the fishing season. In KPANDU (Ewe) 'hard-working lads are rewarded at dinner with extra meat, and pants and shorts or shirts and singlets are given at the end of working seasons. Those who refuse to work or help their parents are heavily abused or flogged by the father. They are refused meat at meals and are never properly loved; they are looked upon as lazy and useless children. If children persist in refusing to help at work, the parents send them away from home to live with distant relatives.' In OTROWE (Adangme) hard-working children are rewarded with delicacies at meals; 'on the whole, hard-working children are treated with more parental care and love than children who refuse to work'.

The attitude towards children's obtaining paid employment in addition to working in the family is generally one of approval. Older girls are encouraged to trade in the afternoons, after they have returned from school.[1] In TUTU (Akwapim) 'girls between ten and eighteen years of age are encouraged to trade on a very small scale'. In BOMPATA (Asante) there is no child employment among local-born people but among the immigrant families from the Northern Territories, some parents hire out their children. In GOVIEFE (Ewe) children who manage to obtain casual employment or who make money from odd jobs are applauded. In CHRISTIANSBORG (Ga) parents disapprove of child employment, 'as it is likely to create the impression that parents are not able to feed their own child'.

[1] See Plates 121-126.

CHAPTER TWENTY-TWO

PUBERTY AND ADOLESCENCE[1]

> 'When a young man sees a girl whose features appeal to him, he could approach her there and then and give her, say, two or four shillings and say "I love you". If the girl accepts the money, then it shows that she has accepted the boy's offer of love. He may show the girl where he lives and may invite her to come and spend the night with him.'

TRADITIONALLY in most parts of Ghana, the onset of puberty in girls was recognized as the sign of approaching womanhood, and the occasion of a girl's first menstruation was marked by a special feast. This was followed by an elaborate puberty rite, often lasting for weeks or even months, during which the girl was instructed in wifely duties; she underwent a number of ritual purifications, often involving seclusion in a special house and was obliged to keep to an elaborate programme of taboos. At the end of this period, the girl was gorgeously dressed and paraded the town. She was now regarded as marriageable, and if not already betrothed, she was expected to become so soon

[1] The concept of adolescence as a stage of emotional development between the onset of puberty and acceptance as an adult member of society, is not altogether applicable to African tribal society, particularly if it is assumed that it is accompanied by temperamental behaviour characteristic of this stage in European society; that is, moodiness, rebelliousness, irritability, embarrassment and so forth. In tribal society, the period between the onset of puberty and marriage, which usually confers adult status on a girl at least, is often very short, and may be entirely given over to the performance of the puberty rites. It is true that adult status may depend upon the having of children, but even before her first child, a married woman can scarcely be described as adolescent, in the usual meaning of the term. However, with the coming of general education and the intrusion of European ideas, something like a period of adolescence on the European pattern is emerging in Ghana. In this book, the word is used only to mean that period between the onset of puberty and acceptance as an adult, and must be taken to carry no implications as to characteristic forms of behaviour unless specifically stated.

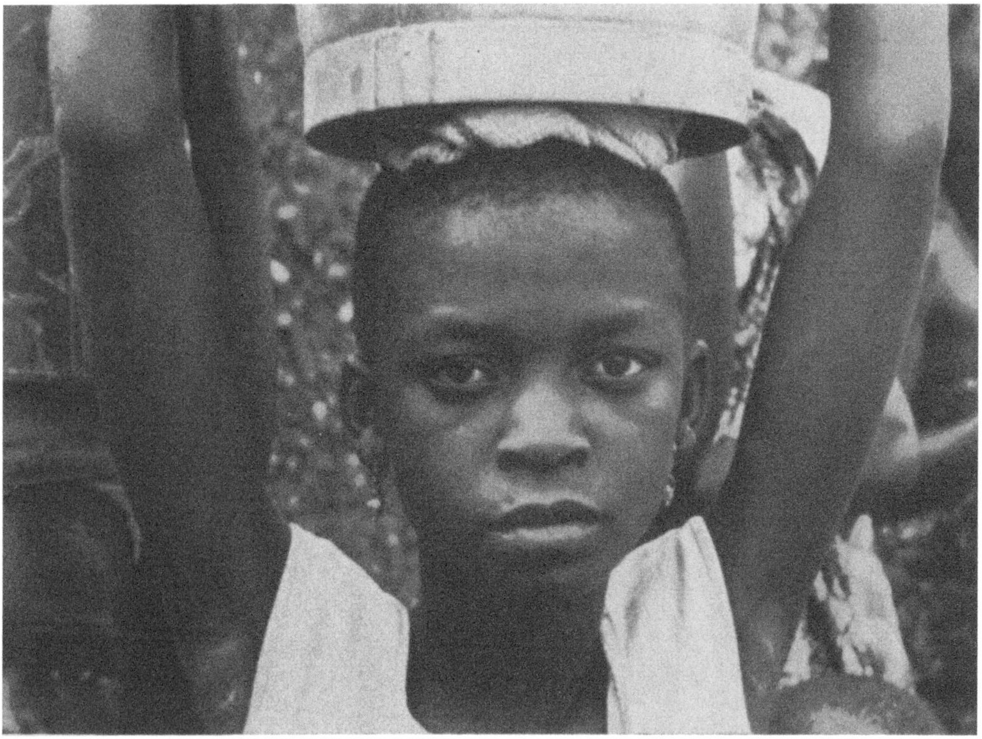

Children's domestic chores. 113. Carrying water home in Goviefe.

114. Carrying water home in Kpasinkpe.

Children's domestic chores. 115. Carrying water home in Winneba.

116. Carrying water home in Keta Krachi.

Children's domestic chores. 117. Young girl, about six years old, carrying water home in Teshie.

118. Carrying water and food home in Ahenboboi, near Cape Coast.

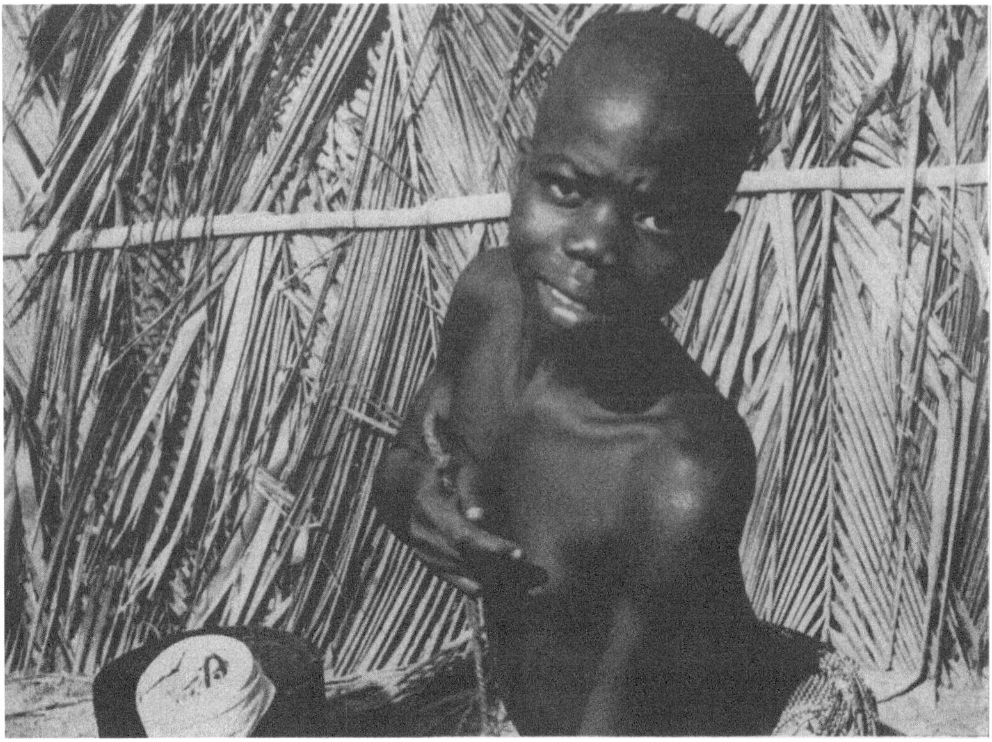

Children's domestic chores. 119. Drawing water from the well in Ahenboboi, near Cape Coast

120. Drawing water from the pond at Komenda

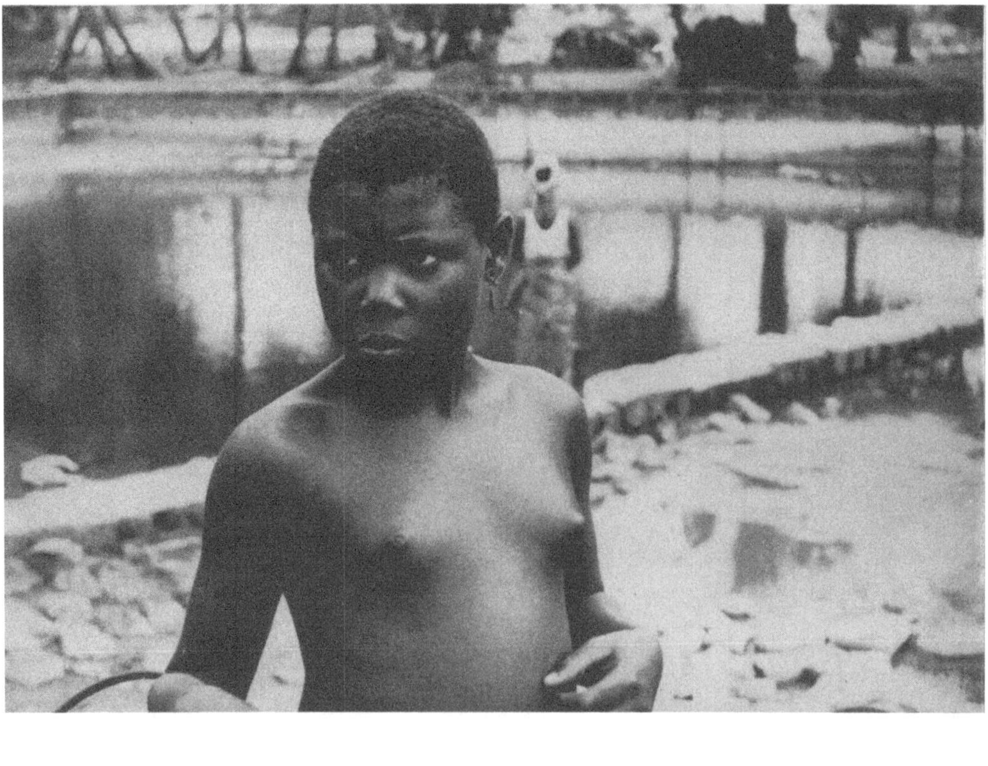

after the performance of her rites. A most important aspect of the rites was the announcement of the girl's chastity, and candidates for the puberty rites who were found not to be virgins were driven out of the tribe or killed, and the whole clan was obliged to undergo ritual purification.

While the puberty rites are still fairly elaborate in some areas, notably the remoter villages, they have lost a great deal of their importance, and in some towns have become little more than a feast and general recognition of the girl's availability for marriage. In some areas, partly on account of the terrible punishments visited on those who become pregnant before their celebration, puberty rites are held a long time before the girls reach puberty; as early as five or six years of age. Among Christian families, the confirmation rite is replacing the puberty rite; the celebration may be a mixture of elements of both rites.[1]

On reaching puberty, girls generally in Ghana have decreased freedom of action. They are said to become self-conscious, particularly in the matter of clothes and self-adornment.[2]

[1] Descriptions of girls' puberty rites among the Akans generally are given by Manoukian in (25) 52; among the Akims by Field in (7) 137-8; among the Ashantis by Rattray in (31) 69-75; among the Fantis by Christensen in (5) 85-6; in Sekondi-Takoradi by Busia in (4) 33-4; among the Gas by Field in (8) 185-91 and (9) 23; and among the Shais by Huber in (23) *passim* .According to Rattray, among the Ashantis 'in times not so very remote, any laxity of morals prior to reaching puberty was commonly punished by death or expulsion from the clan of both the guilty parties; if a man had sexual intercourse with a young girl prior to the appearance of her first period it was considered as an offence for which the whole community would suffer'; (31) 74. According to Wartemberg, in Elmina the illiterate girls still adorn themselves while schoolgirls are exempted from doing so. He also observed that in a number of cases, the rite was performed for girls only after they had been found pregnant; (36) 121-2. According to Manoukian 'in general, it is considered blasphemous and dangerous for a girl to conceive a child before her *kpemo* rites have been performed and in earlier days such a woman and her child were driven from the "town". Nowadays the offence is condoned but the pregnant girl is rushed through an abbreviated form of the rites to prevent the child being born stupid'; (25) 91. Field notices the different importance attached to the puberty rites by Gas; 'two families may be living side by side in the same town, speaking the same language, obeying the same officials, attending the same market, fishing from the same beach, serving in the same military company, dipping from the same well, keeping most of the religious feasts in common—in short, living the same life—yet the girls of one family perform no puberty rites whatever, and the girls of the other would feel overtaken by the greatest possible social disgrace in this world and disaster in the next if they did not'; (8) 185. Busia notes the mixture of Christian and pagan elements in puberty rites in Sekondi-Takoradi; (4) 34. Huber notes that among the Shais, while puberty rites may be shorter, they are not necessarily less elaborate than they used to be, and some say they have become more so; (23) 118.

[2] See Plates 127-128.

For boys there does not appear ever to have been a formal puberty rite.[1] In some areas, acceptance into the Asafo was the occasion for some kind of initiation rite, but this was usually limited to those likely to succeed to high office.[2]

In the Northern Territories, puberty is reached without any form of ceremony for either girls or boys,[3] and even in those tribes in which clitoridectomy is practised when the girls reach puberty, it appears to be unaccompanied by any special rites.[4]

Throughout Ghana, however, the onset of menstruation is regarded as an indication that a girl is ready for marriage.

In ABURI (Akwapim) modified puberty rites are nowadays held in conjunction with confirmation at a Christian Church. In BANKO (Asante) elaborate puberty rites are performed. These are accompanied by considerably decreased freedom of action for girls. Adolescent boys are free to go out as much as they like. Among Christian families, confirmation is taking the place of puberty rites. In BENIM (Asante) puberty rites are held for girls. If a girl becomes pregnant before her puberty rites have been celebrated, she has committed a crime against society and the ancestral spirits. If a girl is not betrothed before the celebration of her puberty rites, she is then expected to become so. In JAKOBO (Asante) as soon as the mother learns that her daughter has had her menarche, she prepares a special dish called *oto* and her relatives are notified. The full puberty rites are performed subsequently and if the girl is not already betrothed, then it is quickly arranged for her to be so. In BEREKUM (Brong) there is a tendency nowadays for Christian confirmation rites to replace puberty rites. In APAM (Fante) 'in the case of school-going girls no fuss is made about their menstruation. The mother or the grandmother may give the girl a present of boiled eggs to eat, and that may be all there is

[1] Rattray says there are no puberty rites for boys among the Ashantis, though an Ashanti father will instruct his adolescent son in sex matters and warn him not to masturbate; (31) 69. Christensen notes there is no puberty rite for boys among the Fantis; (5) 85.

[2] Field speaks of puberty rites for boys; these are only concerned with entrance into the Asafo and are seldom performed except for those likely to reach high office. She describes such a rite in (8) 191-4.

[3] Manoukian confirms this; (27) 74. Rattray says that the Isalas do not have any form of puberty rite; (32) 500. The Gurensis do not have any rites though, when 'a child is old enough, he will be told the clan secrets by his father, in the night'; (32) 238. Fortes says that, among the Tallensis, 'there is no affective or social break to mark a transition from childhood to adulthood'; (14) 198.

[4] Rattray describes the operation as performed by the Gurensis in (32) 168-70.

to it, but the girl from this time onwards is given attention, her freedom may be restricted, and her dressing is now given more care.' The girls from fishing families undergo traditional puberty rites from two to four years after the menarche. In GOVIEFE (Ewe) nowadays puberty rites are much modified and only the procession among the relatives and friends is left. Traditional puberty rites have been replaced among Christian families by the confirmation ceremonies. Girls who have reached puberty plait their hair, and wear adult cloths and a kerchief on their heads. Puberty is accompanied among girls by decreased freedom of action and greater vigilance on the part of their mothers. In CENTRAL ACCRA (Ga) there are no puberty rites for boys. There used to be initiation rites into the Asafo companies, but even then the rites were usually held only for those likely to succeed to an important office. With girls, a special food made with corn and palm oil is prepared for a girl when she has her first menstrual flow, and a feast is held. This custom is dying away as nowadays girls tend not to tell their mothers when they reach the menarche. In some areas, a very modified form of the old puberty rites is rushed through for pregnant unmarried girls, in order to prevent the children from being born stupid. While puberty rites are the exception rather than the rule, the attainment of puberty is marked by a great attention paid to dress and general appearance in both sexes and both boys and girls wear gorgeous clothes and powder their faces. In CHRISTIANSBORG (Ga) a girl's father, on the occasion of her menstruation, gives a fowl to be used for a feast for the girl's friends. Her mother lectures her on the dangers of an immoral life. Girls go through a puberty rite called *Kpemo*. This is a mass rite. The candidates live in a special house under the instruction of an old woman who teaches them home economy and other subjects. They must jump over a chastity rock, take part in ceremonial dancing and are dressed up and paraded. Their brothers may accompany them in their dances and may keep the special taboos pertaining to the rite, but there are no other rites for boys. In TESHIE (Ga) no puberty rites are held in some divisions of the town, though in others there are such rites for girls. Puberty is accompanied by considerable self-consciousness in the matter of clothes. The girls dress up more and the boys are fond of wearing coloured drawers on which phrases are embroidered, such as: 'I love you', 'Love is great', 'Darling, forget me not', and the names of such heroes as 'Joe Louis', 'Roy Rogers' and 'Roy Ankrah'. These underpants are worn under a cloth but are shown to the interested gaze of any girls around. In APIREDE (Cherepon) puberty rites used to be performed as soon as the girl reached her menarche but 'the puberty rite as described is not done nowadays. The egg is still given when the girl has her first menstruation. Drumming, singing and dancing which used to accompany the occasion have ceased; instead the girl's mother goes round early in the morning from house to house to give the announcement, and that ends it.' Among the ISALAS there are no puberty rites, and the transition from childhood to adulthood is a gradual one.

In Ghana, very few girls learn about menstruation from their mothers or other relatives, and most of them learn about such matters from their friends' conversations, or from attending the puberty rites of others. In many areas, girls are expected to report their first menstruation to their mothers. It is widely held for it to be unlucky for this to happen during the day;[1] the most auspicious time is at dawn. They are then instructed in personal hygiene by their mothers, and sexual instruction may also be given. In some areas, girls are prepared for marriage by being told how to please their husbands sexually.[2] In APA (Asante) girls learn about menstruation from discussions with their mothers or grandmothers and from their friends. 'Before marriage the girl is given sex education by her mother and her grandmother. She is taught how to sleep with her husband; and when she goes to the bathroom, she is taught how to wash her genital parts with lime.' In JAISI (Asante) many mothers teach their daughters the facts of menstruation including the menstrual taboos such as that they must not prepare food for men, nor enter a stool house nor a chief's house, nor swear an oath, while they are menstruating. In JAKOBO (Asante) girls are instructed by their mothers how to keep their vaginas clean with lime juice and herbal balls. 'The girls are also instructed in the technique of giving satisfaction to their husbands during coition, which mainly consists of waist-shaking.' They are also taught to recognize pregnancy from the absence of periodic menstruation.

[1] Rattray notes that, in ancient times, a girl to whom this happened was killed; (31) 69.

[2] According to Christensen, Fanti girls are instructed by their mothers in behaviour associated with menstruation, including the taboos to be observed; (5) 49.

In VAKPO (Ewe) the facts of menstruation are explained to girls by their mothers on the occasion of their first menstrual flow. In TESHIE (Ga) girls learn about menstruation from friends; parents never discuss such matters with their daughters nor do the latter report their first menstruation to them. In APIREDE (Cherepon) now that puberty rites are no longer performed, girls often do not know anything about menstruation until they reach the menarche. Among the DAGABAS 'generally speaking, there are no taboos on any aspect of sex and parents are outspoken on sexual matters even when children are present. The result is that before the child reaches the age of puberty, he or she may have acquired information about sex knowledge and menstruation which is quite comprehensive.'

In some parts of Ghana, boys learn about sex matters from discussions with their friends and from overhearing adults' conversation; in others they are told by their fathers. While in some families it is thought wrong to discuss sexual matters in the presence of children, in others no attention is paid to their presence, and indecent jokes and the pleasures of the previous night are all discussed.[1] In DWINYAMA (Asante) boys receive no direct sexual instruction from adults; they learn chiefly from conversations with friends and from overhearing conversations between adults. In SUPOWMU DUNKA (Fante) 'the parents discuss their private affairs regardless of the presence of the children. Owing to this, children learn a good many things about sex and marital affairs which they are not supposed to know.' In AYIKAI DOBORO (Ga) boys learn about sexual matters from friends, both boy friends and girl friends. Ignorance of coition is held to be shameful in adolescence, so older boys instruct them. In DOME (Ga) boys learn about sexual matters from their friends and from school lessons, not from their parents. In TESHIE (Ga) obscene language is freely used before children, and the women in the house discuss the sexual pleasures of the previous night before the children. In AGOMANYA (Krobo) a boy learns about sexual matters from his father; 'from pubescence the answers to his questions are frank and straight-

[1] According to Christensen, among the Fantis there is no formal sex instruction for boys, who acquire knowledge by listening to the conversations of older boys and adults; (5) 99. Fortes says that, among the Tallensis, 'there are no taboos on conversation on sex matters. . . . Men, women, and children are all outspoken about sexual matters, though young women are apt to use euphemisms and to talk more circumspectly than men'; (14) 251.

forward'. Among the ISALAS 'the boy's chief source of sex knowledge is from friends and other adults who talk loosely about sex practices in the presence of them. Parents seem to pay no regard to the presence of children when they talk about sex among themselves.'

Chastity can mean two things in Ghanaian society; chastity before the celebrations of a girl's puberty rites, and chastity after the celebration of her rites, but before her marriage. In former times, both were thought important, and if a girl failed in the first, she was killed or expelled from the tribe. Nowadays, this is still thought important and in some areas, girls who conceive before their rites are rushed through an abbreviated ceremony or a public ritual of purification may be performed. The attitude towards post-pubertal but pre-marital chastity, however, has undergone a marked change in many parts of Ghana, and, particularly in schoolgirls, such chastity is not always expected.[1] In APA (Asante) a girl who becomes pregnant before her puberty rites have been celebrated is known as *kyiribra*. *Kyiribra* couples are punished with stripping, being mocked at and smeared with various substances. Sacrifices are made to purify the village and the family and the couple are driven away. Girls may be more leniently dealt with if their menarches were reported to the Queen Mother. In BOMPATA (Asante) people expect 'chastity before marriage but in practice it is rare among girls in Bompata once they have undergone their simple puberty rites'. The prospect of being confirmed acts as a deterrent against the loss of virginity, as large sums

[1] According to Fortes, among the Ashantis, 'it is a sin and a crime, for which both parties are nowadays liable to a heavy fine and to public obloquy, for a girl to conceive before her puberty ceremony. But after this ceremony no disgrace follows premarital pregnancy, if the girl has not been promiscuous'; (11) 265-6. Rattray says that, for an Ashanti to have sexual intercourse with a girl before her menarche was held equivalent to murder. If the menarche had been reached but not disclosed, the couple were made to undergo a purificatory rite; (30) 298. Christensen says that, among the Fantis, a premium is placed on virginity at marriage, and promiscuity in adolescent girls is punished by beatings, the application of red pepper or ginger, and other threats; (5) 49. Field reports that, of the Gas, 'I am told "not one girl in a thousand is a virgin". . . . Schoolgirls are said to be the least chaste of all and frequently sell their favours for small sums of money'; (9) 39. Busia says that, in Sekondi-Takoradi 'it is considered a great disgrace and the breach of a taboo for a girl to conceive or be married without having the puberty rites performed, and any girl who is so married is often reproached with the fact . . . a heavy taboo . . . formerly rested upon pre-marital sexual relationships. These have, however, considerably relaxed. Pre-marital sexual relations are common, and the celebration of the puberty rites is no longer indicative of virginity'; (4) 33-4. The Tallensis, according to Fortes, 'attach no value to prenuptial chastity'; (14) 100.

of money, averaging as much as £15, are collected by girls during confirmation rites, which are nowadays fulfilling the function of puberty rites. In JAKOBO (Asante) until recent years, most women were chaste when they were married. If a husband found that his wife was a virgin, he presented her relatives with cloths and money. 'Nowadays, however, things have so changed that there are practically no virgins among adolescent girls.' In the olden days, if a man had sexual intercourse with a girl before the onset of her menarche, it led to their death or expulsion, since it involved the breaking of a taboo. Nowadays, if a girl becomes pregnant before her puberty rites have been celebrated, a sheep is sacrificed and the couple are expelled from the village for the course of the pregnancy. They are allowed to return three months after the delivery. In KOFORIDUA (Asante) 'I have often heard a mother say of her pregnant daughter, when an enlightened father or relative remonstrates with the girl for being pregnant, "Oh, leave my daughter alone. Don't scold her. After all she is a woman and must bear a child for me. What is the use of education without a child."' Many girls become pregnant, especially schoolgirls. 'As there is no marked restrictive training for the girls as well as for the boys, the girls congregate at Nkwantanan and mix freely with the boys until very late at night. Sex passion grows and many girls fall victim, they become pregnant, especially those of them who are schoolgirls.' Among the DENKYERAS chastity is still very important and girls known to be lax in their morals find it difficult to get married. In AYIKAI DOBORO (Ga) chastity before marriage used to be rule; 'it was the pride of parents, it is now regarded as shackles of the past'. Nevertheless, it is generally supposed that if a girl is made pregnant by a lover, whom she subsequently does not marry, she may find it difficult to get another husband. In AGOMANYA (Krobo) no emphasis is placed on chastity except in Christian homes. However, parents are concerned if their daughters conceive before the puberty rites have been carried out; girls who nevertheless do have lovers before the puberty rites are said to be 'smuggling' and they dress their hair in a characteristic fashion. Chastity is expected in Christian homes and from teachers; 'the glorious aim to postpone sex experience and to produce better cultured children is often not achieved'. In APIREDE (Cherepon) chastity before the menarche is held to be important; after the celebration of a girl's puberty rites 'she can now love and marry'. Among the DAGABAS there is 'no emphasis on chastity; a boy or a girl may have illicit sexual relations with a friend long before he or she marries'.

Sexual intercourse appears to be widely practised among adolescents, often as a result of games played on moonlit nights, but also from assignations made at school and church meetings and elsewhere. This behaviour is not condoned by most parents, though many know of it and feel that they cannot do anything about it. In some areas, however, children who are known to have had sexual intercourse are severely punished. There is some evidence of male homosexuality. Fathers in matrilineal tribes are responsible for their sons' debts arising out of sexual misconduct, and for this reason they may warn their sons against pre-marital sexual affairs. On the other hand, the attitude of a girl's clan towards her illegitimate child may be permissive if not actually approving.[1] In TUTU (Akwapim) 'occasionally boys and girls play together far into the night in the street without any censure from their parents, and at other times they play separately. Sometimes, having played separately for a considerable time, the boys often attempt to disturb the girls and they rush on to disorganize their play. It is during such periods that they practise sexual intercourse. The boys and the girls run in different directions and each couple, a boy and a girl, in a hurry to avoid the risk of discovery, have coitus standing; sometimes the girl supports her back against a wall, at other times the girl may crouch on her arms and legs.' In BOMPATA (Asante) occasional sexual intercourse takes place, usually arising out of love games. Among adolescents of fifteen to eighteen years of age, 'confessions of homosexual activity are not easy to obtain, but it is said that early in the period of adolescence intense homosexual friendships are made by boys'. In JAISI (Asante) sexual intercourse is a common adolescent activity. This is unknown to the parents, and if discovered the boys are reprimanded and beaten if persistent; the girls are severely beaten and pepper is put in their vaginas and eyes. In

[1] Christensen notes the need for a Fanti father to impress upon his son the necessity of abstaining from pre-marital sexual relationships, on account of the fact that the clan of a girl with whom he had sexual relations, may sue the father for indemnification; (5) 99. According to Fortes, Tallensi boys of from about fourteen to about twenty may experiment with sex, particularly with younger girls of the same clan. 'With them they can indulge in sexual play, not always stopping short of intercourse, without criticism'; (14) 249. Field, somewhat obscurely, alleges that incest is 'very common' among the Gas; see (8) 168.

Children's work. 121. Child in charge of a cooked food stall in Komenda. Estimated age: ten years.

122. Girl selling food outside her house. Taken in Tamale.

Children's work. 123. Boy looking after a food stall in Kpandu market.

124. Girl selling drinks in Bawku lorry park.

Children's work. 125. The tailor's son in Winneba.

126. A young boy selling plantains in Komenda. Notice circumcision.

Adolescence. 127. Adolescent girls dressed in their finery. Notice the elaborate dressing of the hair. Taken in Teshie.

128. An adolescent girl wearing a tunic or 'cover-shoulders', skirt and cover-cloth of the same material, which she is wearing as a shawl. As may be seen, she is very pleased with herself. Taken in an Ashanti village.

KPANDU (Ewe) 'nowadays, sex activities are common and almost out of control in the clan and in the state. Young men who are under eighteen years of age and are known to be misbehaving with girls are not punished in any way in the house by the parents or dismissed from school. Young men in school of sixteen to eighteen years keep girls in their parents' houses, bring forth children and still attend school. About the girls, things are even worse. Parents interviewed, said conditions are such as they cannot control easily. They pitifully said that they do not sanction the immorality of their daughters, and that as the daughters set off to school, they are met by any character on the way, receive love letters which they can less control, attend to trunk calls occasionally, never reach the school when they leave them, as they the parents also leave for their farms. That those daughters who are in boarding schools have their own boxes, and secret presents given to them cannot be seen or less controlled; that the present form of dressing, and the Church Ministers' insistence on the girls covering their heads with headkerchiefs before services, make the young daughters appear attractive and more like women of age, making the men chase them and so spoil them. The parents also complained that those companions or friends they may not like their daughters to go with are those very ones they meet in the schools, and that confidences about early love are kept secret from them, and known only to their fellow schoolmates. That in a mixed school, the male teachers are sources of danger to their daughters attending it. That in a girls' school, the daughters tell them that they are sent by the female teachers to their lovers with letters or parcels and there contract the bad habits. The mothers said that they could not tell whom to blame in the matter and that if their daughters who were attending school conceived and they still kept them in their premises, it was because there was no alternative and it should not be taken as their sanction to the immoral life of the present day. There are thirteen girls in the clan who have stopped schooling because of early conception. Two children of such condition have no known fathers and are now adopted by the chief of the clan. There is only one family in the whole of the clan where strict morality is kept and all the five daughters are reputed to be chaste girls and free from pollution. Even in this very family, the four sons are ill-spoken of with regard to their immoral behaviour.' In

AGOMANYA (Krobo) 'it is common to see a group of adolescent boys relaxing by the street. If one of their number strolls to join up the group, they greet him with a shower of questions and comments; "You, where did you sleep last night? Oh, he has been to his girl's; your waist must be strong for such regular visits." I sat a whole afternoon watching a group of young men idling in the shade of a tree. As they sat, they passed remarks on each girl that passed by. I heard them portioning out a group of girls who were approaching. "It would be a good idea to have connection with them tonight", one remarked, and he went on to allot the girls among them. As the girls passed by, two boys rushed out, one stretching out his hand and tapping gently the head-belt of the girl he chose, whilst the other also stretched out his hand, jerked up the cloth of "his" girl, to look at her genitals. Though the girls resented this horse-play, they never took it as as serious offence. "Oh, take this foolishness from me", "Oh, I do not like this", were the rebuffing remarks made rather with laughter. There was an uproar in which all participated. All kinds of jokes, some quite obscene were used.' 'When the breast is budding, a girl may have suitors and thus may indulge in sexual intercourse. A girl who has already been initiated may have two or three boys. A girl who has not undergone the puberty rites signifies that with the hair dress. Though she may indulge in sex experiments, she is "smuggling" at the risk of being banished from home and family should she be pregnant in this unprepared state.' When a boy reaches puberty, 'though he had hitherto been enjoying some freedom in sex experiments, he is from this stage encouraged by the sisters especially and to a lesser degree by the mother to take a girl friend. The sisters more often are the mediators. This he does and thus enters into a loose marriage, *pla*. Most often early child-birth is prevalent and these boys become fathers rather early.' In LARTEH KUBEASI (Guang) parents 'often complain of laxity in sexual morality among adolescent schoolgirls and boys. Abortion among schoolgirls is reported to be a growing evil.'

Adolescents' first love objects tend to be of the same age as themselves, though they may subsequently, if they are girls, see the advantages of an older and therefore wealthier man as a permanent mate. In BOMPATA (Asante) early love relationships are likely to be of the same age, though 'such friendships are said to be short-lived. As the girls grow older, other qualities in them other than the mere ability to satisfy the sex urge begin to appeal to them. For practical purposes, they realize that the friendship of an older or working man who can clothe her and give her substantial presents is better than one of their own coevals who may still be supported by their parents. "What can these 'knickers' boys (implying that the boys' possessions consists of only a pair of knickers) give you if you 'deal' with them?" Girls are often reminded of the inability of younger adolescents to support them if the girls continue to befriend the boys.' In DWINYAMA (Asante) boys are likely to befriend older girls, girls younger boys, in their first love relationships. In JAKOBO (Asante) first love objects are likely to be of the same age, though they cannot marry, since boys are not economically independent until the age of eighteen or so.

The behaviour of some adolescents in Ghana, notwithstanding what has been said above, tends to be the typical behaviour of adolescents elsewhere; they become moody, irritable, rebellious; they become religious, they adopt radical ideas.[1] Nevertheless, it is generally agreed that adolescence is a very happy time. In APA (Asante) 'there is often a complete change in the girls' conduct at the age of adolescence. They very often want to have their own way, and so become obstinate, disobedient, disrespectful, impatient and have less regard for their elders, including even their parents.' In BANKO (Asante) adolescents are commonly called 'those who cannot be stopped from action'. They tend to rebel against authorities, to quarrel with their parents, especially over going out at night. 'At Banko, religion plays an important part in the lives of adolescent boys and girls.' It is regarded as an unhappy time since it is easy to get involved in an affair which may disgrace the clan or family. In APAM (Fante) 'the freedom boys and girls enjoy in their love affairs does not give rise to any show of "storm and stress", though there is a lot of self-assertiveness, impulsiveness and a display of masculinity among the boys. Apart from such outbursts, the young men are usually quite well-behaved and submissive to both school and home or parental authority. Most parents show sympathy to their children at this period, and as they are anxious to see how their children will fare in life, they leave their love

[1] Field says that, among the Gas, if an adolescent goes through a period of difficult behaviour, this may be attributed to fate; (8) 96-7.

affairs alone, and so adolescents here seem to enjoy this period of their life immensely.' In AYIKAI DOBORO (Ga) it is believed that the strength of their desire is such that lovers will go to any lengths to sleep with each other. Adolescents are said to become unruly, and self-opinionated and to adopt radical ideas, and this is attributed to their sexual experience. Adolescence is generally regarded as a happy time. In TESHIE (Ga) 'at this period of the girl's life she becomes emotional, irritable, shy and awkward; she suffers from moods for no apparent cause, and generally it is at this period that many parents come to complain to the teachers that their girls have become difficult. The boys at this stage become shy and reserved, and moods of boastfulness and aggression may alternate with moods of diffidence. He too, like the girl, becomes difficult.' Adults always say that adolescence is the happiest time of one's life.

In Ghana generally, adulthood is reached with marriage, though boys may be regarded as adults when they earn their own livelihood. In BANKO (Asante) a girl becomes an adult once she has menstruated. Boys do not become adults until they have the means to keep a wife. In BEREKUM (Brong) boys are regarded as adults after they have married; girls, after child-birth; barren women, after about the age of thirty. In KPANDU (Ewe) 'a young married man of even twenty-eight years will first be served before a fully grown unmarried adult of say, forty years, who is a bachelor'. In DOME (Ga) a woman is regarded as an adult when she had brought forth a child; a man, when he earns a livelihood.

BIBLIOGRAPHY

I

Students' Theses

In the following list, the students' theses are listed by towns and villages in the order in which they are dealt with in the main text. This list is followed by a bibliographic entry for each thesis, arranged in alphabetical order of the students' names. The spelling of place-names adopted here and in the text is that of the 1948 Census, even where the spelling in the thesis itself may be different.

Central Accra, see Lamptey, S. A.
Ayikai Doboro, see Addo, W. A.
Christiansborg, see Fleischer, G. E.
Dome, see Pappoe, J. A.
Tema, see Asihene, J. B.
Teshie, see Acolatse, M. G. A.
Agomanya, see Ocansey, P. K.
Kordiabe, see Doku, C. W.
Otrowe, see Caesar, G. V.

Aburi, see Owusu, A. A. S.
Mampong, see Addo-quao, S. G.
Tutu, see Asiedu, W. T.
Apa, see Cudjoe-debrah, G.
Banko, see Opoku, J. E.
Benim, see Manu, R. A.
Bompata, see Kyerematen, E. A.
Bosofo, see Ofori, B.
Dwinyama, see Ahinful, T. E. K.
Jaisi, see Forson, W. G.
Jakobo, see Kwofie, B.
Koforidua, see Sam-amavih, G. K.
Berekum, see Anane, F. K.
Apam, see Wright, T. S. D.
Komenda, see Annan, J. E.
Supowmu Dunkwa, see Nicholas, T. A.
Ayanzili, see Amuzuah, J. K.
The Denkyeras, see Mensah, A. K.

The Kwabus, see OSAFO, S. L. A.
Gblede, see MORTTY, G. G.
Goviefe, see DZANSI, Y. T.
Kpandu, see DZIDE, A.
Vakpo, see DOGBE, F. H. K.

Apirede, see KORANTENG, F.
Larteh Kubeasi, see OTU, W.
Winneba, see MENSAH, J. S.

The Dagabas, see ANDOH, M. D.
The Isalas, see EGALA, I.

ACOLATSE, M. G. A. *Child Training in the Kle Division of Teshie.* Typescript, foolscap. Pp. 112, bibliography, children's drawings, map. Illustrated by photographs. No date.

ADDO, William A. *Child Training in Ayikai Doblo: a Village in the Ga State.* Typescript, foolscap. Appendices in manuscript. Pp. 99, bibliography, children's drawings, pressed leaves of herbs, maps. Illustrated by photographs. Achimota, 1954.

ADDO-QUAO, S. G. *Child Training in Mampong-Akuapem.* Manuscript, foolscap. Pp. 133, bibliography, children's drawings, map in pocket. Illustrated by photographs. Achimota, 1956.

AHINFUL, T. E. K. *Cultural Training of the Child at Dwinyama.* Manuscript, foolscap. Pp. 133, children's drawings, map in text. Achimota, 1953.

AMUZUAH, J. K. *The Home Education of the Eletile Nzema Tribe.* Typescript, quarto (copy of manuscript original?). Pp. 70. Achimota, no date.

ANANE, Fred. K. *Child Training at Berekum in Ashanti.* Manuscript, quarto.

ANDOH, M. Dawson. *Child Training among the Dagaba, N.T.s.* Manuscript, foolscap. Pp. 80, children's drawings, map. Illustrated by photographs. Achimota, 1953.

ANNAN, J. E. *An Investigation into Child Training in Komenda.* Typescript, foolscap. Pp. 125, bibliography, children's drawings, tables, maps. Illustrated by photographs. Achimota, 1956.

ASIEDU, W. T. *Essay on Child Training.* Manuscript. Pp. 168, bibliography, children's drawings (loose), map on back cover. Illustrated by coloured drawings (initialled 'A.O.') and photographs. Achimota (1954?).

ASIHENE, Juliana B. *Child Training in Tema.* Typescript, foolscap. Pp. 113, bibliography, children's drawings, maps. Illustrated by photographs. Achimota, 1953.

CAESAR, Grace Violet. *Child Training in Otrɔkpɛ*. Manuscript, foolscap. Pp. 168, children's drawings, map. Illustrated by photographs. Achimota, 1956.

CUDJOE-DEBRAH, Grace. *Child Training at Apaah*. Manuscript, foolscap. Pp. 135, bibliography, children's drawings, maps. Illustrated by photographs. Achimota (1956?).

DOGBE, F. H. K. *Child Training in an African Society, Vakpo, Togoland under U.K.T., West Africa*. Typescript, foolscap. Pp. 121, bibliography, children's drawings, map. Illustrated by photographs. Achimota, 1955.

DOKU, Charles Wesley. *Child Training among the Shai People of Kordiaber*. Manuscript, foolscap. Pp. 154, children's drawings, map. Illustrated by photographs and diagrams. Achimota, 1954.

DZANSI, Y. T. *Child Training in Goviefe, Togoland under United Kingdom Trusteeship*. Manuscript, foolscap. Pp. 185, children's drawings, pressed leaves of herbs, map on back cover. Illustrated by photographs. Achimota, 1954.

DZIDE, Ambrose. *Child Training in Kpandu Tsakpe within the Akpini State, Trans-Volta Togoland*. Typescript, foolscap. Pp. 111, children's drawings, pressed leaves of herbs, maps. Illustrated by photographs. Achimota, 1956.

EGALA, I. *Child Training in Sissala Culture*. Manuscript, foolscap. Pp. 65, children's drawings. Illustrated by photographs. Achimota, 1953.

FLEISCHER, Gilbert Ebenezer. *The Home Education of Children in the Ga Tribe (Osu: Asante Blohuŋ)*. Manuscript, foolscap. Pp. 117, bibliography, children's drawings, map. Illustrated by photographs. Achimota, 1953.

FORSON, William Gabriel. *Child Training at Jiasi via Konongo*. Typescript, foolscap. Pp. 178, children's drawings, map. Illustrated by photographs. Achimota, 1955.

KORANTENG, Florence. *Child Training at Apirede Akwapim*. Typescript, foolscap. Pp. 160, illustrated by photographs, children's drawings, pressed leaves, maps. Achimota, 1957.

KWOFIE, Beatrice. *The Training of the Child in Jacobu*. Typescript, quarto. Pp. 93 [plus children's drawings, coloured and drawn illustrations in foolscap, map. Achimota, 1953.

KYEREMATEN, Emmanuel Amankwa. *An Essay on Child Training in Asante Akyem Bompata*. Manuscript, foolscap. Pp. 213, illustrated by photographs, children's drawings, map and plan. Achimota, 1955.

LAMPTEY, S. A. *The Training of Children in Central Accra*. Typescript, foolscap. Pp. 105, illustrated by photographs, children's drawings, maps. Achimota, 1955.

MANU, Rebecca Agnes. *Child Training in Benim, a Village in Ashanti.* Manuscript, foolscap. Pp. 99, illustrated by photographs, children's drawings. Achimota, 1953.

MENSAH, Alfred Kwamina. *The Home Education of Children in the Denkyera Tribe.* Manuscript, foolscap. Pp. 83, illustrated by photographs, plan and map. Achimota, 1952.

MENSAH, Joseph Sampanny. *A Study of Childhood and Youth at Winneba.* Typescript, foolscap. Pp. 148, illustrated by photographs, children's drawings, maps. Achimota, 1955.

MORTTY, Godfried Geormbeeyi. *Child Training in Gblede an Ewe Village in British Trust Togoland.* Typescript, foolscap. Pp. 188, illustrated by photographs, children's drawings, map. Achimota, 1953.

NICHOLAS, Theodora Alberta. *Child Training in Supowmu Dunkwa.* Typescript, foolscap. Pp. 64, illustrated by photographs, children's drawings, map. Achimota, 1957.

OCANSEY, P. K. *Child Training at Agomenya in Krobo.* Typescript, foolscap. Pp. 130, illustrated by photographs, children's drawings, map. Achimota, (1954?).

OFORI, Betty. *Child Training in Bɔsofoɔ.* Manuscript, foolscap. Pp. 127, illustrated by photographs, children's drawings, map. Achimota, 1957.

OPOKU, Johnson Ernest. *Child Training at Banko: a Village in the Sekyere-Mampong Area of Ashanti.* Typescript, foolscap. Pp. 97, illustrated by photographs, children's drawings, map. Achimota, 1955.

OSAFO, Sophy L. A. *How Children are Brought Up in Kwabu.* Manuscript, foolscap. Pp. 55, illustrated by ink sketches. Achimota (1951?).

OTU, W. *Child Training in the Esentere Section of Kubease, Larteh, Akwapim.* Typescript, foolscap. Pp. 140, illustrated by photographs, children's drawings, pressed leaves of herbs, maps. Achimota, 1955.

OWUSU, Alice A. S. *Child Training in Atweasin-Aburi.* Manuscript, foolscap. Pp. 186, illustrated by photographs, children's drawings, maps. Achimota, 1955.

PAPPOE, Jessie Aku. *Child Training in Dome Village.* Typescript, foolscap. Pp. 62, illustrated by photographs, children's drawings, map. Achimota (1953?).

SAM-AMAVIH, G. K. *The Home Education of the New Juaben Child.* Typescript, foolscap. Pp. 33, illustrated by photographs Achimota, 1952.

WRIGHT, T. S. D. *Child Training in Apam.* Typescript, foolscap. Pp. 75, illustrated by photographs, children's drawings, pressed leaves of herbs, map. Achimota, 1954.

BIBLIOGRAPHY

II

References

1 ACQUAH, I. *Accray Survey*. London, University of London Press, 1958.

2 ARMITAGE, C. H. *The Tribal Markings and Marks of Adornment of the Natives of the Northern Territories of the Gold Coast Colony*. London, Harrison, 1924.

3 BECKETT, W. H. *Akokoaso: A Survey of a Gold Coast Village*. London School of Economics Monographs on Social Anthropology No. 10. London, London School of Economics, 1944.

4 BUSIA, K. A. *Report on a Social Survey of Sekondi-Takoradi*. London, Crown Agents for the Colonies, 1950.

5 CHRISTENSEN, J. B. *Double Descent among the Fanti*. New Haven, Human Relations Area Files, 1954.

6 DANQUAH, J. B. *Gold Coast: Akan Laws and Customs and the Akim Abuakwa Constitution*. London, Routledge, 1928.

7 FIELD, M. J. *Akim-Kotoku: An Oman of the Gold Coast*. London, Crown Agents for the Colonies, 1948.

8 FIELD, M. J. *Religion and Medicine of the Gã People*. London, Oxford University Press, 1937.

9 FIELD, M. J. *Social Organization of the Gã People*. London, Crown Agents for the Colonies, 1940.

10 FORTES, M. *The Dynamics of Clanship among the Tallensi*. London, Oxford University Press, 1945.

11 FORTES, M. 'Kinship and Marriage among the Ashanti'. *African Systems of Kinship and Marriage, ed.* Radcliffe-Brown, A. R., & Forde, D. London, Oxford University Press, 1950, pages 252–84.

12 FORTES, M. *Social and Psychological Aspects of Education in Taleland*. Supplement to *Africa*, 1938, XI, No. 4. London, Oxford University Press, 1938.

13 FORTES, M. 'Time and Social Structure: An Ashanti Case Study'. *Social Structure: Studies presented to A. R. Radcliffe-Brown, ed.* Fortes. Oxford, Clarendon Press, 1949, pages 54–84.

14 FORTES, M. *The Web of Kinship among the Tallensi.* London, Oxford University Press, 1949.

15 FORTES, M. & FORTES, S. L. 'Food in the Domestic Economy of the Tallensi'. *Africa,* IX, 1936, 237-76.

16 GHANA, Government of. *Education Statistics,* 1958 Office of the Government Statistician, Accra, Government Printing Department, 1958.

17 GOLD COAST, Government of the. *Census of Population, 1948: Report and Tables.* London, Crown Agents for the Colonies, 1950.

18 GOODY, J. 'The Fission of Domestic Groups among the LoDagaba'. In *The Developmental Cycle in Domestic Groups, ed.* Goody. Cambridge Papers in Social Anthropology No. 1. London, Cambridge University Press, 1958, pages 53-91.

19 GOODY, J. *The Social Organization of the LoWiili.* London, Her Majesty's Stationery Office, 1956.

20 GRANT, F. W. *The Nutrition and Health of Children in the Gold Coast.* Chicago, University of Chicago Press, 1955.

21 HAYFORD, C. *Gold Coast Native Institutions.* London, Sweet & Maxwell, 1903.

22 HILL, P. *The Gold Coast Cocoa Farmer.* London, Oxford University Press, 1956.

23 HUBER, H. 'Initiation to Womanhood among the Sɛ (Ghana)'. *Nigerian Field,* 1958, XXIII, 99-119.

24 LAWSON, R. M. 'The Nutritional Status of a Rural Community on the Lower Volta, Gold Coast'. *Journal of the West African Science Association,* 1957, III, 123-9.

25 MANOUKIAN, M. *Akan and Ga-Adangme Peoples of the Gold Coast.* London, Oxford University Press, 1950.

26 MANOUKIAN, M. *The Ewe-Speaking People of Togoland and the Gold Coast.* London, International African Institute, 1952.

27 MANOUKIAN, M. *Tribes of the Northern Territories of the Gold Coast.* London, International African Institute, 1951.

28 PURCELL, F. M. *Diet and Ill-Health in the Forest Country of the Gold Coast.* London, H. K. Lewis, 1939.

29 RATTRAY, R. S. *Ashanti.* Oxford, Clarendon Press, 1923.

30 RATTRAY, R. S. *Ashanti Law and Constitution.* Oxford, Clarendon Press, 1929.

31 RATTRAY, R. S. *Religion and Art in Ashanti.* Oxford, Clarendon Press, 1927.

32 Rattray, R. S. *The Tribes of the Ashanti Hinterland.* 2 vols. Oxford, Clarendon Press, 1932.

33 Sarbah, J. M. *Fanti Customary Laws.* London, Clowes, 1897.

34 Tait, D. 'The Family, Household, and Minor Lineage of the Konkomba'. *Africa,* 1956, XXVI, 219-49 and 332-42.

35 Taylor, A. 'Understanding Children'. *Gold Coast Education,* 1954, I, 4-26.

36 Wartemberg, J. S. *Sao Jorge D'El Mina.* Ilfracombe, Stockwell (195?).

37 Westermann, D. and Bryan, M. A. *The Languages of West Africa.* London, Oxford University Press, 1952.

INDEX

Reference to important sections in bold type, thus: **200–12**. Reference to plates in parentheses, followed by a page reference number, thus: (85) 160 f., i.e. Plate 85, to be found in the section following page 160. Reference to footnotes by index numbers, thus: 90[2], i.e. in footnote [2] on page 90. Isolated references in successive pages shown by, e.g. 114, 115, 116; continual references in successive pages shown by, e.g. 114–16.

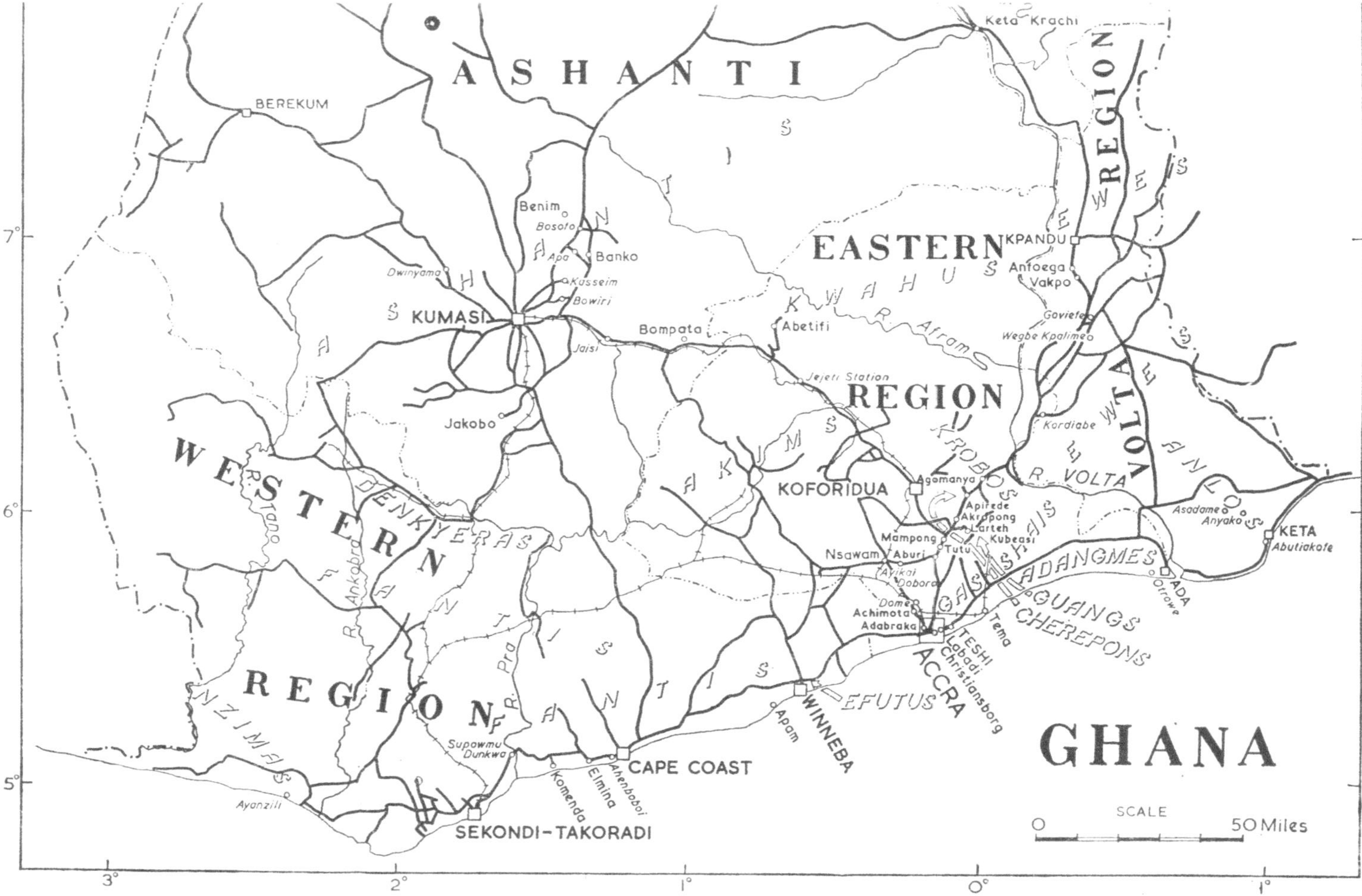

GHANA
ASHANTI
EASTERN REGION
VOLTA REGION
WESTERN REGION
BEREKUM
KUMASI
Benim
Bosoto
Apa
Banko
Kusseim
Bowiri
Dwinyama
Jaisi
Bompata
Abetifi
Jejeti Station
Jakobo
KOFORIDUA
Agamanya
Apirede
Akropong
Larteh
Kubeasi
Mampong
Tutu
Aburi
Nsawam
Ayikai
Dobora
Dome
Achimota
Adabraka
ACCRA
TESHI
Labadi
Christiansborg
Tema
ADA
Otrowe
KETA
Abutiakote
Asadame
Anyako
Keta Krachi
KPANDU
Anfoega
Vakpo
Gaviefe
Wegbe Kpalime
Kordiabe
R. Volta
R. Afram
KWAHUS
AKIMS
KROBOS
GAS
SHAIS
ADANGMES
GUANGS
CHEREPONS
EFUTUS
ANLOS
WINNEBA
Apam
CAPE COAST
Ahenboboi
Elmina
Komenda
Supowmu
Dunkwa
SEKONDI-TAKORADI
Ayanzili
NZIMAS
DENKYERAS
FANTIS
R. Pra
R. Ankobra
R. Tano
SCALE
0
50 Miles
3°
2°
1°
0°
1°
7°
6°
5°

For Product Safety Concerns and Information please contact our
EU representative GPSR@taylorandfrancis.com Taylor & Francis
Verlag GmbH, Kaufingerstraße 24, 80331 München, Germany